RETAILS OF THE UNEXPECTED

RETAILS OF THE UNEXPECTED

A CUSTOMER SERVICE TRAVELOGUE

Mark Bradley

First published in 2008 by

Ardra Press
PO Box 243
Beverley
HU17 6AX
United Kingdom
www.ardrapress.co.uk

ISBN: 978-0-9548678-5-0

British Library Cataloguing in Publication Data:
A CIP record for this book can be obtained from the British Library

Designed and typeset by Julie Martin

Printed and bound by TJ International Ltd, Padstow, Cornwall

Cover design and front cover photo/graphics by Ciaron Lee Marlow
www.rockers-going-starwars.co.uk

Back cover photo by Elena Bradley

Some sections of this book first appeared in the following newspapers, website and magazine, to whose editors Ardra Press expresses its gratitude: *Yorkshire Post*; *Bradford Telegraph and Argus*; www.customermanagementonline.com; *Customer Strategy Magazine*.

I've learned a lot about women. I think I've learned exactly how the fall of man occurred in the Garden of Eden. Adam and Eve were in the Garden of Eden and Adam said one day, 'Wow, Eve, here we are, at one with nature, at one with God, we'll never age, we'll never die and all of our dreams come true the instant we have them.'

And Eve said, 'Yeah ... it's just not enough, is it?'

Bill Hicks

I know a bank whereon the wild thyme blows,
Where oxlips and the nodding violet grows
Quite over-canopied with luscious woodbine,
With sweet musk-roses, and with eglantine

William Shakespeare[1]

---

[1] Although, admittedly, he does not explain which bank he is referring to and whether they offer online current accounts and unsecured loans.

For Ana, Luis & Elena

In memory of Barrie Clayton

Contents

Thank you

I owe a debt of gratitude to the following friends for their support, inspiration and endless ribbing. In fact one of them suggested that if I were to stretch the *thank you* list out to a whole page, I could personally thank everyone who bought my first book, too.

With a support group like this, how could I fail?

So here's the roll of honour.

First of all, an affectionate shoulder-charge for Ronan Fitzsimons at Ardra. Well I say *shoulder-charge*, but it's more sort of a big, fat *abrazo* really. I hope I can repay your confidence with book sales. But if that fails, we'll just open another bottle of *Gran Sangre de Toro*.

My sincere thanks are due to Jonathan Lel at City Speakers International (www.cityspeakersinternational.co.uk) for helping my star rise in the public speaking world and for curbing some of my less commercial tendencies.

Thanks to Andy Baker (Spanish Pirate) for his 'coaching' and for alerting me to the hitherto unknown activities of the Gas Police.

I would also like to thank Tom Richmond for allowing us to re-print articles originally published by the *Yorkshire Post* and Steve Hurst for allowing us to include some of my online contributions to *Customer Strategy Magazine*.

Big thanks also to Darren Bernstein, Pat Brown, David Warren, Doug Smith, Xander Leijnse, Iain Wilkinson, Fran Montgomery, PY Gerbeau, Cathy Long, Pete Sowden, Steve Weston, Anne Dowle, Rich Cundill, Ciaron Lee Marlow, Michelle Delaney, Andrew McKenna, Jonathan Buck, Jon & Pauline, Sean Jarvis and Colin, Lisa and family – and all my e-Newsletter subscribers (see www.bradleyprojects.com) and customers too.

Love to Mam Kathleen and Dad Michael, as well as to sisters Catherine and Sarah and their families: Martin, Tom, Jack, Dylan, Ruby and Peter.

I also owe a big debt of thanks to UK customers everywhere for sending me their real-life customer service experiences. Just when I think it can't get any worse, Jolyon tells me about the waiter who announced, 'would you like the house wine, sir, or something decent?'

Finally, thanks are due to my own lovely family: to Ana, Luis and Elena. I've a feeling this journey isn't over yet.

Foreword

PY Gerbeau

Bonjour!

In my professional career I have been fortunate enough to travel the world and experience some of the best and worst customer service around. Sometimes I've encountered warmth, engagement and beaming smiles, while on other occasions I've been greeted by empty faces staring back at me like dogs watching a card-trick.

Believe me, with a background in theme parks and over 25 years in the leisure industry, I not only understand the importance of a great customer experience but I also know its value to any progressive organisation.

As a French person living in the UK I believe there is a perception that my countrymen are not top of the list for user-friendly customer service – *Vive l'indifférence* maybe – but I wasn't sure if the Brits were that much further ahead. I got my answer when I met Mark Bradley at a tourism conference in Manchester and it's not good news. Customer service has a disastrously low profile in the United Kingdom.

It's a simple message, but one that tends to elude those organisations that fail to see things from the customer's perspective. You see, I've listened to *experts* who dazzle us with terms like 'internal service profit chain' and 'applied business process improvement methodologies'. Now I'm not arguing against these important concepts. I'm simply stating that unless you take the customer view as your starting point, you're missing the point.

By the way, these experts almost always have a PowerPoint slide with a complicated-looking pyramid graph on it too. Few presenters seem able to explain it, but it does lend an air of academic *gravitas* to their pronouncements.

Mark was different. In the conference foyer he told me that everything would become clear once he'd told me his *coffee house* story. He was right. By the time he finished it, everything was clear – the room was completely empty. Then he started on a story about the M6 Toll Road, so I smiled, made my excuses and tried to catch up with the others.

The fact is that we live in a fast-moving world, where customers' expectations are on the increase and other countries 'do' service better than the UK. We should be aspiring to the exemplary standards set by our friends in the US and the Far East but unless we learn to take a long, serious look at service from the customer's point of view, we'll always lag behind.

Retails of the Unexpected is a good starting place. *Bonne chance, mes amis.*

PYG
July 2008

Introduction

In popular music parlance that *difficult second album* is usually a consequence of a thrilling debut. Expectations are set so high that, inevitably, the creators of the first work are unable to match it with the second. That shouldn't be a problem for me, as I understand both of the people who bought my first book only thought it 'ok'. One uses it as a draught excluder and the other finds it handy for scraping ice from his windscreen.

In *Inconvenience Stores* I decided to travel in 'the customer's shoes' and record my experiences. As it happened, I didn't come back. My aim of raising the profile of customer service in this country appears to be best served by continuing to document consumer experiences, so I've stayed in that metaphorical pair of well-worn shoes and continued the customer travelogue.

Where once the phrase 'put yourself in the customer's shoes' seemed such a throwaway remark in any customer service training session (i.e. always said, never taken seriously, or only discussed at extra-curricular gatherings supported by lashings of Marks and Spencer's buck's fizz and prawn sandwiches), the fundamental need to institutionalise this activity – this mindset – in British retail businesses has never been more important.

*

Customer service is not core activity in the huge (landslide) majority of the organisations I encounter. Posing simple questions like 'do you know who your customers are and what matters most to them?' provokes contrasting reactions that either (a) signify a complete failure to regard customers as important or (b) represent a Damascene moment that is usually closely followed by 'emergency executive visits to the branch network,' a lot of hand-wringing and an outbreak of customer-facing employee incentives. Either way, few organisations truly engage with the concept of differentiation through the quality of the customer experience.

But when they do, one not so obvious benefit accrues. If I tell you that customer service improves when you find out what your customers think, your minds are full of images of an elderly relative sucking an egg and bearing a sarcastic expression. It's no great surprise to learn that upon engaging with customers and beginning to explore their experiences, opportunities to improve emerge by the hundred. But it's the third, less obvious, revelation that wakes you up with a metaphorical squirt of lemon juice in the retina. When you start to see things from the customer's point of view, you begin to uncover the reasons why customer service does not thrive in these Islands. Customer service has an incredibly low profile in this country and one way or the other, it is slowly bringing us down.

Let's think about it for a moment. When we start to contemplate my soapbox beseeching, we do so from the perspective of an employee. After all, most of us work for one, single employer, with all of the dumbing idiosyncrasies that such a state implies. But we're customers of hundreds, maybe thousands of organisations.

So, frighteningly, when it comes to the need to improve our business performance, we rely on our 'employee' head to provide the answers. Our failure to replace this internally fixated vessel with the brutally objective perspective of the 'customer' means that our increasingly blinkered view of work blinds us to the possibilities of seeing our existing and potential customers as partners – true contributors to the success of our organisation – rather than lumped-together punters with a shoal mentality to price alone.

Therefore, in the hope of raising the profile of customer service and providing some fast food for thought, I've brought together a collection of essays, articles, arguments and stories. Some are short, some are long and some may bear no relation to the others whatsoever. In fact, if they were people, you'd want to avoid the pub where they gather.

What distinguishes them, if such a verb doesn't over-egg the pudding, is that they offer a *customer* view of the world, rather than a business view. They are offered as an antidote to the malaise affecting many UK organisations – a basket of symptoms including a lack of perspective, a surfeit of internal fixation and an unstinting belief that they know exactly what's best for the customer. And that's when they regard themselves as being *quite good* at service. Don't even get me started on the rest.

I cannot detect an improvement in the overall level of customer service in this country, but I can more accurately pinpoint the factors that have brought us to this place. Some are easily identifiable and often just as easily addressed.

Other factors, such as the criminally low profile of service in this country, are partly a cultural issue and those causes are more deep-rooted. Others, such as the tendency for large double glazing companies to regard customers as opponents, need to be overcome in any way possible. (I heard of a friend who was quoted £17000 by a large Northern double glazing company. Another company offered to do the work for £3000. When the former heard of the latter's offer, they haunted the potential customer, finally agreeing to do the work for £8000, perhaps spotting some basic maths flaw on the part of the customer. Happily she opted for the latter company, who did her a fine job, but her loathing for any form of organisation who would regard her as someone to 'rip off' has left a scar.)

I've examined many individual sectors (as the double glazing one would be too easy to have a good go at) and have built the book around a series of essays and observations. Among other areas, they deal with the challenges of the UK retail industry and how the low profile of customer service in this country has tainted it to the extent that when a colleague told her co-workers that her daughter was embarking on a retail career, many offered their commiserations.

But think about it. Every time you enviously glance up at the latest 'Dragon' on TV or at the luxury lifestyle of the latest celebrity entrepreneur, their talent will, as likely as not, have been honed throughout a career in retail. Where else can you accumulate the complex and diverse skills and experience necessary to be able strategically to carve up a huge slice of British customer spend for yourself?

So my travels extend to UK retail financial services and, in particular, the challenge facing our apparently recalcitrant UK banks to restore trust and faith among their battle-hardened customers, as well as words on public transport, dentistry, postal services, retail, restaurants and education.

Some of them argue specifically for change, others marvel at the astonishing contradictions we create and, occasionally, I've even been distracted by some of the wider social issues affecting our times, taking in the travails of the family unit, the devaluing of foreign languages and the traditional British fear of the unknown.

I think all are relevant to the context. That said, maybe the bit on dentistry was stretching things a bit. But then again, the tooth hurts. I don't share Deming's ultra-sharp vision, but like him I can see something intrinsically good behind the customer-centric models at play in those few proud organisations who truly *are* delivering fantastic service (which for the purposes of this book translates as: more often than not).

I sense it starts with the right kind of leadership – and one of the reasons we've got to where we are today is largely through our institutionalised tendency to approach business solely in economic terms – rather than recognising that any successful business is based on aspiring to the creation of a community of leaders, employees and customers.

We've reached an age when the achievements, passion and vision of the sadly missed Anita Roddick are admired universally and espoused through company values, mission statements and internal communication campaigns. And yet, at the same time, the customers I encounter and the employees I talk to describe a different world altogether – a 'talk' not transparently 'walked'.

Business is viewed through a prism where selfism defeats values, *do as I say, not as I do* characterises many of our leaders and, as a result of all of these mixed messages, we reach that inevitably British scenario – which somehow sums up our deep-seated inability to take good work seriously: the time when we celebrate most in the workplace is when someone leaves.

Mark Bradley
April 2008

1

Very Cross Country
September 2007

I arrive at the railway station in Leeds at 0520, far too early for the 0600 to Birmingham (and thence to Plymouth), but I'm a paranoically punctual sort of bloke. There might be a rush at WH Smith or the station concourse might have been closed as a result of a stray multi-seed bagel causing a customer to lose his footing, fall and render the place closed to customers. This might sound like further paranoia, but then again, having seen women almost wrestled to the ground for trying to take lipstick through airport security lately, I feel it's justified. But, the M62 might be blocked. It usually is.

The station car park at Leeds has been designed for people with bendy cars. It is nigh on impossible to enter the station without veering out to the right to attempt an unlikely left-hand turn. Even owls would baulk at the degree of neck swivel required, while futurists muse over the introduction of a third side of the road. As it happens, leaving is even worse. In order to line yourself up to insert your parking ticket in the machine by the exit barrier you have to either get out and walk or produce another exaggerated manoeuvre, involving a stretch of the arms that would have tested Eugene Tombs, that bloke from the *X-Files* who could squeeze through your pipes. Thankfully, the station car park is peopled by the friendly Yorkshire-type who's only too pleased to come out and open the gates for you – but it does seem to defeat the object of the automated gates.

McDonald's is open. Normally I wouldn't. But it's the only place open at this time of the morning. The trendy Italian coffee bar is closed. The French baguette shop is shrouded in darkness, with M&S and Starbucks yet to open. I look at the time, take a deep breath and enter McDonald's. I look up and order a bagel. Can I have a receipt? The request is met with a frown. It will have to be hand-written.

As I leave McDonald's my guilt increases. Everywhere is open now. It seems they were all crouched in darkness waiting for me to enter the golden arches. Just to spite me.

But the train leaves on time, full of yawns, billowing newspapers and the faint whiff of coffee. Mobiles chirp, laptops chime into life and the announcer welcomes us to Monday 10th September 2007 – with an apology. *We haven't been able to show the seat reservations this morning, ladies and gentlemen, so if you could stick to your reserved seats, that would help.* His assistant, the snack bar manager, is next on the line. *I'm afraid we have no hot water on the train this morning, so we'll only be able to serve cold drinks.*

I look at the time on my mobile phone. I have twelve minutes to make the connection at Birmingham. But we proceed in a stately manner through West and South Yorkshire, through Derbyshire and into Staffordshire, as Burton and Tamworth lurch up to the train out of the early-morning mist. On time.

Just short of Birmingham, realising that there's a chance we'll arrive at the advertised time, the driver slows the train down to a crawl – or at least that's the impression this frustrating delay causes. The speedo falls as my heart-rate rises. Twelve minutes becomes ten and ten becomes eight with the depressing certainty of an evening watching mainstream TV. Finally, we snake around past St Andrew's and enter New Street station. I alight with impressive speed and discover, from a jovial platform assistant, that my connection is the next train into the very same platform. If this is the biggest problem I'll face today, I can sit back and enjoy the journey.

We arrive ten minutes early into Plymouth at 1141 and I go about my day, relaxed and energised by my own unique interpretation of a power nap on the train. This involves lurching from side to side, muttering incomprehensibly and allowing my lower lip to droop horrifically chest-wards, as the Lush moisturiser I applied to my entire head this morning transfers effortlessly to the inside of the train window. Every time my head moves involuntarily up and down, the window squeaks like a startled Guinea Pig.

My work complete, I'm dropped at Plymouth station for the return journey. Far too early even for my train's departure time to be on the monitor, I take a seat in the Pumpkin Café (which sounds like it should have been serving Hobbits in the Shire), order a latte and emit a sigh that compels all present to recall the sound of a large tyre deflating. Twenty minutes later I check the screen. My train, the 1825 to Leeds is direct, thank the Lord, so once I'm sat down, I can relax. *Re-lax*.

The train has been cancelled. The station manager explains that the train hasn't made it as far as Plymouth, so they are providing a bus to take us to Tiverton, from where we will be ferried to our various destinations on the original train. No delay, he said. No hassle.

I get on the bus and enjoy the views as the A38 threads through the Devonshire countryside, the Teign estuary glistening in the distance. Around me passengers text and call, as those less familiar with English attempt the phrase 'Tiverton Parkway' to bewildered respondents. I explain my predicament to my wife in a text. Helpfully, she responds: *Try 'three coins in a fountain,'* referencing Steve Martin's unsuccessful attempts to entertain his fellow bus passengers in *Planes, Trains and Automobiles*.

Tiverton Parkway is a strange destination. Certainly nowhere near Tiverton, it nestles at the end of a country lane, past two farm shops, a driving range and next to a pond. As we swing into the station car park, the driver makes the observation that the train is due out in one minute so we should get a 'move on'. In our mass panic, the door then fails to open, adding several unnecessary seconds to our misery.

Happily, the train is several minutes late. As we wait by the whitethroats, pied wagtails and willow warblers, an automated announcement advises passengers not to board a train if they do not intend to travel. We nod to each other, agreeing that this is, indeed, sensible but somehow redundant advice. We begin to speculate that perhaps, several years ago, a group of bewildered shoppers meant to go out for bacon but found themselves irresistibly drawn to the 1045 to Skipton. The message continues to advise us that we should avoid boarding trains when we do not intend to travel, as this can cause delays and inconvenience. Immediately we share stories.

Funny how we've all had those moments: I was at home preparing dinner for the kids, when suddenly I had the urge to nip down to Tiverton Parkway and board the 1939 to Leeds, even though I didn't want to go there. Can you imagine the delays and inconvenience? Er, yes.

On the train, the manager cheerfully announces the destination stations while the snack bar manager counters this cheer with the news that he's closing. Never mind, it's only 1945. Immediately the train manager takes the crackling mic again. *I'm afraid that this train has failed and will be taken out of service at Bristol Temple Meads. There is, however, a replacement train and this will be waiting for us once we reach Bristol.* Ho-hum.

At Bristol, we board our third vessel and within minutes we're off again. I notice that we're actually still on time. Due in at 0100 hours. Late, but manageable. It means I've managed Leeds to Plymouth and back in a day. Quite an achievement, especially since the only other attempt to do that ended as another section in this book.

We're not exactly motoring along and hunger begins to bite. I look back towards the snack bar. The shutter is down and it looks like they've closed for the night. The train manager passes. He explains that all of the snack bars on Virgin Trains close at 2000 every day. I make a face not unlike my tomcat's when he's watching us eat seafood. *If you could just see your way to passing a few prawns down here.* He takes pity on me and retrieves what I take to be a 1st class snack pack from the silent snack bar and hands it to me. *Here, that'll keep you going.* It contains some fruitcake, a kitkat, some dried fruit, some orange juice and two *Tuc* cheese sandwich biscuits. Other passengers look on in horror, anticipating the gastro-intestinal chaos that is likely to ensue from such an imbalanced repast. But just as I bite into the fruitcake, the train manager takes the microphone again. *I'm sorry to announce that this train has also failed and will be taken out of service at Birmingham New Street.* He adds the now routine advice that another train will be waiting for us further down the platform and gives another apology. No supper, one bus and three trains – and I'm not even half way home.

Remarkably, among the debris of today's return journey, the seat reservation signs are flickering the correct data at passengers – so each stop ends with me arriving smoothly at seat D58, albeit with someone different in the seat behind me each time.

Train number three has a nice surprise for me. The occupant of the seat behind me is playing his music very loud. It's a rough DJ mix of 'Because of You', presumably recorded to see how many times the f word could be included in a song – and broadcast at just sufficient a level to make everyone else in the carriage strain their necks to stare at me. *Me? It's HIM behind me*, I try to convey with an unconvincing facial expression. I can't say anything, as he might stab me. His phone calls betray a certain frustration with the world, resulting in him leaving his girlfriend to take some time out in … Chesterfield. Chesterfield? Home of the Spireites and, one presumes, many more rejected urchins with a penchant for violent rap.

At Tamworth, just about everyone gets off, apart from the Wu Tang clansman and me. We're in adjacent seats. I reach for my magazine and perch nervously, waiting for the inevitably unpleasant racket to continue. At this point, seeing an opportunity to entertain us even further, the train manager announces that we're taking a diversionary route to Chesterfield, which is where I'm certain my fellow passenger will be leaving the train. Just as my feelings of unease rise, so the train manager's visits to the carriage decrease. But gloriously, the Lord intervenes, as we discover the intended destination is blocked. We revert to the main line and my friend disappears into the Chesterfield night, presumably to howl his anguish at the North Derbyshire moon.

Another text from Ana arrives: *Flintstone, meet the Flintstones!* I don't laugh.

It's now 2351. I have been on one bus and three trains and travelled from Plymouth to this unimpressive siding short of Sheffield. I look at my phone to check the time. Unbelievably, we're still on time, but we receive another call from the train manager.

It's 2356 and we've reached a place called Woodhouse, but we're subject to a points failure (now). This time there's no spare train down the line, or hope of any specific time to this delay. But they will keep us posted. At this point I notice two or three other fellow travellers. Maybe like me they've paid £122 for a saver return. Maybe they've paid the standard open return rate of nearly £200. God help them if they've paid nearly £500, which is what I was quoted for a first-class return from Leeds to Plymouth.

I look down at my newspaper. I've read it and re-read it several times now. As madness descends I start to see if I can detect any hidden messages in the type. Looking at the last letters of each line of the front-page headline I nearly make out the word 'leper' which would appear to have some relevance to my experience. But then my excitement is shattered upon discovering that the headline on page 2 reads 'rrkefs', which admittedly somewhat resists analysis.

The train manager visits us and shares the news that he has no idea how long we will be waiting here. *Until the maintenance team get out to help us*, he explains, *I only know as much as you do*. It's not been a good day, I offer innocently, trying to lighten the gloom. *It's been awful for ME*, he responds. Does he know who he's talking to? He might have had a 'bad day' but I'm spiralling into despair – and the contents of my stomach are now only minutes short of inevitable combustion.

I take a trip to the toilet – which has clearly been used as a secret smoking den, evidenced by the little stogie among the bogies – forgetting my troubles as I press the various automated door closing / opening buttons. The train lurches forward and I fall against the toilet door, pressing my new spectacles into my forehead. I take them off, return to my seat and inspect my face in the reflection of the window. It looks like I'm still wearing them. Two lifeless eyes gaze back at me from within a pair of ugly thick Eric Morecambe frames – except the frames are in my hand.

Things brighten up. We're now officially late, and the last encouraging text from my better half has suggested applying for compensation. Perhaps I *can* get my money back. So I'm a little disappointed that we've started again. It might have been fun in Woodhouse. I could have sold some shower curtain rings in exchange for a night in some out-of-town redneck motel. Or a Premier Inn. Or a Travelodge. But don't get me started on them. Last time I stayed in a Travelodge, there was a note explaining how they'd been able to keep the prices down. Many unnecessary extras had been removed from the rooms to allow a fair price for a minimalist experience. This included, as I discovered upon trying to sit down at the desk to work at my laptop, a chair.

At 0015 we're back on track and careering recklessly forward, Sheffield in sight. I look for a 'John Candy' to take joyfully home to my kids. We pass the tram depot. They all proudly wear the motif NOT IN SERVICE, as if to emphasise the pointlessness of UK public transport. Curiously, these signs are all lit up on individual trams.

Has there been a spate of bewildered Sheffielders trying to board inactive trams after the hours of darkness? Or do these people really not care about saving electricity?

Sheffield station moves slowly into view. There are only two more journeys on the screens, one of which is mine. When the last train to Manchester leaves, presumably the signs change to *no more trains; it's night time, you idiot* in bright neon letters. An announcement is made: *a warm welcome to those customers who have joined us at Sheffield. This is the 2359 train. If you do not wish to travel, please make your way back to the platform.* Yeah, yeah. Don't get on if you don't intend to travel. For that inevitable crowd of carousers who've appeared at platform 7 but don't know why – and who find themselves strangely drawn to our deserted carriage. Don't get on!

As the train reverses out of the station back whence we came, intent, one imagines, on making the little known Sheffield to Leeds journey via Whitby, a regret occurs to me. *Don't get on?* I wish I'd taken that advice this morning.

Written in real time on the laptop from seat D58 (three different trains)

2
Retails of the Unexpected

One of the analogies that occasionally stirs my audiences from their deep sleep concerns the proud parents of children who have announced their interest in pursuing a career in medicine, law or architecture. Every decisive step towards fulfilment of such dreams embeds the parental dream further. The dinner parties! The retirement cottage in the Cotswolds! The pride rushes around the psyche like a child on Christmas morning, but soon evaporates when your youngest delivers the following stern announcement: 'I'd like to work in retail.'

But surely retail work endows the individual with a refined cache of entrepreneurial know-how. It's not just a question of making eye contact and smiling (although, admittedly, that would be a start). It's about sales, marketing, merchandising, stock management, people management, inspiration, determination and imagination. A successful career in retail requires a combination of strong operational knowledge with an appreciation of the intangible, that is, that which makes customers come back and spend more. It's no coincidence that the likes of Theo Paphitis, one of the more instantly likeable and pragmatic *Dragons* from the TV series, has made his own particular fortune in this very sector.

*

The current boom in retail has provided some remarkable opportunities, whether you're a school-leaver, unemployed or already in the industry, to the extent that in one major UK city's central shopping mall, there are over a thousand vacancies over any one year. Every development presented to bewildered council officials contains at least some reference to retail space while new entrants into the market see opportunities everywhere.

Academically, new and innovative opportunities are emerging for youngsters wishing to excel in the industry while recent Government initiatives, such as the National Skills Academy, seek to combine knowledge and resources to unify progress and increase opportunities on the foundation of a strong skills set. And yet our hearts drop when our kids tell us they're doing 'till work'.

We've demeaned customer service in this country to the extent that the single most representative signal of a strong economy occupies the lower rankings on the 'most favoured career' lists and is blighted by a pall of aspirational indifference. Or at least, that's what my travels have uncovered.

I know it's an easy remark to make, but I believe that culturally we're not able to appreciate the true meaning of customer service and its role in our society. We're British and, by definition, non-confrontational. This may seem dimly relevant to the point about retail's low profile, but bear with me.

As any foreign visitor attending a British restaurant will attest, we are shy when it comes to offering constructive criticism. Our waitress will circle the table, often at inappropriate times like just before the starter has been served or shortly after coffee, and ask 'is everything all right for you?' Of course, that's only if you're lucky enough for your waiter to be anywhere near. The *Observer*'s restaurant critic, Jay Rayner, once memorably attributed the lack of attendant waiters in one restaurant to the immense size of the dining room ('perhaps they were obscured by the curvature of the Earth').

We may be contemplating a piece of fish so underdone that it is still making arrangements for the rest of the evening, but are we likely to make a fuss? Er, no. Unlike the situation over the Atlantic where, by this time, the customer will have called his lawyer, begun to take pictures and started to record conversations with his *cell phone*.

One critical area of business best practice that suffers as a result of this is customer feedback. Anyone knows that sound businesses are built upon a detailed knowledge of what matters to customers and how well (or otherwise) they are engaged by your service offering. Feedback surveys abound and almost every coffee shop I've visited lately has left small feedback cards for us to fill in. Where did they get that idea? Perhaps they've been to America recently. Not in the UK though, since I've heard that only a tiny percentage of these cards ever find themselves being completed – and often then only by a small, sad man with a form-filling fixation.

The other day we visited the Yorkshire Sculpture Park, a vast rolling array of striking artistry, some works at peace with their surroundings, some at odds. The sharp angles of the galleries give way to undulating pasture and there's a lake at the bottom of the valley. It's a good place to go *blackberrying* (a word, unsurprisingly, questioned by my no-doubt Home Counties-based spell-checker) and when the sun shines, as it did last Sunday, there can be few better places in the north of England for such invigorating fresh air and art.

But even this diamond in the sceptre of West Yorkshire cannot resist catching the bug. Having parked the car we paid for a parking ticket at the machine. I glanced up. There was a list of forbidden activities. Prohibited pastimes. Not one, not two, but more than several. No dogs off leads, no kite-flying, no this, no that. In such a great visitor attraction I felt let down. I'm proud of our immediate surroundings here in Yorkshire, but sometimes that negative instinct just can't help pushing through to the surface. It's as if Titus Salt, that great Victorian philanthropic industrialist whose kindness was only tempered by his fear of anyone ever actually *enjoying* themselves, had been resurrected as a signage consultant.

It would have been nice to read about something that we could do (like go to the visitor centre to get change for the car park). I recall a friend from Visit Britain telling me about the signs at the wonderful Eden Project. Instead of telling people 'don't walk on the grass,' the sign shows a little cartoon of someone nearly treading on a flower. As the flower shouts 'eek' the message is: *please keep to the footpaths*.

There are so many simple ways to improve the UK customer experience, but few organisations have taken those simple, yet decisive steps. There must be a reason why and I think my travels in UK customer service have begun to clarify an explanation.

In previous ramblings I've explored the high profile of customer service in other parts of the world and compared it with the paucity of passion here. In North America, there are many explanations for the better-than-average customer experiences reported. They range from the 'new frontier' rationale, which reasons that the aspirational nature of 'making it' has driven immigrants over the years to have a higher work ethos. Those who do, quickly establish the value of great service and put the theory into practice. Others argue that it is the tipping culture that creates the memorable visits while others say that American customers are much more demanding than their British counterparts.

What is clear from my research is that North American customers are much less tolerant of poor service. What is less clear is whether service over the water is as good as we sometimes make it out to be.

Teri, who says she works for a major clothing retail company, wanted to share what it's like to be 'on the other side of the counter.' She said she felt the need to 'defend customer service.'

'The truth of the matter is we do much better than we are given credit for,' she wrote, 'but the bad experiences are so easy to point out.

'We strive to provide the best possible customer service as that is what drives our business, but there are limits on what we should tolerate from customers. I will bend over backwards to make it right for you if you are polite and explain what outcome you are expecting. [But] I have been yelled at, cursed at and had my lineage questioned by angry customers. I can tell you that the experience is quite common. That type of customer can take their business elsewhere and I will not consider it a loss.'

This begins to clarify the situation as it clearly identifies one of the key drivers of the higher profile service enjoys in North America. The fact is that customers are far less tolerant of poor service over there than over here. Here, indifference is routinely greeted by an awkward smile whereas in the States recently, one unhappy customer reacted to slow service in his local diner by using the ketchup dispenser to write his frustration large on the formica table before him, before leaving to shorten his life elsewhere.

And if that didn't cheer you up, let's talk to Gary in Connecticut. He feels that 'customer service is dead,' believing that 'the lack of indispensable service is appalling today, but we allowed people to give us poor service for so long that many people do not even try (or possibly even know how) to provide even the basic good customer service [sic].'

Gary likes Nordstrom and McDonald's, though. 'The counter person who waits on me most mornings will always have my medium

black ice coffee waiting on the counter – before I even get in the door.'
Heartening indeed. Now were I routinely to visit the ubiquitous burger bar in the UK for breakfast, I could at least expect an icy stare, if
not an iced coffee.

Let's meet Leta, who handles technical support in North Carolina.
She says she constantly deals with customers who use 'loud, abusive
language'. She also gets calls from people who expect miracles from
her – in her opinion. 'We're technicians, not magicians,' she explains,
somehow forgetting that the rest of us out here believe that our laptops do indeed possess some dark magic, perhaps via a team of sprites
who live beneath the keyboard and see to it that my email works.

But with her customers' shoes on, Leta does have some issues with
customer service. 'I'm really annoyed that it takes me up to ten menus
(press one for sales, two for customer support, etc) to finally get to a
warm body, only to find that the warm body not only doesn't speak
English well enough to understand what I'm saying, but they are even
more ignorant of the problem than I am! Big business needs to be will-
ing to hire knowledgeable customer service representatives that thoroughly know the company's product and can talk to the consumer in
everyday English that is understandable.'

It's interesting that Leta appears to be answering her own question.
Given the increasing number of similar experiences I've suffered in
recent months, it would not be surprising for me to un-cage my pent-
up frustration in the vicinity of a representative who doesn't really
deserve it. Leta's explaining the context and letting all her fellow technical helpdesk colleagues know that the majority is spoiling it for the
minority. And speaking of minorities, it would appear that in the
USA, just as in the UK, it's the overseas contact centres that are causing the problem.

Let's fire ourselves across to the North West Pacific coast, Google
Earth-style, to Seattle, home of Frasier Crane and the currently splut-
tering Seahawks. David owned a camera store in the Seattle area for
36 years before retiring. His views reflect those of the other people
interviewed.

'Where is customer service? The consumer voted with his or her
wallet and opted to shop box stores, catalogue sales and the Internet.'

David believes that many of his customers would come in, pick the brains of his sales people and then order the item on line or from a discount store. The argument continues – if we want to keep our 'local corner gas station, clothing or book stores' then we have to start valuing service as well as price. And this coming from a resident of the country that proved that point in the first place.

Back in the UK, Martin Brampton offers some insightful opinions on why there are so many frustrated customers around. He argues that it's not to do with outsourcing, but a result of some bigger issues. A couple of years ago you will recall BT accusing its customers of racial prejudice towards its Indian call centres. This is distracting, in Brampton's view, as it takes us away from the fundamental problem. 'The whole question of how large organisations interface with their customers needs an overhaul.'

Brampton's view, which has some currency among those of us who have worked for any length of time in a large organisation, is simple. 'The fundamental problem, as we all know, is that for all the talk of the supremacy of the customer, most large companies want to take the maximum amount of money for the minimum amount of deliverable. And customer service fails because it has little connection with achieving that minimum amount of deliverable.'

Martin (www.silicom.com) continues: 'For the most part, people do not contact organisations such as BT until there is a problem or a question. We are then forced to deal with a group that is clearly at arm's length from the functional areas of the organisation. The geographic separation of outsourced "service" centres only emphasises the operational detachment that affects even UK-based centres. In the specific case of BT, only a minority of employees seem to understand the company's service offerings.'

Sadly, all of my experiences underline the points above. BT appears to exist purely to spite us. The fingers of colleague after colleague, friend after friend, visibly twist into unnatural knots of fury, as they recount amazing tales of failure. One friend received a letter confirming his impending house move. The only problem was that he wasn't planning to move. However, simply contacting BT to point out this error set him on the inevitable path of confusion: broken English, broken promises and, ultimately, one broken spirit. Others are simply frightened to pick up the phone, even when things are going wrong, as they fear they'll be similarly stung. Again and again BT makes unscheduled appearances in the consumer pages, lambasted for service failures. Again and again (and, on my reckoning, at least on a biennial basis and as recently as February 2008) it blames problems on a 'new customer management system'. At least we've pinpointed the incompetence as residing among the folk who approved the 'upgrade'.

But let's not single out BT, as it appears there are other telecoms companies equally bent on a frenzy of failure, incompetence and stubbornness. Take Talk Talk (and I wish someone would). Last night my wife received a phone call. 'We've got some good news for you,' said a lady, apparently far away geographically (and equally distant from the English language). 'Because you're such valued customers of Talk Talk, we're going to give you free telephone calls and free broadband for life – for £20-odd a month.'

As my wife tried to reconcile the multiple mentions of the word 'free' with the phrase 'monthly cost', it occurred to her to explain that we were currently half way through a broadband contract. At this point the caller simply told my wife she could pay a charge to get out of that contract. 'But I'm happy with it,' protested Ana.

Sadly – but not surprisingly to anyone who has accidentally picked up their telephone at home in the evening – the caller would not let it lie. 'I'd rather leave it for six months and then re-consider,' said my wife. 'Why would you do that when you can pay a charge to get out of your existing contract now?' continued the caller. 'Because I don't want to,' responded my wife. This exchange continued until the point when my wife asked if she could end the phone call as she didn't want to carry on. The caller ignored this, but a third party stepped in and ended the call. What was Martin Brampton saying about the maximum amount of money for the minimum deliverable?

Insistent cold callers are becoming a nuisance. Not because the call itself is unwelcome (and I know I could register with the Telephone Preference scheme) but because an increasing number of callers will not take a polite decline as an answer. The fact that increasing numbers of us now prefer to share a far less polite form of decline with them is surely a testament to their falling levels of professionalism.

If someone calls, I listen and then share my conclusions. I allow them to attempt to 'overcome objections' or to clarify that I've understood the offer. If they still insist on peddling their wares after this point I advise them that I'm about to hang up. When I inevitably do hang up, it usually catches the caller mid-sentence. And I derive no pleasure from this.

The most recent recalcitrant caller belonged to Southern Electric. Having offered to beat my current package, I explained that I was not interested. She was astonished that I would not simply go with the cheapest provider, but preferred one that provided a half-decent service. Curiously, in continuing to debate the issue, she demonstrated how far away Southern Electric were from delivering a half-decent service. If politeness and respect is such a difficulty, imagine how hard it must be for them to send some electricity down a tube towards me. I asked to end the call, but she insisted. I asked again. She kept going. I put the phone down and emailed a complaint using the contact page I found on the offending company's website.

A day or so later a polite response explained that they hadn't appreciated I was on the Telephone Preference list and they apologised for calling me. Unfortunately, they were responding to someone else's complaint, as I'd made no mention of this and didn't subscribe to this service anyway (otherwise I wouldn't be able to share my wonderful adventures with you all).

Perhaps they'd been sold some algorhythmically enhanced automated-response software by some enterprising IT firm, but they got it wrong again (and it doesn't work), so I emailed a second time. This time the serious response kicked in, with promises of an investigation. Reassuring perhaps? No. I wouldn't touch any organisation that is obviously putting its outbound callers under so much pressure that they believe this sort of behaviour is acceptable.

Another irritating tradition is the daily 'silent' call. Every day I receive at least five unwanted 'outbound' calls. Two of them result in the phone being put down the minute I answer, one falls into the Southern Electric bracket and one unsuccessfully charms me with extended silence. The silent calls are very annoying, especially as some are intent on withholding their number, so you can't identify them when you dial 1471. The ones that hadn't thought of that can usually be found via a quick Google search – and usually featured on a consumer website advising people of scams, sales tricks and worthless offers.

The fifth one at least allows me to exercise my anger in a therapeutic fashion. This is the call that, in order to save money (one imagines), consists solely of a pre-recorded message, usually delivered by the same woman that resides in your SatNav and opening with the phrase 'Were you aware …?' I don't know how the call continues, because by this point I have usually responded with an impressive tirade of obscenities.

And the worry is – they're all at it. Take the focus of follow-up calls that banks, for example, make, ostensibly to collect your feedback on a recent transaction, for it is indeed one of these calls that has just roused me from my laptop.

My view of the state of the majority of 'outbound calling' operations in the UK is that it is run by incompetent, morally corrupt, spineless speculators. I've only avoided registering on the Telephone Preference Scheme to allow me to collect examples and complete my research, but if someone were to offer technology that would allow me to send a massive electric shock, James Bond-style, back up the phone to the Head of the organisation calling me, I'd pay top whack for that.

But what of the less shady operators, such as our leading banks? Recently, I managed to key in my Personal Identification Number (PIN) on my NatWest Gold Card incorrectly for the third time. As the equally bewildered readers out there will no doubt have learned to their dismay, this is an all too frequent occurence. I offer a simple solution to the bank: do not produce Maestro cards and Gold cards in exactly the same colour and style. I'd taken out my Gold card by accident, thinking it was my Maestro card and proceeded to enter the wrong PIN. After I'd repeated this feat twice further the card was automatically blocked at a time when my charge card was dangerously near my monthly limit. At the time I was in Marks and Spencer's looking for some boots for my daughter. I rang my wife to see if she had access to NatWest's website and to see what I should do to have the PIN unblocked (you see, I know all of the terminology). She explained that I needed to call their Customer Services team, then gave me the number and a kindly M&S employee gave me a piece of paper and a pen so I could write it down.

So, at approximately 5pm on Wednesday 9th January 2008, I made the call. The IVR kicked in and I had three simple choices. I dialled the appropriate number and waited ... and waited. After around 30-40 seconds a recorded voice apologised for the delay, reiterated the importance of my call and returned me to the frenetic classical refrain that accompanies such interminable waits. Again, another 30-40 seconds passed, the apology repeated itself and I slumped against an equally bored-looking mannequin on the second floor of the Oxford Street branch of M&S. Thirteen further automated apologies were received before a man picked up the phone and dealt with my query in a matter of seconds. Do the calculation yourself (please). You'll discover I had a wait of 10 minutes.

So now, two days later, I am roused from my laptop to answer a polite enquiry about my 'recent transaction with NatWest' – probably by an employee of a third party contractor who's won the feedback business by undercutting all of the other bidders. The conversation is pleasant, the approach professional but the questions are so closed and so plainly designed to elicit such easily computable results, that I find it difficult to explain why the assistant could not have done more when I called – but why I gave the experience 3 out of 10.

Your people are great – but I don't think it's acceptable for a Gold Card customer to have to wait 10 minutes, on a mobile phone, at 5pm on a winter's evening, just to have his PIN unblocked. There are several questions asking if I wouldn't mind being approached by NatWest in relation to other products and services (no) or whether they could add my data to other information they have about me (yes) but no opportunity to provide a freeform reading of the big disappointment factor. Yes, it's great that you ring customers to get their feedback, but you've designed the process completely to meet your own internal convenience, rather than making it easy for the customer most accurately to convey the tangible and intangible elements of their recent experience. Hats off to you for ringing so closely after the event – I can recall it all with blinding clarity – but who's concluded that the length of time the customer waits before being put through does not count among the most significant customer 'moments of truth'?

Elsewhere, particularly in the car industry, the effectiveness of the feedback call process is rendered 'nil' by the fact that salesmen routinely explain, upon handing over the keys to your new car, that you will shortly receive a feedback call. If you give them top marks, they beseech you, then they will receive their bonus. Irrespective of the dire service one may have received up to this particular point, your personal expectations and perceptions must now be relegated, for fear that the smooth-talking shyster sat opposite you may not have enough cash to upgrade to HD 1080.

Two colleagues have recently bought cars at two different dealerships in the north of England. At each 'hand over' this incredible cameo is played out. How on earth can this car company expect to derive any value from this process when it is being subverted by its own people – presumably concerned that the 'typical' customer experience may lead to expressions of indifference, once the dreaded call is made. Only a short step from here to salesmen ringing the third party outbound-calling company and offering them a bribe to 'fix' the data.

The problem is that, for one of the customers, the salesman had made the promise that he would make a follow-up call to the customer 'every two weeks' during the period of time required to deliver the car, just to reassure the customer. The calls never came, but the customer was still presented with a request to provide positive feedback.

The noise you can now hear is the sound of my head being banged against my desk as I've suddenly realised that our polite British approach requires that we oblige these salesmen and give them the feedback they have requested. What an effective process! How many senior automobile executives are enjoying the benefits of this artificially inflated customer feedback? The richer they get, the poorer the service their companies give.

Friends visited the other evening and the conversation quickly turned to cars. I'd spotted that one of my guests no longer had her

Mercedes, but now drove a Volkswagen Golf. Being male, I drew a series of conclusions largely focusing on the penile prowess of such a vehicle: its horsepower, trim, extras, etc. The response should not have surprised me. It was due to the poor level of service she received when she first bought the car. On one of the many occasions it broke down, she was given a Smart Car as a replacement, but one containing the unexpected bonus of cigarette debris and a cushion of dog hair (and the accompanying fragrance).

Upon complaining, she received a dour refrain of disenchantment from the assistant she was addressing. He explained that BMW treated their staff better, implying that she should not be surprised at the poor level of service. Before Mercedes' lawyers get on the phone, let me hasten to add that I've no reason to predict that current service levels will be as bad, but as the old saying goes, better buy good service than a 'good' car.

Easy to sit and criticise (I hear you criticise) so let's put this to the test. We needed a new car, so instead of leaping before we looked (a tendency that's produced a series of hysterically inept car choices), we opted to perform as the 'investigative customer' and spend some time looking into our options. This we did during August 2007, having narrowed down our list to SEAT, Audi, BMW and Volkswagen. We needed a reliable car, so that we could run the kids around, shop and pick up from school easily (our P-reg Polo having started to investigate its retirement options). Yes, I know we should be walking (or gliding around zeppelin-fashion beneath a cushion of inflated plastic shopping bags), but no one goes to their closest school anymore.

We started at SEAT, having discovered through some reviews that one or two of their models ran the Golf close for performance. Here, as everywhere, the 'look and feel' of the establishment is strong: a sharp, attractively designed showroom, peopled by a couple of employees sitting at desks. Having walked around one model and displayed some early 'buying' signals, we were disappointed not to be approached by an assistant. We had to go to them to ask them questions. From the opening exchange, it was clear that we would have to push the conversation and engineer responses by explaining our detailed needs. There was no attempt on the part of the employee to understand our fundamental needs. How many miles do you antici-pate driving? Will it be a motorway car or a 'round the doors' vehicle? How long are you likely to want to own the car? None of these ques-tions was asked; we were simply pointed to a range of vehicles in a bright, printed brochure and told what the prices were.

At no point – and I stress this – was the employee indifferent or unhelpful. They had simply entered 'passive' phase and were not going to expend the effort required to make a full understanding of their customer's needs. The conversation was conducted standing up at a form of reception desk. No drinks were offered; nor were seats. Nothing to keep the kids occupied either. In and out in a few minutes.

From there we went to the Volkswagen franchise where we were met by a more enthusiastic salesman. 'Take a seat,' he offered, the minute it became clear we were interested in a particular model. The kids were shown to a small recreational area in the showroom and we were invited to have a coffee, while Daddy internally speculated over the wisdom of responding to the statement 'take a seat' with 'but I want a Volkswagen.'

At this point a more natural example of 'conversational selling' took place. Interested in what we did, what our company was up to and what our plans were, the salesman made us feel that any recommen-dation would be based on a comprehensive knowledge of 'where we were at'. We felt comfortable with the advice and felt under no pres-sure to commit – we should continue our research and come back with any questions. It was clear from a comment my wife made that this car was currently occupying the top of the list, so the salesman could let us walk off with some confidence that we would return (and he had all of our details as an extra layer of security).

At the BMW showroom, where we were showing some interest in the 1 series, the response was eager and focused, though infused with a touch of complacency, it has to be said. We'd not visited a BMW showroom before and were naively staggered at some of the vehicles on show. But within minutes of displaying some interest in the 1 series, we were outside, about to take the keys of one and sizzle around the streets of the town. The car felt great and drove well, but size-wise, we could have had more space. The boot seemed small, even when contemplating a week's shopping, never mind a trip abroad.

Getting to a deal was quick – almost vertiginously so. Within seconds of establishing a budget, deals were on the table, eager to befriend us. Taking a deep breath and recognising the benefit of the quality of the drive but seeing the space as a problem, we explained that it was something we would think about.

'Have you had a chance to think about the car?' came the call from the BMW salesman, just a few days later. He meant business, but by now we'd committed to the car that ticked most, if not all of our boxes (the box remaining empty being the *ridiculously cheap* one).

Audi was a more relaxed experience altogether. Our host had charm and an exotic accent, which added to the memories I'm recalling now. He found us out in the car lot inspecting one of the vehicles, invited us in, sat us down, offered coffee and, again, started to assess what it was we needed from our car. Having shared our mental tick-list with him (and emphasised the *ridiculously cheap* box), it quickly became clear that when comparing the A3 with the Golf, the latter was giving us more car for the same price. Impressively, he came to the conclusion openly and honestly, suggesting that when the time was right, we check in and think about upgrading to an A4.

From here, we went back to the Volkswagen franchise to open negotiations and also my wallet (from which flew the obligatory solitary moth). As I mentioned previously, we were told that we would receive a fortnightly update, between ordering the car and the car being delivered to the dealership. To show good faith, we left a deposit (paid by credit card) and congratulated ourselves on having, at least, pursued a semi-serious assessment of all of our options, instead of lurching forward at the first car to present itself.

Two weeks passed and there was no update. I began to wonder what the update would actually be. We knew it was going to be about 12 weeks before the car arrived, so would the update be a human, calling to tell us '8 weeks now', '6 weeks now' etc. While the customer focus is admirable, perhaps we were talking 'redundant' here. Nevertheless, in the hope that the update might be some unexpectedly exhilarating experience, we waited. I'd like you to believe that we were there, poised by the phone, every week, with bated breath, but to tell you the truth, the frenzied excitement soon simmered down to an irritated concern, followed by absolute indifference, as no calls were received.

The exact chronological position of what happened next eludes me now after so many months, but, in a nutshell, we were called and asked for our deposit. 'But we gave you the credit card details when we ordered the car,' I protested. 'Yes, but we weren't able to process them, since the law only allows us to hold on to the card details for a month and it's been more than two since you ordered the car.' And yet, we had been under the impression that the deposit was a deposit, to be debited and used towards the purchase. 'No problem,' I continued, 'take them again.' So perhaps the update calls would have uncovered this little flaw in the process and made things easier for organisation and customer alike.

*

Making things easy for customers has always, for me, been a central principle of good customer service. 'Easy to do business with' – that's a strategy for which we'd all happily vote. And yet, our experiences continue to present numerous examples of organisations whose processes tie both themselves and their customers in knots of Gordian proportions, the like of which would baffle the creator of the Rubik's Cube.

Later in this book, in what was originally one of my *Yorkshire Post* columns, I reveal the experience of my pal Andy and what happened when shortly after ordering and paying for a new cooker, he opted to return to the till and buy the matching cooker hood. As you may have guessed by now, we may have put a man on the moon, but the company were unable to unite both items in a way that had them delivered to the customer in one dispatch.

Our experiences reveal contrasting approaches, from the obvious focus on ease of our major supermarkets (reward-card points can now be collected with a key fob, to make it easier for us and we can check out our own goods, if we want to, and if we're in a hurry. Easy!). But if anyone has ended up seeing a purchase through at Ikea and been directed to their 'warehouse' they'll know things don't always go so smoothly.

Ikea has, for me, always been a bit of a curate's egg. My family quite enjoy making the three-mile trip down the M62 to our nearest store, but I've always had a problem (thus possibly rendering me incapable of objectively assessing the organisation). For most of us, the working week precludes visits to places like Ikea, as we're simply so busy. So we go at the weekend and the experience is chastening. My memories of Ikea are clouded by long waits outside car parks and scenes reminiscent of rush-hour tube chaos, with hundreds of us fighting over tiny plastic teaspoons which, everyone concurs, are 'a bargain and well designed, too.'

Recently, at the behest of my considerably better half, we returned, to purchase some shelves and (yet) another extension to the CD bookcase. Trying to contain my insane mutterings, we walked in on a quiet Tuesday morning, late November 2007. Inside we calmly identified the items we required, breathed a massive sigh of satisfaction upon discovering we wouldn't have to go to the separate warehouse and made our way to the tills.

Our purchases came to about £35, so I offered my credit card. Basking in the satisfaction of having proved that I could get around Ikea without whingeing about something, I smiled at the cashier. 'There's a surcharge on all credit card payments' she asked. I can't remember what the figure was, but felt confident to correct her. 'I imagine that's when you use a card to spend less than a fiver, isn't it?'

I was wrong. 'No,' she continued, 'it's for all purchases regardless of the amount.' 'Why?' I asked, as my wife began to sink disconsolately into depression. 'It seems a bit much,' I added, referring both to the cost and the cheek of it all. 'Well,' she continued, drawing closer to us as if to impart a secret, 'the *powers that be* (her emphasis) have decided that this is for the cost of administering credit card payments.' Proudly I marched back to the car. 'If you say *what did I tell you* once more, I'll be forced to run over you in my new car,' declared my darling partner, while I struggled to stifle a large bout of self-satisfaction.

What was interesting about this particular experience was the concept of employees openly sharing concerns about a recent 'innovation' at their organisation. It's happened in a number of places: from football stadia, where we've been warned by stewards that the food is 'over-priced and not very good,' to a recent visit to Debenhams, where they've decided to drop their membership of the Nectar Points scheme and launch their own reward system.

I would have misgivings with this, as one of the only reasons I ever go to Debenhams, is when there's a sale and because I can get some points (sad life that I have). When sharing this observation with the lady serving me last weekend, she agreed. 'If you could use it at super-markets and to get petrol, I'd go for it,' I began. 'Yep, that would be good, but it's only going to be for purchases here.'

Having concurred that the Nectar card met this particular cus-tomer's needs and that the new system would probably lead to us not visiting as regularly, I wondered how the thinking behind the new scheme had evolved. Surely, apart from confirming how gullible we customers are, one major success of reward-card schemes has been in their omnipresent use via multiple-partner schemes. To go back to one and one only, may turn out to be a retrograde step for Debenhams in more ways than one.

In fact, as I inspected some of the cologne on sale at Debenhams, I found myself thinking aloud, 'Might be the same price at Boots, but I can use my Advantage card.' Now, in itself, that might be contradicto-ry. I'm arguing against single-establishment reward schemes, but opt-ing for one right now. Fair point, but the fact is Boots got there first, and the need to visit Boots very often (children and all that) means that it's in my mind when I shop there. Debenhams isn't a regular des-tination for me and this recent move certainly hasn't been designed to have me returning with any more frequency.

Ease of doing business has become one of the great differentiators since I penned *Inconvenience Stores* and a quick analysis of our shop-ping habits reveals one or two fundamental changes.

In fact, the two main changes are the words 'Abel' and 'Cole'. The reader may recognise these words as completing the title of one of our organic vegetable delivery services, but our attachment to the business is more to do with ease than it is with some middle-class environ-mental bent (as much as I'd like you to try and believe I'm middle-class). Previously, we'd collect our vegetables from a local farm, about three miles away – a small, family business with a narrow but suffi-cient range of seasonal produce. We'd collect our box, use the veg, return the box and repeat, probably spending about ten pounds a week. There was the added attraction of the family pet, a dog rescued from the streets and who loved children (especially seasoned with salt and pepper). As is often the case with organic food, we'd often be let down by the odd dodgy onion or would unpeel a garlic clove to reveal a soft, grey centre (novel, but unhelpful when preparing dinner), but we used the service – letting them know a week ahead if we would be repeating the order or if we were away.

Having come across Abel & Cole in a newspaper article and read something about being able to order on line and make up your own vegetable box, Ana and I spent a few minutes on a quick recce, navi-gating through the website and discovering that you could go as far as nominating those vegetables that you didn't like, so they would never be sent.

As my son pointed out, we were not helping the environment by travelling 6 miles every week to collect the vegetables, so we gently let the current suppliers down (the hardest part) and had a 'test flight' with our potential future supplier.

At the appointed time on the chosen day, the van pulls up (on bio-fuel, I tell you) and a kindly person carries the cardboard box of veg-etables to our door, taking away the empty flat-packed box from the previous week. The quality of drivers does fluctuate, but always flick-ers back and forth within the *polite and courteous* spectrum.

Making changes is easy, but it had yet to face, for me, what is the single greatest opportunity any business faces: how it would deal with a problem or complaint?

As was the case with our previous provider, one of the habitual problems of purchasing organic vegetables is that they don't general-ly match supermarkets and traditional greengrocers for consistency of quality. It's generally been a price worth paying, from our perspective at least, but a few weeks ago, it came to pass that I was unhappy with my celery. No, that's not a misspelling (I'm happy with my income, as you ask, but could always manage more). It was simply a poor-quality batch of celery that had found its way into my cardboard box. Now I know many of you would argue that there are more pressing cases of concern in the world today, but bear with me.

Having checked the website, I discovered that you could email your concerns or complaints, so this I did. What impressed me was the personal tone of the response, which came only a few hours later. Clearly I had not been responded to by any kind of algorhythmically designed complaint robot, but by a real person. One with a sense of humour too, I was subsequently to discover, when I sent a 'thank you' email later. 'No, thank YOU,' came the second reply. Ana looked on, shaking her head as she does when she thinks I've found a new friend.

Strangely enough, as I write this, I receive an email from Abel & Cole suggesting some Mother's Day gifts and recipes. Yep, it's only a few days away (but how did they know I had a mother? Perhaps they just guessed).

The bottom line for Abel & Cole is money and, in this case, the bottom line for us is that we're staying. We know the quality is as good as you can get when buying organic. They're easy to do business with, seem to have a human heart and deal very well with complaints. What did they actually do? They simply refunded the money paid for the celery without question or delay – and asked if there was anything more they could do for us.

With some of our larger organisations, the sense that doing business will be a pain, a challenge or downright impossible, does influence our behaviours. Last night BT called me, offering a good deal were I to keep their broadband package for another 12 months. I think it involved free extra services, a free gift and a home hub (I'll tell you what that is when I see it). So what happens in my mind when I'm presented with these options? Do I conjure up an image of the modern family in their adverts, the knowing winks, smiles and undercurrent of passion? Or, do I think it'll probably all be too much hassle in the end? For me BT is at its best when I'm not dealing with it – and I wonder how many other customers feel the same way. They've never truly pulled the rug from under me, but every time I've changed something, upgraded or simply tried to contact the right person, it's cost me half a day's time at least.

Last night they phoned me with this offer, so I asked if they could email the details as I was busy with my family. Think about it. There was no real reason for me to resist the offer and to conclude it over the telephone but subconsciously I vacillated. Something stopped me and the fact that this happens should sound alarm bells for BT. Perhaps their one advantage, if it can be described that way, is the fact that many other competitors are perceived as equally unreliable. I'll wait for the email (and they quoted the correct email address) and follow the offer through, but with a degree of trepidation. Three months later, it still hasn't arrived.

Many of the more impressive stories of 'ease of doing business' have come about as a direct result of the omnipresence and omnipotence of the Internet. Abel & Cole may be nice people, but the online ordering and account maintenance makes it different. The Internet has institutionalised 'ease of doing business' for a great deal of successful organisations, but it's those whose employees see this principle as key to the customer experience that truly do stand out. And there are, in our experience, very few of them.

It won't come as an exciting relevation for the reader to learn that our rail infrastructure and the companies operating within it are not the easiest to do business with. Indeed several of the articles that follow focus on some personal horror stories. But while they are often the result of infrastructure failings, delays and/or overcrowding, I want to focus on the early stages of the customer journey.

I generally use the term 'customer journey' when extolling the virtues of putting oneself in the customer's shoes for a good length of time, given the previously mentioned benefits of the new objectivity that such activity brings. However, in this case, we really are referring to movement – transport and the act of getting safely from A to B at a good price consistently.

So first impressions count. Imagine, therefore, that you are visiting the UK for the first time and want to travel by train around the country. Elsewhere in Europe, the standard approach of paying one basic fare applies. But not here. It can take the train guard several minutes to explain the complexities of the ticket situation. It may be that some tickets are valid on the train and some aren't. Some have to be booked on specific trains and some don't. You can pay more for a second class open return than an advanced first-class ticket. And that's only the beginning. Given the concerned looks of fellow passengers, as they check their tickets, I often wonder what it must be like for visitors from abroad, who don't have English as their first language. What impression does that give them? But let's return to the present tense to explore how well parts of the transport industry handle problems and complaints – that key part of ease of business.

In November 2007, National Express takes over the franchise for the East Coast mainline from GNER. But the new website doesn't like my laptop and it takes us several weeks to be able to use it. In the process I decide to buy some tickets on line from www.thetrainline.com. Previously I've used it to identify when trains are leaving, before buying over the phone, but as my confidence increases, so does my readiness to transact on line.

As I type in my requirements, I notice that an earlier email address is being held. I try to correct it and continue through the booking procedure. Upon trying to purchase there is a problem and the screen doesn't change and doesn't show the ticket purchase details. I decide to abandon the purchase, wait to see if any email confirmation comes through and try again. My second attempt is more successful. Now holding the right email address, the system obliges me by confirming the purchase of my return journey to London and I await the email confirming this. Moments later two emails arrive. Each one confirms a separate journey. It transpires later that the first order did go through and was confirmed to an email address I no longer have (and the one I tried to correct). The second has come through correctly to the new email address. A duplicate purchase. Panicking, I root through the website to try and find out how to cancel one of the journeys. It's not easy, so I end up calling the appropriate number and am greeted by a distant voice, both in geography and in terms of interest. I explain my predicament in as much detail as I can muster. In stuttering English, the assistant gives an explanation that illustrates plainly that he has not been listening at all. The tone is that it's clearly my fault and I should behave. It doesn't feel 'easy' at all. I do get to cancel one of the journeys, however, and some ten days later, the money is finally returned to my account. In addition to having to wait so long for my own money back, the lack of empathy, familiarity with English and ability to listen were just three of the concerns swimming around my mind.

The Trainline might be a good place to check timetables, but in the ease of doing business stakes, it's a clear case of 'could do better'. The Internet is capable of endowing a sense of simplicity and convenience, but it must be matched by the employees themselves. This experience is painful, regardless of whether we may attribute it to 'overseas contact centre' syndrome.

When I do take the train, my destination is usually a hotel. Sometimes, it's out of necessity, as I might be away for two or three days. Often though, it's because it's cheaper to travel late in the day, stay overnight and come back, than to take the morning train to London with an open return. From where I am, it would cost at least £150 to get an open return, leaving in the morning and coming back in the afternoon, whereas I can get two singles for about £20 each and a night in a hotel for £90. Add a restful night and a lie-in to the package (and get one first-class advance single ticket for an extra tenner) and you have a good deal. I hope you're paying attention, as there'll be a quiz later.

The hotels are therefore enjoying a boom period. Budget chains such as Premier Inn and Travelodge are experiencing good times and a number of other competing brands such as Purple and Days Inn are taking their share of the market too. So let's explore some of my recent hotel experiences.

There's nothing quite so dispiriting as having your hopes dashed. Perhaps your recently promoted football team has begun a relegation dogfight somewhat ahead of schedule. Perhaps you've bought the new Eagles album (and then listened to it) or shelled out the £900 it costs to operate one of those new iPhones. It all sounded so alluring, yet deflating in delivery. Apple, it's claimed by its US-based detractors, used to represent an anti-establishment Microsoft, but now it's become as depressingly money-oriented as the people it once stood against.

Following this theme, it's also quite wearing to discover that the *Oxford English Dictionary*'s description of a hotel is *an establishment providing accommodation and meals for payment.* But my guinea pig hutch could equally be described that way. My little ginger beast gets meals and accommodation and, in exchange for this, the kids get to take him out, put him on Dad's head and speculate about how this remarkable new hairpiece would be received in public. But before the Guinea Pig Defence League start to surround my semi-detached, let me point out my main contention here. Hotels may only provide accommodation and meals for payment, but in order for us to return repeatedly, they need to do a little more by way of customer engagement. And from recent experiences, some of them need to do a lot.

In November I was invited to speak at a conference in South Wales. It's one of my favourite parts of the country, as it's almost exactly like my native North East England with its mining heritage, great sporting rivalries, friendly folk and an accent that no one else can fathom. The company who booked me to appear kindly provided accommodation at a local hotel, part of a well-known national chain. We were all to meet there the night before the event, dine together and relax. One of the party had planned ahead and booked a table, so at the appointed time, we left the bar en masse and moved to the restaurant. It was quiet. 'Ah, good,' I said to myself. 'At least we can rely on their full attention.'

I wasn't wrong. Within seconds a waitress approached the table. With the demeanour of a woman who could start an argument in an empty room, she surprised us with a pair of direct questions: 'Who is the leader of this group? Who's going to be paying? We don't want you all wandering off.'

A simple *hello and welcome to our hotel restaurant* would have sufficed, but perhaps they'd been sponsored to perform their own interpretation of *Tenko* for Children In Need. Being British, we meekly acceded to her dramatic request and pointed out a rather bemused-looking senior manager, before sitting back nervously and preparing to receive more orders.

The food itself was fine, albeit dressed in a sort of language designed to lift it above the drudgery of ordinary life: like a Gregg's savoury on an undercover visit to a Michelin-starred restaurant. In the real world, my favourite is called 'Corned Beef Pastie' but in

Hotel-world it adopts the intriguing soubriquet of 'Cured Beef Pâté Nestling in a Case of Mille Feuille pastry'. Such was the case with my dessert. Called 'Nutmeg and Custard Tartlet with raspberries', it turned out to be a mini-custard tart (possibly one of a pack of four). More *feuille* me!

A more descriptive menu might have read: Sour grapes served with spilt milk accompanied by a bitter tart. Now that feels better. For dessert? Have your cake and eat it.

Elsewhere in the restaurant a concerted effort to distract guests from the futuristic extras and welcoming décor was under way. Opportunities to engage were missed. A box of poppies sat on the reception desk, but no one made reference to it or used it to generate a warm exchange. One felt that the fact that we'd secured a group discount meant that somehow any additional human extras were now no longer part of the package. One guest complained that his bedroom smelled of ammonia. I think the bitterness was simply a natural indication of their preferred ambience.

And yet recently I returned to Tyneside and stayed in a Premier Inn. To the uninitiated, this used to be a Travel Inn, before beginning a *Doctor Who*-style regeneration and becoming a Premier Travel Inn. The ladies on the reception desk were warm and engaging, as a series of visiting Irish Sunderland fans requested taxi information. Breakfast was a delight. It was set out buffet-style, but a friendly and pro-active woman stood by, asked us what we *didn't* like (interesting opening line, but it speeds up the process no end), served us and asked us what we were doing for the weekend and if we were having a good time. All of this and a view of the revitalised Tyne too.

Back in the *Hotel de Gloom*, I pondered the differences between the more expensive hotel with its sophisticated technological extras and modernist décor and the minimalist Quayside residence. It was the latter whose basic offering most closely matched the *OED* description, but it was the unadvertised but necessary extras that made us want to return soon.

Versions of the above scenarios have been played out over a number of recent hotel visits, with the result that the budget chains have recognised that price alone will not sustain their market share – they must compete on service. Given that their business model does not predicate hundreds of staff (you don't see bellboys at a Premier Inn, unless they're there on a stag weekend), the pro-action, engagement and ownership required of the few staff present must be top-quality.

With the more established, more expensive hotel chains inarguably possessing the better facilities, from the quality of the room to the 'extras' (like the kids' goodie bags you could pre-order from the Marriott at Regent's Park and which made such an impression when they were handed to our two tired but excited children), there would appear to be something for everyone. But some of the more established chains appear to believe that the 'extras' mean that service is less important.

Many would tut and point to past success with corporate reservations, but the budget chains are now offering corporate accounts and, to my eyes at least, are increasing their share of this valuable market. *Past* success indeed. But the future may see a different picture emerging as companies tighten their belts in response to the current general economic uncertainty.

Ease of doing business is therefore a key to success. Customers will trade other perceived benefits for the convenience of the hassle-free experience. But the Internet is not the only pre-requisite. Human ownership and a willingness to sort out problems must be present. And present it was last week when I sat plotting Ana's Valentine's Day at my laptop.

Picture the scene, if you will. It's the evening of Tuesday 12th February 2008 and I'm spending a distracted couple of hours at the laptop. Life is hard, especially when you're trying to work, keep abreast of the Live Update section of the Sky Sports website and hoping (but failing) to avoid opening iTunes and sampling a bit of something you read about in *Mojo*. And, on top of that, I'm thinking about how to make sure Ana has a memorable Valentine's Day, while I'm chairing a conference in London. Come to think of it, my absence would probably be a start ...

But I decide to send some roses, courtesy of the Interflora website. Twelve beautiful stems (and a little pink teddy bear for my daughter) look lovely, so I'm soon keenly (and surreptitiously) keying away, for my sweetheart is but ten yards away, upstairs having a bath. The only other person in the office is Cheddar, our guinea pig, who's been brought indoors (from his penthouse in the garage) to survive his fourth Bradford winter. Normally, his ferreting about doesn't bother me much, but on this occasion, every time he jumps or squeaks, I lurch forward to cover the laptop screen with a piece of paper, should Ana be about to enter the room. Carefully, I negotiate each section of the website, keying in the detail and checking back to make sure I'm following the instructions correctly. I enter my chosen message for the gift tag, enter my credit card details, and like a speeding gazelle in graceful flight, Ana flies downstairs and begins to ask a question of me as she approaches the office door.

Looking back, my reaction is comical, if not somewhat effective. I push the laptop screen down, to avoid being caught *interflora*grante. As it turns out, she doesn't enter the room, but walks off in the other direction. My sigh of relief is so audible, neighbouring residents hurriedly check their gas pipes for leaks.

I lift up the screen. I've gone off-line. I curse audibly. Neighbours relax, but I don't. I've managed to cut off the connection at the moment of paying. I re-connect to the Internet and refresh the page. No confirmation of order is displayed. I check my emails and nothing has arrived. Confidently I repeat the operation from the start. Happily, the website has retained some of my details, so I quickly proceed to payment. I enter my card details again and press 'purchase'. This time, a confirmation screen appears. I congratulate myself on my technological expertise and nonchalantly print off the order, secreting it between some sheets of paper that will accompany me to London tomorrow morning. Stretching back into my faux leather office chair, the sweet tinkling of my inbox alerts me to the email confirmation … er, two email confirmations. Forlornly, I acknowledge that even though I did not see a confirmation screen, this was, in all likelihood, a result of my prematurely ending the transaction, rather than some complex website glitch.

I pick up the phone and before I can select any options, God lifts up my skylight window and throws a metaphorical used bag of cat litter at me. The message is: 'As we are so busy with processing

Valentine's Day orders, I'm afraid we cannot cancel any existing orders at this time.' The small fluttering in my stomach is slowly evolving into hysterical flapping. I calm myself by imagining the look of surprise on my wife's face as numerous bunches of roses arrive simultaneously on the big day. Then contrast that burst of joy with the recognition that my credit card balance will soon equal the national debt of … er, the UK.

I start to feel an unjust sense of loathing towards Interflora. It's not their fault after all, but someone should recognise this is a duplicate. Surely. Searching around their website I come across an email address – to which you can send enquiries – and I put my story in writing and press 'send' more in hope than expectation (having requested a 'read receipt').

The following morning, after walking my son through the February gloom to his bus stop and moving all of my emails to a separate file, in case they should be spotted, I log on and, sure enough, someone has read my message. At around 8 a.m. the phone rings. Thinking this will be some domestic issue, I pick up distractedly. A woman's voice announces herself, and explains that they've received my email and will be cancelling one of the orders and refunding the money to my credit card account. My gratitude is fulsome and deserved. Someone's 'broken the rules' on pre-Valentine's Day non-intervention and decided to intervene to put things right.

In London the next day, I break for lunch, switch on my mobile phone and discover the following message from my little daughter. 'Mum loves the flowers. She was even happier when they arrived again in the afternoon.'

*

There's something lasting and memorable about the warmth created by a human intervention when things are going wrong. Ease of business can be a double-edged sword if you confer it in its entirety to the strange and beautiful magic of the Internet. Systems aren't flexible, you see. But humans are.

You may have gleaned from this chapter that the balance of recent years has been more positive than when I first put pen to paper to share my frustration with UK service, but I need to stress that these few examples are the ones that restore my faith, as the majority of experiences still make me wince. We'll end this treatise on the current state of UK retail service with a day's shopping. The day in question: Saturday 16th February 2008. The location: a large shopping mall in the north of England.

Having established that ease of doing business is a key customer requirement, let's add in to the mix an ability to engage with the customer, some technical product knowledge, an ability to overcome issues and sort problems out and, finally, a talent for creating sales – in fact, much of the profile of those who are now our leading business entrepreneurs, but strangely of little interest to our youngsters who increasingly see retail as a default career.

In taking out the magnifying glass and the notebook, we're also aware of the opportunity to count up the number of *moments of truth* there are in a typical day's shopping. By this, of course, we mean those little milestones in our journey that influence our perceptions and control our levels of engagement and potential buying behaviour. Whether the wallet comes out depends on a number of minuscule factors, making up the totality of our experience. And we know that just as many of these are outside the control of the businesses we visit as are directly manageable.

Let me set the scene. It's a fine day. My son is staying at his mate's house for a couple of days and they're off to walk around Ingleton Falls. I'd sooner be there, but instead, find myself behind the wheel as we dart down the motorway. I'm certainly more relaxed than on a typical Saturday – or rather, when my beloved football team is playing. Today, they won't lose, simply because they aren't involved in a game. I can relax and enjoy the day.

We do have a small list of objectives for the day. My wife needs a couple of items of clothing, while my daughter also needs some new clothes. Each of these tasks has its own particular challenges. In order to buy clothes for my daughter successfully, one requires resilience, tact and a degree of persuasion. What we regard as 'modern, stylish and appropriate' is some distance away from her own imagined catwalk gear. She often requires softening up, perhaps with an impromptu show of humour from Dad, from pretending to try on a bra in House of Fraser to accommodate his 'man boobies' to dancing 'uncle-style' to the latest pop combo in the entrance to Zavvi. Actually, upon recalling each of these moments, she tends to 'walk away' rather than 'soften up'.

Back in the car, the iPod is on shuffle, while we discuss the day ahead. Dad has one or two main requirements, including lunch and a visit to any music retailer in the vicinity. If he gets time, he will also peruse any new football kit he may find intriguing, even though he has now happily passed the phase of wearing a football shirt to family weddings.

The drive is straightforward and the entrance to the Centre easy, in spite of the curious driving habits of the woman in the Citroen in front of us who veers back and forth across the two lanes like a greyhound on LSD. But, while this could sink further into a lasting state of bitterness, impacting on everyone's day, it does provide an example of one of those moments of truth that the retailer cannot control. (I can personally see the value in adding programmable neon signs to the tops of cars so that you can type up sarcastic messages and direct them at other drivers, but it ain't gonna happen.)

We quickly find a space in the lower car park, right by Debenhams and enter through the nearest door, straight into the ground floor. The women's and children's sections are above us, so we move around quite rapidly until we split into two groups. I wander off towards the men's clothing section, while my wife and daughter move upstairs.

As I wander from section to section, pretending to know my Sonnetti from my Ben Sherman, I begin to think about my sister's impending wedding. There is always the default suit, of course, but perhaps I should try and make a statement. Hawaiian shirt, spats and leg warmers, perhaps, set off with a fine pair of 80s pixie boots. I begin to take an interest in the clothing around me. Having lost a little weight around the leg region –no, I haven't had my feet amputated, but have been visiting the gym – I consider the appropriateness (or otherwise) of a pair of skinny jeans.

Unfortunately, I have no idea which designer makes which jeans, so I need some help. There is no one around. Occasionally a young woman comes dashing past, adding new clothing to the rails and removing other items. She's probably already mentally computed that the solitary man in the jeans section is lost and needs to be accompanied back to his minibus and given a flask. I sense that the service may be passive here. You have to make the moves. I make one upstairs to find the rest of my party. The girls have identified a couple of items, and as they do, they march around holding them, displaying a conviction to purchase, but just before leaving, they put them back on the rails again. Curious.

Upstairs I study the cologne and aftershave. No one approaches me. I begin to wonder how the ladies having impromptu manicures had got there, if no one ever approaches customers. I don't know of anyone who walks up to a beauty counter, sits down and expects to be manicured, painted, scraped or otherwise, but here they all are, lined up, with brightly coloured eyebrows, flapping like awnings on a windy day.

We leave and continue our walk along the upper floor of the Centre. We stop in at Ted Baker, where we're immediately approached and asked if we need help. Cool. We wander into Accessorise and also Russell and Bromley. They're at the end of their sale period and Dad has an account with them. I wander in. There is one rack of men's shoes left in the sale. There must be about 20 different styles available, but none of the shoes are in my size – a very common 9. As if to make a point I repeat this conclusion to my wife but, again, no one comes over. Perhaps all they can do is to confirm that 'everything we've got is out,' but you never know.

Upstairs in Zara I am approached and asked if I need help, but in Monsoon, the person serving is busy filling out a credit account application with a couple. I've found what looks like a decent suit here, but need to check a size. No-one around, so I leave and go downstairs, where I meet up with the rest of the party and we go to the till to buy a couple of items. We're greeted with a smile and the transaction is processed swiftly. We're asked if we're interested in opening an account. We decline. It won't be the only time today that we're asked about opening an account before – and almost to the absolute exclusion of – being asked if we found everything we were looking for (which, in itself, seems to have become UK Retail's very own version of our banks' 'is there anything I can do for you today?').

As we pass the discount perfume shop on the corner, Ana suggests that I try Boots for my aftershave. 'You can use the Advantage Card and get some points,' she sensibly suggests, 'and they were quite good the last time we went.' We arrive at Boots and Ana enters into deep, prolonged negotiations at a particular beauty counter. As I walk away towards the aftershave section, I catch the beginnings of a warm conversation.

This time I begin an assault on the tester bottles, whipping out those little paper sticks, spraying with abandon and converting one section of the store into a house of ill repute, given the sickly combi-nation of tones affecting the air. I spot a new brand. Narciso Rodriguez. Sounds alluringly Hispanic. 'That's a new one,' comes a voice from behind me. A woman presents herself, smiling. 'It's very nice. I can recommend it.' At last, someone is attempting to engage. I politely decline as, to tell you the truth, I've been hooked by the new Chanel one, Allure Sport. She doesn't follow me back to the section where that is, but it isn't on offer, is very expensive and if I were to spray on too much and walk past the recalcitrant smokers gathered outside, they might spontaneously combust.

As we leave the store, Ana having made a purchase, we summarise the morning. There's been very little pro-action anywhere, bar a few attempts to flog store cards – not even an attempted upsale. It strikes me as surprising, since the environment is conducive to shopping. We're not outside, everything is close together and people have come here to buy, one assumes. So it shouldn't be too difficult to engage with people and move them politely towards a sale – and yet there's been a noticeable hesitancy, perhaps reflecting my concerns about Retail's low profile.

Lunch is always a good opportunity to take stock of levels of UK service and in this particular Centre, customers are spoiled for choice. We make our way to Pizza Express, but at the door we're told there'll be a twenty-minute wait for a table and then a further thirty-minute wait for food. It's good that we know, as I'd rather have the option of leaving than waiting endlessly for what would inevitably be a Stroppy Giuseppe, if Dad starts to get hungry.

In the afternoon we visit several shops, among them the newly reconstituted Zavvi. Formerly the Virgin Megastore, this business was subject to a management buy-out and is now, along with HMV, one of the two major high street music and entertainment retailers, apparently (according to most retail commentators), finding themselves in Sisyphus's shoes, rolling the stone up that hill.

My intended purchase is not intentionally oblique. I'm looking for the Scott Walker box set *Five Easy Pieces*. It's not inexpensive, so probably better bought on line, but one does encounter sales of box sets around this time of the year, so I go in.

Having bought a couple of 80s Brat Pack films for a friend's 40th birthday present, I fail to locate any box sets at all. Disappointed, I walk up to the till, where a woman greets me and processes the sale.

'Did you find everything you were looking for?'

It's that question again. The same old song, that familiar refrain, that call with no response, its frequency redolent of an industry that has little concept of customer service. But wait a minute. I *was* looking for something. Let's see how it goes.

'Actually, yes, I was looking for something,' I respond, with a smile. 'I couldn't find your box sets.'

'What are you after?' she asks and I explain.

'I see. Well we did have that in stock some time ago, but I think I would have to order it for you now.' She looks at her screen, does a couple of searches and locates the item – and its £44 price tag.

I make some excuses about it being probably cheaper to buy on line, she nods her agreement, I thank her and leave, somewhat chastened by the unexpectedly positive response to a question I expected to be 'appended' rather than 'genuinely meant'.

Zavvi also holds the record for being the only entertainment store ever to check the age of the intended recipient of a DVD. As it happened, it was for my son, who was with me at the time and just beyond the 12 certificate of the item in question. The assistant looked nervous when he asked, but it was encouraging. Usually, staff find it difficult to ask those embarrassing questions (unless it's: *are you interested in saving whatever percent today by applying for our new, exciting store card?*) but this youngster had clearly received an explanation of the context, had encountered the circumstances when the questions should be asked – and did so in a polite and professional manner.

Elsewhere, there is a visible distance between shop assistants and customers. It's as if our retail industry is trying to replicate the conventional 'coldness' of the Brits, by actually establishing some distance between us. Alternatively, it could be because people don't have the skills and confidence to open up a conversation, or it could be that no one has taken the time to explain the context – and to reinforce the value that strong first impressions have on customers' likely buying behaviour.

Lush has, for some time, stood out for this reason. There have been a few times, when I've wandered in to be gloriously asphyxiated by the products and have found myself in a warm conversation almost immediately.

A couple of years ago I did a mystery shop of Belfast City Centre for the local BBC radio station. The intention had been for me and a radio reporter to experience 'under cover' the levels of customer service at several city centre stores. It was clear from an initial chat with the producer that the good folk of Belfast were a tad disappointed by levels of service, so my little piece of research should at least shine a light on some of the issues, without claiming to be anywhere near a statistical assessment. Incidentally, I have a real problem with the concept of a statistical assessment: I just can't say it. The two of us set off towards the centre of Belfast, the reporter giving me some background while I set down mental 'post its' of where I might profitably browse CDs once the job had been completed.

The first shop we went into was a bookstore. My task? To ask for a copy of *Inconvenience Stores*, that well-known (in some deprived neighbourhoods) tome on UK service. At the first stop – a national chain – I wandered downstairs to the customer service desk and waited … and waited … and waited. I looked around, but even if there were other employees around, they were obscured by the massive shelves. The only chance I would have had of getting served would have been if Suleiman Ali Nashnush was on the payroll. Yes, that's him. The tallest basketball player ever to have lived. He was so tall that my spell check just asked me to replace the word 'was' after typing his name, suggesting 'were' instead. He's so tall he's plural! Mr Nashnush was conspicuous by his absence, as was everyone else. I waited five minutes and could find no one. I left. Outside, the reporter enjoyed my brief description of the experience, finding that their fears were being confirmed. Having gone a metaphorical goal down in the first five minutes, we continued afoot.

Another bookstore. This time I entered an independent one and waited in line at the desk, while one employee did his best to process an enormous queue while his colleagues hid between the bookcases. Time passed. Finally, through the couple of hours' growth of beard that had swamped my face, I finally got to splutter out a question about the book. This time, the assistant did a check, using the ISBN number and located it. 'It's not in stock,' he confirmed, 'so would you like to order it?' I declined, opting to search around the city a bit longer to find it (as if). Again, the performance was a let-down. Some encouraging shots on goal (via an attempt to make the sale via placing an order) but we were now two down and it was not even half time.

Next, I walked into HMV. My aim? To locate a new Squeeze compilation, which I understood might not be released until the following week. I searched the shelves fruitlessly (I usually carry apples when searching shelves). No sign. I approached the till and was immediately greeted with a smile. 'Yes, you're right. It doesn't come out until next week.' And then, amazingly, he demonstrated that he'd been listening. 'Is that too late for your sister's birthday?' I nodded, my tissue of lies extending by the minute. 'Well, there are a couple of old Squeeze compilations in stock and one of them is in our sale.' Wow. I made my excuses and left, having determined to go elsewhere to buy the unreleased and unavailable item for my sister (actual) whose birthday it wasn't and who doesn't like Squeeze. Boy, these lies can weigh you down.

But an excellent outcome from a store obviously keen on ensuring their customers leave with something. I left with my confidence high. Here was a place that got us a goal back. Whether we were to produce a last-minute equaliser depended on Lush. Yes, the very same smelly, hand-made cosmetic emporium mentioned above. As the reporter nervously concealed herself in a nearby coffee house, I wandered in. Again, my comprehensive preparation had produced a very interesting scenario. The last time my better half bought her favourite item from Lush, the seasonal nature of their produce (for all the right reasons) meant that it would no longer be in stock by the time I made this 'mystery call'. If things were to go to plan, I would enter, fail to find said item, be engaged by a helpful employee and then be offered some similar products (one of which my wife had identified was the 'right' answer). And, low and behold, the above did come to pass, with almost unsettling similarity to the vision we'd hoped for. We broke our cover.

In the conversation that followed, the girl who served us explained just how much customer service was 'core' to the Lush strategy. 'We get out and mystery shop our competitors as much as we can. Sometimes we go inside, sometimes we look at what they've got in the windows but we're always keeping an eye on how well they're treating their customers. It gives us ideas and it keeps us on our toes.' I could have kissed her. If I had done, the evidence would have been hard to remove, given the overpowering aroma of cosmetic, but the proof was there. Their focus on customers was a direct result of their focus on competitors: getting different perspectives helps you understand what you do well and where you need to improve. In most businesses this is the preserve of one or two managers, whose visits to other businesses are often seen as jaunts, rather than learning expeditions. What Lush appears to be saying is: let the team itself do the visits and the team will make the necessary changes. It's a healthy switch on the routine 'external benchmarking visit' and one that augurs well for their future. And an equaliser in the last minute too.

Later that afternoon I explained my adventures to the taxi driver who took me back to Belfast International. In his engaging Ulster drawl he described a recent visit to a furniture shop. 'Being a taxi driver, I can be flexible, so I went in one mid-morning and spent about ten minutes looking at the table I wanted, without anyone coming over to help me. They were all about 30 yards away. There was a group of 3 or 4 of them and they were enjoying a little chat, a coffee and a break.'

As he continued, he drew a lengthy sigh and looked at me. 'You know what?' he continued, 'I went over to ask them for some help. The first one looked at me with a baffled expression on his face. He said *are you in a panic?*' We laughed, but it was the laugh that precedes a good cry.

Retail suffers by association with poor British customer service. Culturally, we avoid confrontation, believing a justifiable complaint about poor service to be akin to personal insult, thereby dishonouring the most sincere of feedback collection schemes and making nonsense of the ubiquitous feedback card. Customer contact by phone is brutal, condescending, often incomprehensible and rarely focused on the individual customer needs. Again, this desecration of customer service seeps into expectations of the retail experience, regardless of their innocence when it comes to outbound calling. Our children see retail as a default career – at best a 'stop gap' career, at worst a punishment for not trying harder at school.

The retail experience itself displays all of the resultant wounds. Employees lack the confidence to engage, the skills to sell conversationally and the attitude to be flexible when an opportunity to rescue a problem emerges.

Management on-site appear distant, unengaged with employees and 'outside' of the customer experience, perhaps more engaged in operations than experiences.

Training, more often than not, focuses on the procedural, when the point of differentiation is emotional engagement and organisations struggle to develop a meaningful customer service ethos.

However, my positive experiences reveal that several organisations have both understood the benefits of customer service and committed to the step-change required to deliver them, while the majority complain about the quality of school leavers. And yet, paradoxically, it remains the best career option for any would-be entrepreneur.

There are steps afoot to change the retail landscape, with the National Skills Academy, a new Diploma for Retail and the recently mooted, regionally-based skills shops. But these will take time to change the view from here.

In the meantime, we can't count on British consumers to overcome their reticence and foment a customer service revolution. We need plainly successful organisations, visibly differentiating through service, to make that point loud and clear.

At the moment, they're shouting, but we can only just hear them above the din of indifference.

3

Badly Overdrawn Boy

It's a frosty February morning and I've roused myself early to make sure my son gets up in time to catch the bus to school. I fumble about in the dark of the kitchen, locate the light switch, stand on the cat, plug in the kettle and turn on my radio. As I slowly stir the porridge (not a euphemism), the business news bleeps into focus with a story about Barclays' unexpected £7bn-plus pre-tax profits. I listen attentively and anticipate the 'take' on the story. Regardless of what the reporter actually says, I hear a sharp, predictable shower of phrases: banks 'ripping off' customers, charges increase while profits double, fat cats celebrate while branches are closed, etc.

We've all been there. Like a corporate PR machine in our psyche, we're ready with the prepared sound bites. It will take little persuasion to convince us that banks are the personification of evil on our high streets. But in recent years, there's been something of a charm offensive (a phrase capable of being reversed to convey an alternative reading). A couple of years ago, HBOS plc (Halifax Bank to you and me) announced a considerable investment in new branches both in the UK and in the Irish Republic, while NatWest has embarked on a long campaign to persuade us that there is a 'different way' to do your banking – and that generally involves choosing one or more of their products. Such attempts at reconciliation with the public are long overdue.

Until recently, banks and building societies have been paying out millions of pounds in returned administration and penalty charges, while pinning their hopes on a pending court case or an Office of Fair Trading-sponsored compromise. It appears that banks have been able to apply for special dispensation to refuse to respond to customers' bank-charge complaints until legal certainty has been established.

Everyday account enquiries are being re-routed to contact centres which, it's claimed, are often located in distant solar systems, manned by aliens who communicate via a series of intermittent beeps. Some banks phone you. You answer and then an automated voice starts up a conversation. I suppose they don't sound too hurt when I tell them to 'do one', so that's consoling.

ATM networks (cash machines to you and me) are sold off at a huge profit to operators who install them in motorway service stations and charge £1.85 for every transaction, while people in 'areas of poverty' have to pay a 15% surcharge to access their own limited resources, or effectively pay a surcharge to travel to the nearest machine.

The message from the media and consumer groups has been clear: retail banks are disingenuous operators in a marketplace generated by inertia where a creeping *cost cutting* ethos has combined with clandestine fee outbreaks to line the already gilded pockets of the few.

All of this combines to create a climate of mistrust, culminating in the events played out recently at embattled Northern Rock branches around the country, where queues of disenchanted and frankly distrusting customers waited to withdraw their savings (and now speculate about the delights of a nationalised future).

Prior to this quickly shifting context, banks' profits, paradoxically, appeared to expand in reverse proportion to the quality of service provided.

To those of us interested in the plight of the consumer, our arguments for change would have been much more persuasive in the past if banks were being stung on the balance sheets and not scooping record-breaking profits. The poorer the service our banks provide, the higher the profits they enjoy. In the past, unfortunately, there's little evidence of this scenario evolving. Now, however, when consumers think banks have gone 'too far', cataclysmic effects are possible.

Branches in small towns and villages are closed (see National Australia Bank's swooping sword of mayhem and its effect on Clydesdale and Yorkshire Bank's networks and HSBC's swingeing removal of offices, to name but three).

Banks are being criticised for failing to provide support to the less well off in our communities, while unscrupulous loan sharks fight well-meaning neighbourhood co-operatives for market share. Another 'there, I told you so' for the mid-evening pub debate.

But our financial services providers try to meet all of this growing disenchantment on the front foot. *Stratospheric executive bonuses are but an irritation when compared to the money raised for the Exchequer through these enormous profits*, they could (and arguably should) say. What's one man's unmentionable fortune compared with several new hospitals and schools? Branch closures are argued as being an attempt to get closer to customers (often attributed to 'changing customer needs'). So is there any hope for the retail financial services consumer?

Let me offer the fruit of some initial research. Having moved accounts three times in the last 7 years, I greeted the invitation to meet my new account manager with a large ladleful of scepticism. The fact that the person calling to make the appointment couldn't tell me what we were going to discuss magnified my concern. Had we gone overdrawn without permission?

'We could probably do with some help with saving for the kids' future and possibly the help of a business expert,' I announced positively to my disbelieving wife, as we approached the branch. But what followed demonstrated the full dysfunctional glory of 'customer lip service'. As I prepared for a few conversational openings (having worked for a bank before) I was asked two very direct questions: *what is your largest monthly outgoing?* and *would you like to consolidate your outgoings into an unsecured loan?*

What was most dispiriting about the experience was that the person in front of me had earned a wall full of service awards, presumably for implementing this fiercely sales-driven policy. And yet there was absolutely no attempt to identify our needs and aspirations before striking.

This policy was also evident on a recent trip to pay into my kids' savings accounts at a different provider. On this occasion my attention was drawn to the new higher rate of children's savings accounts, but having established that I didn't appear to represent a good 'sales lead', the cashier made no mention of the offer, in spite of my perfect suitability. In fact, she said it all by saying nothing at all, in a fruitless pitch for a role in the next Ronan Keating video (unless we're spared).

On a more recent (and the subsequent) visit to the bank where the savings are held, I arrived at 11.40 a.m needing to be somewhere else in town at noon. There were three cashiers serving with three tills deserted. There were eight of us in the queue. Tesco wouldn't allow this, I'm sure, so what's going on here? At 11.55 I finally approached the till as a fourth cashier deigned to join the fray. She apologised for the queue. 'Are you short-staffed?' I asked, having failed to squeeze a miniature-shepherd-related joke out of that phrase. 'No,' she replied glumly, as if disappointed that I hadn't tried. 'What with holidays, lunches and everything, it's really hard to keep the service going at lunch time.' Now if that were 1856 I could believe her, but this is October 2007 and, if I'm not mistaken, the idea of staggered lunches did occur to our greatest business minds some time ago. At least she had the presence of mind not to ask me 'is there anything else I can do for you today?' otherwise I might have said something requiring an urgent visit to the confessional booth.

On a subsequent visit, I once again presented my kids' passbooks to an indifferent-looking youngster. The silence engulfed our little section of the counter. I sighed. She looked up, flashing one of those half-hearted smiles you get at passport control. Had she had some life experience – or, indeed, a basic level of human interaction skills – she could have picked up on the fact that I had the kids' savings books. She could have said 'You spending the kids' money again?' I would have smiled and passed a comment like, 'Yeah, they've got more than I have.' From there to a potential cross-sale is but a hop, skip and jump. However, from the lifeless mundanity of the transaction to a cross-sale, for her, is like getting to Plymouth by train (see previous chapter).

Believe me, UK banks know we're not enamoured with their service. Research shows that most of us suspect that we could get a better deal elsewhere, but as inertia has been rampant in this country, we stay with our provider. Banks say that when they try to offer their existing customers a better deal through the post, we throw it in the bin, so why, it is implied, should they make the effort?

Banks also complain that stringent regulation restricts their activities and makes it difficult to apply flexibility – regulation which only needed strengthening in the first place to stop them using the concept of endowment mortgages to rip us all off.

So what of the regulatory bodies? The Financial Services Authority, for one, has moved from the imposition of rules to the promotion of principles, aimed at encouraging cultural change instead of knee-jerk process changes and furtive track-covering. So are banks right to blame their constraints on an overly legislative government? Is it possible to practise great service delivery in a regulated environment anywhere? Or is the reality that banks are somehow the embodiment of human evil, hell bent on lining their pockets from our repressed misery.

But banks helpfully point out that research shows that one out of three customers would happily recommend their bank, as if that's a good thing, since presumably two out of three would do anything other than advocate their own provider. And I use the word *happily* as it's certainly more positive than *under duress, if paid to say so* or *if subjected to torture*.

The two out of three, if anything like me and the compelling majority of all my friends, are mostly concerned with one contextual dark cloud – and that is the perceived perfidious stance of championing service publicly, but privately (and in everyday interactions) only being interested in selling. As I type this, I receive a call from one provider, offering me a new and exciting credit card. Politely, I let the man finish, especially as he's struggling with his English (or his script). The benefits described? Simply the interest rates – and little more – based, one assumes, on the fact that most of us simply want to shift our balances around to reduce the interest.

Banks are in both camps here: using assertive direct-selling techniques to recruit your balances – while bemoaning the fact that customers are much more attritional than before. I can say confidently – and without any recent research to hand – that trust in UK financial institutions is currently at a low. Even though their concern was well founded, it was difficult not to interpret the queuing around Northern Rock branches as a mass expression of mistrust in our financial services providers.

The FSA (Financial Services Authority) exists to regulate financial service bodies, with the ultimate aim of protecting consumers. It recently introduced a set of principles designed to assess how fairly providers were treating consumers. *Treating Customers Fairly* sets out a series of precepts by which assessment could be made, and several banks and building societies have undergone checks. This is good news for consumers, but where are the results?

From a cursory glance at www.fsa.gov.uk nothing was to be found. Sure, there is a lot of very useful consumer protection information and advice and the website is worth a look. But how well are UK banks and building societies doing on the *trust* score? We should be told, I think.

Check out a random selection of banks' and building societies' websites. From the dozen or so that I checked, only the Britannia made a great play of its commitment to fairness on the home page of its website. Elsewhere, a worrying silence. No data on how fair they are perceived to be by their customers. No national league table. Sure, it's all about perceptions and they're not always indicative of certainty or the truth, but the wall of reticence surrounding the majority of our banks and building societies is a source of growing concern.

It's tempting to drag one's laptop aboard this accelerating bandwagon and join the chorus of dissent. But as a seasoned servicewatcher, a consumer writer, a fully paid-up member of the banking community (having spent 12 years working at one of our largest) and, as the archetypal son of the Irish Catholic diaspora, too prone to guilt to risk a hurtful comment, I feel a balanced assessment is due.

Banks genuinely acknowledge the importance of the walk-in customer, as it offers the 'conversational selling' opportunities upon which to build a lifelong relationship. And yet, to date, the one difference I've seen is the cursory question 'is there anything else I can do for you today?' being appended to each and every transaction. Unless we're all to retort 'open more *effin* tills,' something needs to be done.

*

When you read you begin with a-b-c and when you sing you begin with do-re-mi, Julie Andrews once helpfully pointed out. How she would have conveyed the fun of banking in the UK is less clear, but thanks to some furtive phone calls and a friend of a friend in the music publishing industry, I've discovered a little-known out-take from the original cast recording. *What the hell is an originator number?* explores in rich, emotive detail the frustration caused by the jargon encountered in querying a failed direct debit payment.

Yes, it's easy to make fun of antiquated, traditional, bureaucratic behemoths like our banks, especially if it's in an area such as service, where to me, there may be a case to answer. But before we embark on our tour of duty, let's consider a couple of important questions: what is good service and is it in the banks' interest to provide it?

What experience has told academics, marketers and business practitioners is that reputation (often described in terms of 'branding') has a proven impact on the bottom line. Until recently, what were less well understood were the factors influencing reputation. Robert Johnston's 2001 study highlighted that of the principal elements creating reputation, the highest-regarded organisations were 'easy to do business with'.

In the excitement of this discovery, forgive me for leaving a dangling preposition, but it implies that over and above factors such as reliability (keeping promises), flexibility (ownership and creativity) and empathy (treating you like a human being), being able to serve up hassle-free experiences and, even more importantly, responding to problems with verve, imagination and warmth, is the key driver of an organisation's reputation. Service is the car that rarely goes wrong, but when it does, angels flutter down from heaven to mend it.

My website ran a web survey in the Spring of 2006 and this appeared to back up the contention that reliability, ownership and handling problems well do represent the elements of customer service that are most important to customers. I therefore declare with some confidence that they're appropriate to UK retail banking too. Providing financial security, growth and investment opportunities for customers is not akin to the moment the little red velvet heart is warmed up before it's stitched into the teddy bear at that Build-a-Bear place.

Banking is not about the joy of opera, the ecstasy of the first day of the holiday or the satisfaction of a fine dining experience. For me, it's about background efficiency with the minimum of fuss, added value at the point where you need some help and, most of all, completeness of trust. So, in the context of banking, what do we mean by trust? Well for me, trust is the cumulative result of a number of elements of the on-going service experience and it operates at a number of levels.

Firstly, it's the sense of reassurance generated by good governance at the provider in question. And while this is broadly controlled by legislation and regulation, banks don't help themselves by pulling all of the diverse areas of their operations together at 'results' time and declaring a great performance, where, in reality, their corporate investment division is holding up the rest of the enterprise and, without that, their retail operation would be exposed for all its weaknesses.

The general public do not expect their financial service providers to fall foul of regulation and, by and large, this has been the story, albeit punctuated by the occasional scandal (hang your heads, all of you). However, the emphasis of the Financial Services Authority in recent years has switched from rules-based regulation to a principles basis. This has been best illustrated by the introduction of the aforementioned *Treating Customers Fairly* initiative, squarely located beneath the 'trust' banner, incidentally. The title of this initiative says it all, but it's the focus on principles that reveals something of the true task, for businesses' (and, by definition, banks') values often shape their customers' ultimate experiences. What do I mean by this?

Simply put, the FSA understands that service is an output of the culture of the organisation and, importantly, the organisation's leaders, practices and habits determine that culture.

As an example, imagine the business whose leader stresses the importance of teamwork, but who publicly undermines a fellow director at the same time (it happens, believe it or not). One may determine evidence of double standards from that – and, when the knowledge that this happens seeps out into the organisation, people know that when leaders say one thing, they generally mean another.

Such confusing signals erode employee engagement and quickly undermine any focus on customers. There's no one ethos or direction. Things are said on a whim and replaced by the appearance of a more interesting-looking whim. We need to throw our whims away (as Tight Fit once sang). But when invited to help organisations improve their service, I focus my initial questions on areas of 'culture', asking employees what the strongest message going around the business is. The leaders say 'service', but the employees have another story, usually with the focus on sales or cost-savings.

I ask about targets. The leaders say service is the most important thing, as that supports sales. But employees show me a list of KPIs (key performance indicators) containing no reference to measurement of service – but several relating to sales, speed and cost-saving. To their credit, they respond by telling me how hard it is to find an objective measure of service, while the rest of UK retail is happily adopting Fred Reichheld's Net Promoter concept (more on that later). What's so wrong with basing your measure on how readily a customer would recommend you?

One can quickly surmise the impact of such internal dilemmas on employees. They know service is important, but the short-term pressure is on sales, with no clearly articulated connection between the two. As sentient human beings, they want to build relationships and have an instinct to do the right thing by the customer. But the pressure is to perform an artificial and largely arbitrary task – to sell.

I ask about promotion and career development. What does it take to get to a management position in this business? Well, in general terms, people tell me that you're rewarded for good performance by being removed far away from customers – before continuing to tell me that political expediency, personal resilience and the readiness to follow orders (even more unquestioningly and rapidly than your predecessor) are the main guarantees of success. This perhaps explains why banking executives are getting younger these days (with policemen no longer having a monopoly on that particular concept).

I ask about what gets rewarded and recognised, on the basis that great businesses design every aspect of their employee relationship to maximise performance. The reality, however, is that only the truly institutionalised reward systems tend to be evident. Sales is much more likely to generate you a reward than practising great customer service.

This was never more evident than in a cameo I saw played out before my disbelieving eyes in a West Yorkshire town a couple of years ago. The branch was closed until 9.30 on this day – a regular feature, aimed at providing some training time for the employees. As two window cleaners polished the branch exterior, one of the employees emerged and tried to sell them each a credit card. Did they fit the profile? Had they expressed an interest? Had someone assessed their account activity to ensure suitability for unsecured credit? No, but someone was probably on a commission for selling them a credit card.

The fact that every transaction completed at this bank's counter is completed with the question 'is there anything else I can do for you today?' does not usher in an age of customer focus. Neither does the 'did you find what you were looking for?' at that music and entertainment store. Service is a product of the culture – and there are too many contradictory values in play for this culture to be created.

Elsewhere a friend tells me that his wife works for a major bank as a cashier. She has a great relationship with the people who come in week after week. She knows all there is to know about them. As a consequence of this, they trust her. Her employers, on the other hand, do not. Each coaching session (and you have to give them credit for introducing an approach that should help increase focus on service) ends with the observation that she hasn't tried to make a 'sale'. 'But I know this customer very well, and one of the reasons they come to me is that they know they aren't going to have a product pushed in their face,' is her considered response. Incidentally, she has a colleague who regularly greets queuing customers by saying, 'I'm sorry for your wait.' Mishear that comment and you're going to start feeling self-conscious about your girth.

The concept of maintaining local branch service to people who solely wish to transact and who want to make more considered purchases on their own terms is a worrying development. But more worrying still is the fact that the majority of us, whenever we transact with our bank, are dealing with an employee who, more likely than not, is looking at a list of potential sales, generated by their CRM (customer relationship management) system.

CRM is generally misunderstood. If I had a pound for every time someone's suggested running a management workshop aimed at 'demystifying' it, then I'd be rich enough to pay to attend. The fact is that CRM has, for many banks, taken the place of the more human instinct to build and nurture relationships. The data is universally unquestioned by customer-facing employees and the need to promote the suggested product or service takes precedence, even when the evidence before the very eyes of the cashier clearly rules out a sale.

For example, today I receive a call from Air Miles. Their reward-points scheme allowed me to amass a few thousand as I made purchases with my NatWest credit card. NatWest then decided to introduce its own scheme, leaving Air Miles in an interesting position – quandary, even. I'm a customer of Air Miles but cannot have a mutually-rewarding relationship with them unless I am a customer of one of their partner organisations. The caller identifies herself and asks how I collect my Air Miles points. I explain that I don't any more, as my main means of collection was via my credit card. What comes next? You can guess. They want to introduce me to a new Lloyds TSB credit card. But I don't need a new credit card. Well, at least not one that requires any of the money back (and that would be a long over-due innovation in the credit card world).

What CRM systems inevitably do is to take away the need to ask us questions, to find out what we aspire to, to ask about our businesses and family and to understand what sort of assistance we might need. This concept, known as 'conversational selling' in some parts, is clearly more time-consuming than simply lifting one's eyes wearily from the paperwork and shouting, 'did you know we have a new credit card?' However, it is infinitely more rewarding in the long term and is, in my humble opinion, the basis for a 'sales through service' business strategy.

And as if to prove the fact, a second call arrives within 15 minutes. This time it's the Nationwide wanting to speak to my wife. I say she's not in, while trying to hide the fact that she's lurking behind me. At least that's our default setting when an outbound call comes in. The man asks if we would like to save money by consolidating our debts. I decline politely, so he moves on to introducing the idea of re-mortgaging. 'We're not up for that right now,' I courteously reply and shortly afterwards, the call ends. Has the CRM system somehow identified that we have debt? Perhaps so. However, does this mean that all of us are perpetually in need of a debt re-scheduling service?

Today, 20th February 2008, I have had four calls. Two silent, and two FS companies trying to sell me things. Is CRM really working well for companies?

And beyond CRM, there are few consolations for the embattled consumer, apart from the fact that if you need to get in touch with your bank quickly by phone, the act of pressing the number that relates to a 'new sale' will get you straight through to an assistant, as they're so keen to sell, whereas opting for 'customer service' may lead to an interminable wait for which, generally, they won't be sorry at all. But console yourself. It's fun hearing the frustration on the other end of the line as you ask for a list of ATMs in mid Wales and challenge their spelling of Macchynleth.

But back to the FSA and their focus on principles. This is no doubt a result of their perception that banks' overt sales focus is not necessarily in the interests of each customer, while declarations of the importance of 'trust' are meaningless, unless you're talking about the Elvis Costello album of the same name, which is really rather grand.

Trust is important, but too few banks understand how to create and sustain it. Further into this book, I'll set out a consumer-led frame-work that could easily address some of the organisational constraints, apparently hell-bent on creating so much mistrust; you'd think Ming the Merciless had just announced them. And trust is not the only issue. Bank charges have been in the news lately, largely prompted by the fine work of the Bank Action Group (now the Consumer Action Group) and the subsequent announcement by the Office of Fair Trading that bank default charges that exceed the cost of the same bank's administration of the charge are deemed to be 'unfair'. Unfair? Once again impacting on our perceptions of trust.

We've had exposés on TV, radio and, spreading like wildfire, the forum on www.bankactiongroup.co.uk. The wider media coverage it has gained has resulted in a huge increase in the number of customers taking their banks to the small claims court knowing that banks will generally not contest the claims as it will cost them too much to administer (in a final ironic twist).

The whole anti-charge movement may not have even been born,

were it not for a blatantly unfair combination of actions from the Bank Action Group founder's financial services provider. In his own words, it began like this:

> One day in 2004 I found that my career was going nowhere and I decided to change job. I found a job that would enable me to follow a career path that was better suited to me and more 'future proofed'.
>
> It did, however, mean a small cut in pay. To cut a long story short, when I arrived at my new job, I found that although the contract of employment stated that I would be paid on a given date by 'direct transfer', the translation into English went along these lines: 'We'll pay you around that date if we can be bothered and by cheque – usually on a Friday afternoon at 17.30, so no hope of receiving the money for another 4-5 days.'
>
> I had, of course, upon receipt of my new employment contract, changed my Direct Debits and Standing Orders to leave my account a couple of days after the new pay day.
>
> This meant that I was charged £32 for each of the 12 Direct Debits I had set up on my account, as the bank simply refused to cancel them; I was charged £15 for a late payment to a loan I had at the time; I was charged £30 for NOT paying a Standing Order for £3 to the Children's Society, and £32 a few days later for paying it. And the £20 fine for not paying my Barclaycard on time as well.[2]

Either this customer's bank pays its administrative staff a large hourly rate, or they're unfairly making money at his expense. Either way, the concept of fairness and, by definition, trust, is as alien to this bank as genuine talent appears to be to *The X Factor*.

And there are lots of subsets of 'trust' that are also performing questionably in my opinion. Bank complaints are on the increase. I understand that for the UK financial services industry they are currently running at something like 300,000 *complaints received* per month. But that in itself is no bad thing.

Anyone with a cursory understanding of complaints management

[2] With thanks to the Consumer Action Group

knows that it offers organisations the best opportunity to build long-term relationships, for research now unquestionably proves that a well handled complaint has the biggest impact on a customer's lifetime value to an organisation. It has also been shown to have the greatest impact on individual customer advocacy.

It's also true that banks have worked harder to remove the barriers to making a complaint, whereas previously, it was akin to obtaining a ticket for the recently heralded Led Zeppelin reunion concert. So even if the media are quick to jump on increasing numbers of complaints as a further symptom of our fractious relationship with our banks, the reality is perhaps different. The reality is – and I should know this, being a regular speaker at Complaint Management events – that banks have become much more adept at collecting customer feedback.

Approaches to gathering complaints data (albeit largely caused through increasing regulation) and generating wider consumer feedback have become more sophisticated and more effective over the last 5 years. Put simply, banks need to know what matters to customers, whether in the way a complaint has been handled or in the wider delivery of service. Those who act upon it, using a transparently open process to make visible consumer-generated changes, will prosper. But unfortunately few, if any, banks practise this level of feedback management.

Let's take this back to the start. If you really want to empower service to impact your 'bottom line' you would start by asking who your customers are and what matters to them. What *really* matters to them? The point is that if you can consistently deliver what each individual customer really values, then their relationship with you will, as a minimum, not be threatened and may even deepen.

Deciphering their responses needn't be a complicated affair. After all, you want to find out what's most important to customers. Key to understanding this is gaining an appreciation of the detail of the customer experience. It seems simple enough, but how many organisations out there genuinely do this? Most, it seems, just ask us how satisfied we are and, in recent years, banks too were intent on increasing satisfaction, but this is a misnomer.

For me, it's a term only relevant to the effectiveness of the product range from somewhere like Ann Summers, where being truly satisfied does probably accurately reflect the state of arousal introduced by their particular brand of 'clothing'.

Retail banking is not a temporary backdrop to life, like education, childcare or buying Girls Aloud CDs. It sneaks on us post-adolescence, and underscores most of what happens from then on. While it matches the emotional boost of the first dip in the Mediterranean when it approves your mortgage or personal loan, that's only because you see the house become a home or the boneshaker become a neat coupé. And when you're bereaved, separating or having debt problems, the underscore becomes the main theme, as you negotiate probate, re-mortgaging and bankruptcy.

Retail banking can aspire only to the supporting actor Oscar: always the bridesmaid, never the bride. That's why Robert Johnston's work hits the nail so squarely. Retail banking should be easy, especially when we have a problem. By relying on 'ease of business', 'reliability' and excellent 'service recovery' do we have enough of a service spectrum to embrace retail banking? It's an interesting question, as most people I know in banking truly know that products alone do not generate advocacy and loyalty. However, when banks announce their profits, few commentators stretch their analyses beyond product range and asset management strategy.

They say that you need to ensure you practise the right 'service' for the proposition you offer. A hairdresser, for example, may trade on their approachability, friendliness and access to the neighbourhood's juiciest tittle-tattle. But a lawyer needs to cut quickly to the chase, perhaps working *for* the client, before the concept of working *with* them hits home.

Heaven knows how the Co-op Group copes. Financial services, a dairy business, convenience stores, holidays and funeral services. I'd normally encourage businesses to move people around to give them the best perspective on the business and the best opportunity to learn. I do worry sometimes about the potential banana skin that lies ahead of the holiday rep who's been seconded to the funeral parlour ('the plot has a southerly aspect and is three minutes from the beach'). But one of the Co-op's businesses, www.smile.co.uk, has an entire proposition based on differentiation through great service. So if I ask, 'is it in banks' interest to provide great customer service?' then clearly the Co-op believes it is, but they're probably in a minority.

With banks not renowned for their philanthropy (at least not to me), there must be a financial reason to invest in improving service – a silver lining in that cloud of uncertainty, perhaps. We know who our customers are, but do we know what's most important to them? An interesting question whose import often eludes our financial services strategists.

Take this case study, for example. Having established my business I take the advice of a friend and open an online business account with a former building society. The advice was as follows: it's hassle-free and doesn't cost anything.

To be fair to this organisation, I must say that it has worked out that way. I never need to withdraw cash from an ATM and, most of the time, my clients pay by BACS. It costs me nothing, and I've only had to call them once in the first year to sort out an online password problem, which was quickly and efficiently dealt with.

Unexpectedly, the biggest bonus was the faux-leather-bound business account file that they provided. As I'm sure you'll agree, there's nothing like the smell of faux-leather to get you through the morning. Big enough to hold records of all of the clients who owe me money, it's meant we can keep everything together – and its maroon colour matches my desk diary (and also my face, if I've been carrying it around). Happy as a sandboy, I've had a sense of remote warmth, only punctuated by that niggling feeling that there could be something more. Something more? Well, a business charge card, a personal business manager and the ability to access funds via an overdraft, as you ask.

The business is young and I would benefit from not having to conduct all of my business expenditure through my current account. So, as a consequence of this (and without, I hasten to add, closing the first account), I make enquiries about a second, at another bank. Here I can still have free business banking, or at least for an initial period of 18 months or so. I can have all of the benefits of the online account, with the added boon of over-the-counter service and a personal business manager. At this point my mind was racing back to a comment written on a female colleague's appraisal form by her Chief Clerk ('I've tried Fiona in a number of positions around the office, but find she performs best on the counter').

Free banking is something of a misnomer, since the provision of a charge card (i.e. like a credit card but you must pay it off in full every month) requires that a guarantee be arranged and this will cost £30-odd. Never mind, at least we've got our nice new leather-bound file to look forward to. You've guessed it. There isn't one. Neither do any cash cards arrive, so how do I move money from the business account to my current account? Apparently by turning up with a cheque book and a passport for ID and smiling beguilingly at the cashier. We opt to have some cash cards authorised to simplify the process, but are surprised that they didn't appear as part of the original application.

Finally the big day comes. One of my clients actually pays an invoice. I rush to the bank to pay it in over the counter. 'How long do you think this cheque will take to clear?' I ask meekly. 'Five working days, probably, but that depends on how you plan to access the money,' comes the faintly baffling answer.

This is interesting. With my online account, a cheque received on Saturday, usually reaches the account by post by the Tuesday and is usually, at least as far as recent memory goes, clear by the Thursday. With my second business account, the cheque is handed over the counter and takes even longer than the postal, online version, not clearing until the Friday. I point out the anomaly.

'But at least your banking's free now,' she replies.

'It was free before,' I retort.

'Oh, sorry,' she composes herself, 'but at least it's service with a smile.'

Fair point. You don't get that with an online account, but it does show how little some banks have understood what their customers want. This account will cost me after the first 18 months and yet it appears to offer so much more in terms of hassle and so much less in terms of pro-activity than the free online account. It's early days, and I plan to give it more time, but first impressions have not been good.

The main differentiator for me was going to be the business manager and, so far, he's put himself out to assist with the application process, coming around to our house to collect and complete forms, etc. It would appear the supporting processes are letting him down. I hope they don't stop him giving time to customers[3]. But, would better service be worth money to the bank in question? At a personal level, it would actually save them money, since they're in danger of losing out on any fees I would pay as a result of these early complications. So customer service is valuable to a bank if it prevents money from being lost.

Elsewhere a friend of mine, with an online account, discovers that he's got slightly less going in to the account than going out via direct debits and the like. To fix this, he drops in to a branch of the business that owns the online bank and hands £40 across the counter in cash.

'Sorry sir.' It was fairly predictable. 'You can only pay money into that account by post or transfer.'

No way is my colleague going to put cash in the post, so his unauthorised overdraft remains for a further few days and another bank contemplates the loss of a customer's business through inflexible processes.

Now given my particular role as Mr Customer Service, I have to practise what I preach. So, if I don't get decent service from an institution I'll move to a different one. Not a policy applied by many of my fellow UK consumers, which in itself is a big part of the problem, but one that hopefully maintains my integrity and allows me to provide dispassionate comments about the whole industry. If I'm honest, my integrity should be called into question, since many planned mini-service revolutions founder in favour of watching a re-run of *MOTD2*.

Would the provider of my current account several years ago now step forward? Yes, for it was here that I first experienced how poor service can be. Having a mortgage and a current account with the same institution might not be the best advice, but, you would hope, it would ensure that they had a good appraisal of your credit-worthiness

---

[3] They did. I never heard from him again

and ability to repay, in the event that you requested an overdraft extension.

Mine was around £500 at the time and I asked for an extension of £100. No mortgage arrears ever and very few occasions of borrowing in the form of an unauthorised overdraft. I did this by phone to my provider's telephone bank.

'I'm sorry sir, but we can't authorise that today,' comes the predictable reply.

'Why?' I respond. 'I have a mortgage with you. I have a good record. And I only need this for a short-term problem.'

'Sorry, sir. It can't be done, I'm afraid.'

I press on in the vain hope that something might change, but the operator goes on to explain that there is a daily floor level set by their computer over which they have no discretion. I explain again the nature and length of my relationship with the bank, but to no avail. Eventually, I explain my frustration and the operator empathises.

'Sometimes we can't understand it either, but it makes no difference when we talk to our managers, so perhaps you could get in touch with our Customer Relations department. Perhaps if you write a complaint to them they'll finally start to listen.'

A bit candid perhaps, and possibly naïve, but it was the last act of this customer at that bank. They lost my mortgage and my current account.

In an interesting footnote to this story, I receive a phone call from them in June 2007. The voice is distant, both sonically and geographically. It sounds like an overseas call. I'm a valued customer, apparently, so they'd like to ask me some questions to see if I would be suitable for one of their new credit cards. Somehow, my departure and associated levels of dissatisfaction have come to be interpreted as 'value'. I politely decline the offer.

It reminds me of a recent experience with an online anti-virus software provider, who failed to resolve a problem in spite of several emails and phone calls. When I finally did get through and asked if the operator would pass on the details of my unfortunate experience to their senior management team I was told 'I'm sorry. We're not allowed to speak to the management team, so we recommend you contact them yourself.' Oh, the joy of the liberated employee!

So, while I explore all of these issues in much more detail further into the book, the initial impact is to erode further our feelings of trust in our banks, a situation that appears to be getting worse – or at least more evident – as time moves on.

*

So, if improved service can positively impact the banking 'bottom line', how does a bank go about creating the conditions for this to happen consistently, day in and day out?

At this point I'm about to introduce a phrase so hackneyed and unsurprising that you may be forgiven for closing the book, drawing a heavy sigh and deciding to take up entomology instead. Yes, folks, it's all about having a 'customer-focused culture'. Proven beyond reasonable doubt within both academic and actual business fields, the fact is that an organisation's culture determines the quality and effectiveness of its service.

The fact of the matter is that UK retail banking has yet to shed a culture that is no longer appropriate for the times. If, as some clever clogs once said, we spent as much time remembering the future as we did the past, we'd realise that banking has changed, consumers are king and we need a big Allman Brothers-sized 'shake down' if we're going to get it right.

To understand how retail banking culture has evolved, we need to take a look at the recent history of banking. In this way we'll understand the DNA of UK banking, we'll recognise its characteristics and we'll be able to offer a guess at how it may respond to certain situations in future.

To do this, the grizzled, decrepit figure hunched over this laptop will have to transform miraculously into the sprightly, fresh-faced 16-year-old version of the same person. Oh, the memories. 'Picture This' on yellow vinyl is one that springs to mind. As does the Specials' first single and a pink vinyl copy of 'Cool for Cats'. And *Rust Never Sleeps* – which seems all the more relevant. But one specific recollection does shuffle to the front of the queue.

One of my first abortive attempts to move a relationship on from simple hand-holding to full on 'mouth to mouth' ended in failure, as they were wont to do, at deep mid-wicket, with a slightly damaged trombone. However difficult it may be to conjure up an image of the moment, it still sticks with me. The knowledge that the move was ill-timed, the premise ill-starred and that the trombone, an unusual though possibly surmountable obstacle, denoted other less carnal intentions, does not dim the memory of that midsummer evening by Beamish and East Tanfield cricket pitch.

That relationship, like many others struck up through living-room windows as I delivered the *Evening Chronicle* in 1979, ended there and then, tragically just short of my sweetheart's transformation from junior orchestra member to fully subscribed, snakebite-quaffing Hawkwind vamp.

In fact, the only lovebite I received in that barren year came from a particularly amorous Yorkshire terrier who attacked my ankles as I thrust my paper through one of the doors on Masefield Avenue. The terrier itself went on to create a new world record for non-assisted flight when its next quarry responded by 'converting' it between the posts of two adjoining chimney-breasts.

My first banking relationship (with Barclays) flowered upon my arrival at Sheffield University in 1981. Well, I say 'flowered' but this was not a personal choice. It came about through necessity upon receipt of my university grant.

For those unfamiliar with the concept of state aid for students, this amounted to about £1500 and was designed to get me through my first year in Sheffield. I now understand that most 'modern' students require at least this amount to pay for their concierge service and accompanying swimming pool (believe me, I've been back to the University quarter in Sheffield since).

In those days, I don't recall seeing bank ads on TV. I think I went along, as this was where my parents had their accounts. How embarrassed I was to discover upon my arrival at Sheffield that an essential part of 'intro week' was the Anti-Apartheid demonstrations outside Barclays' branches. Lost my cool straight away. Actually I'd lost my cool within 24 hours of arriving by declaring that I thought Anti-Apartheid was what Italians had before the main course when they ate dinner (Auntie Pastie being a friend of my mother's who works at Greggs). Once you'd paid for your university accommodation, there was little left, and Barclays, showing a degree of prescience rarely glimpsed in UK banking, surmised that I didn't represent a good risk and resisted any attempt to provide an overdraft.

Life with my bank back then was easy, precisely because they weren't particularly interested in me, nor I in them. ATMs were making their first shiny and intriguing appearances on the streets of the UK and, following the riots of 1981, distracted us from concerted attempts to overthrow the government or, in my case, the pursuit of new and exciting adventures in food (garlic!).

In fact, my first memories of UK banking are almost entirely of late-night visits to the nearest ATM in order to satiate the predictable thirst for cheap Student Union beer. As often as not, the £5 weekly allowance I'd promised myself didn't stretch to more than the occasional pint, but in those early days of ATMs it wasn't unusual for one of them to pay out more than it should. The late-evening sorties were therefore excusable.

After a couple of uneventful years I was picked to go on a student work exchange. Some unfortunate from Canada would come and work in the UK for a year (being immediately unique in 1981 on account of being in the UK and having a job at the same time), while I would work in Quebec province. A nice arrangement, I thought at the time, but difficult to complete without £350 for flights. So, I summoned up the courage to go beyond the stony-faced cashier at the counter and asked to see the manager for an overdraft.

Sadly, I don't recall my strategy that day. I'm told that I forewent the usual St Etienne home shirt, dirty jeans and sandshoe combination in favour of a shirt and tie (plus dirty jeans and sandshoes). Spying the assistant in the shadows cast by my rampant freakish acne, I may have begun by apologising and thanking him for his time. In reality, I showed the assistant the letter from the Canadian Employment and Immigration Council, complete with the estimated weekly income of somewhere in the region of 150 Canadian dollars, confirmed that my accommodation was included and fired off a smile, full of confident nonchalance, as if I actually believed the overdraft was to be granted. However, for the first time (and possibly the only justifiable occasion) I was clearly being viewed first as a suspect, and second as a customer. This may not have been helped by my unique sense of style in those days. Oh, and did I mention the moustache?

My letter from the Canadian Employment and Immigration Council was examined and prodded as if it lay on a Petrie dish. Questions were asked. The assistant concealed a series of complex calculations behind his hand and, eventually, a £350 overdraft was granted. I paid scant attention to the conditions, admittedly, and disappeared happily amongst the Canadians to busy my time shelf-stacking and trying to avoid listening to Bryan Adams' ubiquitous 'Summer of 69'.

After 5 of the 8 weeks had passed I'd spent so much time with the hosts, a kind family named Ouimet, there had been little chance to spend my earnings, so I'd accumulated sufficient to pay back the over-draft in full, probably twice over. Unfortunately (for Barclays) I then met another Brian, who had a business hoovering the bottom of peo-ple's swimming pools and that soon set my personal financial strategy spinning off course. Fearing that his 'hoovering' was some cryptic euphemism for deviant practices, I kept him at arm's length initially (about half the length of a pool hoover, incidentally). But soon we were as thick as the detritus at the bottom of Mrs Le Brun's *piscine*, passing the evenings playing cards, discovering that you could 'shoot' pool as well as hoover it and being introduced to the pleasures of Labatt 500, the beer of the Canuck sophisticate in 1983.

However, as 'Wherever I Lay my Hat' rose and fell from the num-ber one spot back in the UK, and Robert Plant's languid 'Big Log' shrank back down the charts (let's see that get past the proof-reader), so did my bank balance. I returned to the UK in time to organise trav-el to Catalonia where I was to spend my study year abroad, without, I now confess, repaying the overdraft. Perhaps I was ahead of my time anticipating that this was, in fact, a limit to be used when necessary, rather than the loan, which I suspect it actually was.

Nevertheless, it was several months later when, during a weekly call to apprise myself of Sunderland's latest performance, my parents shared their concern over a letter from Barclays, addressed to them, presumably in my absence. OK, so I'd probably been a bit lax, but the added intervention of one's parents does tighten the focus on such occasions and I duly organised for a bank draft to be sent to the UK.

Barclays finally saw the last of me towards the end of my time at university, but not before another interesting adventure. On this occasion, the monotony of watching snails race each other across our carpets was interrupted by the sound of the postman delivering a brand new Barclaycard. I opened the envelope as if it were a longed-for Christmas present and placed the shining card by my bed, gazing at it and imagining its possibilities like a hypnotised hobbit. But, after some indecent plotting, during which I mentally morphed into Gollum, my evil plans were resisted by my innate Catholicism (profound guilt, shame, etc) so I left it there. I left it there until a week or so later, when we found ourselves to be extremely thirsty one evening and needed to procure some drink. Victoria Wines had helpfully opened a branch on the corner of Rustlings Road and Ecclesall Road, so I marched in there, presented my credit card and left with about £30 of various embrocations (but mainly cider).

Again, not being familiar with the conventions of personal lending, I did not notice the non-arrival of the corresponding statement, or the request for minimum payment. Not, that is, until several years later, when my father recalled once receiving a credit card statement that contained a transaction he firmly denied having completed. Such was the vigour with which he mounted his defence that I believe Barclays may have refunded the sum.

Furthermore, as a North East-based sales representative, he'd spent little if any time in Sheffield and, to add strength to his case, he could prove he was playing golf in Heworth near Gateshead with some mates from Walter Willson's on the day of the purchase in question (although I wasn't allowed to share that fact with his employers). Or it might have been Fine Fare.

Some years later, incidentally, he began claiming to have been with a Vivo manager (a North-East-based precursor to Spar), which led me to believe Barclays were still on his tail.

So, as the realisation dawned on me that I had been responsible for said transaction, it occurred to me that the bank's earlier attempt to collude with my parents to secure their money, might have led to them confusing our contact details – and me receiving an additional card.

*

So the camera pans away from the maternal home in County Durham to a young man in Cheshire who was in the worrying few months of establishing his family business. Early signs had been promising, but the usual combination of the need for urgent investment in growing the business and the delays in invoice settlement, meant that the days grew more precarious.

He visited his Barclays branch manager to explain the scenario and seek support. 'Tell you what,' began the be-suited branch manager, as he looked over the company information, 'I think you've a sound business here. So I'll turn a blind eye to the next 100 cheques you draw. Will that give you the space you need?'

As I contemplated the balance of my years with Barclays after university – and could find nothing in the credit side for either of us – I decided to withdraw from the 'World's Biggest Bank' and seek succour somewhere else.

The 'succours' turned out to be NatWest, who administered my financial arrangements until, as an employee of Halifax Building Society, I was lured into opening a card cash account (and then a 'maxim' current account) by the thinly veiled threat that my salary might not arrive if I didn't. How we laughed the day it didn't, but that was just a joke courtesy of a certain senior personnel colleague of mine who took umbrage at my failure to follow a specific order.

Working in a building society in the late 80s gave me a unique insight into service from the provider's perspective as well as my first insight into the culture of financial services providers. In 1988 when I first started working for a large Yorkshire-based Building Society, there were the four main clearing banks for current accounts (unless you had a private banking arrangement with Coutts, for example) and then Building Societies for your saving and mortgage requirements.

The Building Societies' Act of 1986 had begun the process of deregulation, which has continued ever since, with all banks and building societies effectively now competing for the same customers, so in 1988 my employers had just embarked on providing unsecured and secured personal loans, as well as a current account, from a stock-in-trade reputation built on mortgage-lending and savings. However, what few people appreciate is that only a few years earlier, mortgages were only granted after much supplication and effort. So this new world of deregulation, increased customer competition and new technology would spark a revolution to which few traditionally focused financial services organisations could truly commit.

The manifestation of this, not only in my work place at the time, but also in most others, was a maniacal attention to detail and cross-checking, but scant regard for the customer, who, let's face it, was lucky to be even considered for a loan. I believe that this institutionalised mistrust of the customer is at the heart of the current crisis. Manual completion of daily returns, unexpected audits and the pall of fear hanging over someone whose till failed to balance, did genuinely remove the focus from getting it right for the customer to just getting it right.

A result of this was an internal fixation that would have seemed extreme even to a paranoid gynaecologist. There were hours devoted to having several people cross-check and approve a personal loan application, but never time to devote sufficient time to the customer, or at least, to a customer who had come in 'on spec'.

One interesting aspect of this now curious though then everyday focus on process was the meticulousness with which 'staff' product applications were processed. Just as football clubs can sometimes treat away supporters as 'suspects' first and 'customers' second, so banks and building societies in the eighties regarded every employee's application for a loan as an early warning sign that the individual had either been a bag-carrier for Jimmy Hoffa or was about to 'split', possibly in a Latin American direction, but definitely with the proceeds of the loan.

A multi-level hierarchy further burdened this overly internal focus. Cashier to Chief Cashier. Chief Cashier to Chief Clerk. Department Manager to Assistant Manager. Assistant Manager to Branch Manager. There were even District Managers. And, to cap it all, we had the Area Manager based on the top floor of our branch. A decent man, he spent most of the two years we worked together trying to hush up the fact that we came from the same North West Durham mining village.

As a consequence of all these management layers, the concept of taking initiative, fixing something that you recognise as broken or demonstrating anything resembling ownership, was definitely not encouraged. In fact it was actively discouraged. In these modern days of allowing people to make mistakes and learn from them, so as not to extinguish their commitment, it seems strangely alien to think that a business should be based on following orders, but that's how it was. God help you if you'd got something wrong in the Branch Suspense book. To be honest, that didn't happen very often. But then again when you have a cast of thousands to cross-check everything you do, time and time again, that statement shouldn't surprise anyone.

Those junior managers – my peers in 1988 – have had to evolve into customer-focused leaders to meet the challenges of the modern age, but such a restrained Victorian approach to service may have left many of them with damaging vestiges of the famed quadruple check. Is it any wonder they can't see things from the customer's point of view even now? Customers weren't clearly as welcome as they now are, back in 1988 – and it's no surprise if some of us with longer memories regard banks' eagerness to do business with a large ladleful of scepticism.

One thing I did notice, though, was the creeping modernisation of the superficial elements of banking. Up and down high streets the length and breadth of the country, banks and building societies were re-branding, re-designing their branches and embarking on TV and radio ads and getting involved in sponsorship of major sporting tournaments, etc.

For me and my cadre of checkers at my Yorkshire-based Building Society, this meant a change from beige and brown to silver and blue. Quite what the public made of some of our competitors' design changes, God only knows, but I think we were privately relieved to be embracing a colour combination that didn't remind one of a pair of well-lived-in adolescent male underpants.

Although it's easy to make these remarks in retrospect, I think we knew we were designed for our own internal need to satisfy ourselves that correct procedures had been followed rather than for our customers' changing needs and the dawn of true competition.

OK. Fair enough, perhaps we didn't. I'm not going to sit here and present a level of prescience capable of seeing that far forward, but I think we all sensed that customer relationships were not characterised by warmth. They were somewhere between obligation, respect and fear, as if operated by the Bronte Collective.

From the customers' perspective, it would be stretching things too much to imply that they were aware of our failings. Like most of us, when one needs a mortgage, one asks a friend or a family member to recommend somewhere, whereupon one submits oneself to the 'application process'.

You tended to use words like 'oneself' when corresponding with banks and building societies, as if the use of the familiar 'you' would affect your credit rating.

You'd write to your bank or building society, using 'Yours faithfully' and would always don an austere and obsequious facial expression when entering their banking halls, as if being introduced to Don Corleone at a 1950s New Jersey wedding.

You'd submit yourself to the process, resist the temptation to correct, amend or develop any statements or assumptions made, and, with a prevailing wind, several weeks later, you'd be in receipt of your 'product'.

In truth, banking had changed little in several hundred years. Customer inertia had rewarded the tendency to clutch at conventions and large financial institutions faced the future, blinkered and as agile as an aircraft carrier, with its gruelling turning-circle. It wasn't that there was little hope. There was simply no other alternative to the fading watercolour of financial service provision. Something didn't have to change, certainly in the minds of the traditional banking fraternity, but in the rush to differentiate in Thatcher's Britain, something did.

Somewhere in the UK, the Midland Bank (HSBC as it is now) had brought together a group of people, none of whom had any banking experience together, to answer a question: what do customers really want from their bank? Reliability, approachability, ownership, warmth and great problem-solving were among the answers postulated by this maverick band.

In 1989 First Direct was born and years later it was still winning awards (including the Unisys / *Management Today* Service Excellence Award in 2004). According to reports I've seen, over 90% of its customers describe themselves as 'delighted' with its service. Based on the premise of 24/7 telephone banking, with a human always available, characterised by friendliness, ownership and excellent problem-solving, it soon set about trying to change the face of UK banking.

The principle behind the construction of First Direct was differentiation through service and its impact on competitors has been tangible, with most opting to open up a 'telephone banking channel' within 2/3 years of it establishing itself. But few, if any, have come close to matching the renown of First Direct for one simple reason: First Direct was originally designed, developed and constructed with one desired output: to provide excellent customer service. Elsewhere, too many distracting points of focus were troubling the sightline and, quite frankly, the majority of competing financial services organisations were not even aware that a competitor was in their midst.

The competitor, conversely, had begun to notice that its own service was beginning to get noticed, in some strangely engaging ways. Whereas most customers of the four clearing banks would not declare their provider in public, First Direct customers, by way of their recognisable 'black' bank cards, were wordlessly acknowledging each other in supermarket queues with a knowing nod and, it has to be said, a smug wink. First Direct's disowning forefathers consoled themselves by characterising the new kid on the block's emergence as a 'niche' player – and while it's true that the profile of their customers is more M&S than Asda – other 'niche' players (nephews?) followed on in the early 90s.

Virgin Money (née Direct), Tesco Personal Finance, Sainsbury's Bank and Marks & Spencer Financial Services, were soon joined by the Co-op's Smile enterprise, all focused on the possibilities of playing the 'customer service' card. Further along, Rowan Gormley created Virgin One for Richard Branson, with its customer-focused way of benefiting the connecting of current account and mortgage. Ease of access, transparency, warmth, ownership and character all vied for position while the behemoths circled the wagons and erected 'telephone banks' in defence.

In the mid 90s, some of the larger players, including the four major clearers and their slightly niftier ex-building society competitors (including Halifax and Abbey National) appeared to have decided to invoke a further sea change. They saw First Direct as a great step forward, but embraced technology and the web as a means of staging an even more impressive 'great leap forward'. By 1995 it was already possible to sit at home and take a 3D trip round a property rather than visit an estate agent's for the particulars and drive 50 miles to inspect it.

But in the subsequent 13 years in retail banking all of this has come to a desultory 'is there anything else I can do for you today?' at the end of every transaction. British retail banking is caught in a self-made web of stasis. Perspective is conspicuous by its absence; customers' needs are only half-heartedly understood and if the culture were personified it would be as a wolf in sheep's clothing – a bottle of wine for the extra mile, but only real recognition for the sale.

I perceive a defensive industry, shackled by convention, created at a time when we had to go to our banks cap in hand to put our names on the list for a mortgage. The problem was, things switched. They need us now, but the old-fashioned constraints still mist their thinking. Branch design may have improved, web facilities make self-service a reality and the experienced eye can still find some good deals, but every transaction is carried out in the knowledge that someone, somewhere is examining the cross-sales potential of this particular customer – and someone is being coached either to provide the extra effort required to make the sale, or to ship out.

Speak to employees. Ask them to compare what emphasis is laid on their customer service performance with the need to make sales. I have and the results are frightening. Not because I reject the concept of *upselling*, but because so little is done to understand the real needs of the customer.

To start with, how do most retail banks generate feedback from their customers? From a series of recent face-to-face visits to my local branch, the answer would appear to be in the form of a customer service questionnaire – the kind of ten-a-penny A4 sheets that adorn our British shop fronts. They usually contain a series of well-meaning questions, trying to reflect the bank's view of the ideal customer experience and to collect sufficient data to produce an accurate picture of performance for the service provider.

But the first problem has already arisen. The *bank's* view. It's as if the questionnaire designer already had an inkling as to what matters to the average branch customer.

The questions we're asked are recognisable, because we've seen them everywhere else. They ask for ratings – backed by some sophisticated measurement methodology that will produce a figure at the end, to satisfy the market research department and ensure next year's budget is protected. But what do ratings tell us? One thing for sure is that we don't all rate according to the same mental scale. A 4 out of 5 for me might convey the apex of joy, but might be just not good enough for Wendy at Number 12. And then we have the yes / no questions. Like some ludicrous parody of those TV games of the past where you can't say yes or no, except this time, that's all you *can* say.

All this does is reinforce someone else's view of what matters – someone else's view of how feedback should be collected. Probably more related to post-graduate theorising than genuine customer insight. You're rarely, if ever, given the opportunity to provide ad-hoc verbatim feedback, when everyone would agree that this individualises each customer's experience. Why not? Simply because it's difficult for the computer to manage this. *Computer says no*, but this time, internally.

To be fair to most banks, you're also likely to receive a copy of their feedback form through the post, but the same problems dog the process and make achievement of true customer insight about as distant as a Nobel Peace Prize for Robert Mugabe.

If we examine things from the customer's perspective, there are some obvious quick wins for the organisation with perspective. First of all, people who are likely to pick up an in-branch customer service questionnaire and fill it in are in the minority. Some reports put it at less than one in a hundred customers. Privately I believe this demo-graphic also has a form-filling fixation and will therefore be providing less than insightful data. In other conversations I've heard it declared that 3 in a hundred customers are 'stupid', so that belittles the form-filling fraternity even further. Perhaps we could isolate this population by setting up roadblocks at Subaru dealerships, such is my experience with the younger drivers of those particular cars. But that's for another day.

For those returning postal forms, there is usually an opportunity to give an overall rating for service as well as a box offering you the opportunity to say how likely you are to recommend your financial services provider. This is interesting, as from everything I've seen, the responses to this question are proven to correlate to buying behaviour. In English, people's likelihood to recommend is a strong indicator of future re-purchase. To the layman, if they talk to their friends about you, you can expect a return visit.

If I were leading a large financial services provider, I would want to see some real insights into what it is like to be a customer of ours, so the first thing I would do would be to ensure all current customer feedback is proudly displayed on our website and in regular updates to our beloved customer base. Regardless of how well we are perform-ing compared to the competition, the sheer fact that we believe in transparency and want to give service the profile our customers believe it deserves, will give us the edge in some households. I'd be focusing on highlighting what's currently annoying customers, but countering that with details of changes / improvements made since the last posting.

To get around the entrenched obstacles of the form-filling approach, I would be researching two key areas: *making it easy for our customers to provide feedback* and *ensuring we hear the customer's voice*. You may have heard the phrase 'voice of the customer' before, espe-cially if your organisation has set off on a service improvement odyssey, but it usually means more of the form-filling and less of the customer-orientation, actually. A bit like *walking in the customer's shoes*. If it means spending a while wearing that particular footwear, let's recruit a mystery shopper instead.

If I had a pound for every time I've heard it, I'd be buying him some new ones, but the fact remains it's one of the top candidates for this year's 'do as I do, not as I say' awards. Very few people do it. It's rarely institutionalised into organisational activities and if it is, it's usually in the employee's own time. Making it easy for customers to give feedback denotes a call to action, once you've seen how hard the process is for some unfortunates. You may advertise a telephone number, you may welcome feedback and you may have even published a nifty little tome setting out what we should do in the event of a complaint, but getting us to tell you what we really think? Not easy. *Muy difícil.*

In recent years, there has been a noticeable trend towards facilitating the collection of customer feedback. One building society routinely records customer comments at the till and passes them through to their service excellence department, verbatim – in the customer's own words, covering a vast spectrum of themes from interest rates to the colour of the savings passbook. But they are in the minority.

The word 'feedback' is thrown around in corporate conversations as if it were something that could be turned on and off, like a tap, when in reality we need to go stateside if we want it to work. You have to *faucet*. Sorry. But you do have to force it. Feedback doesn't come easily to British customers, as we fear confrontation and find it difficult to be frank. The curious dichotomy of the Brits is that we find it difficult to be frank but privately enjoy being Christine at weekends.

The problem is that we've found ourselves in a place where we congratulate ourselves if, as a bank, we can generate a 20% return on our feedback questionnaires. Doesn't that illustrate an extremely disappointing level of ambition? Why wouldn't the other 80% respond if it were going to lead to improved service? The fact of the matter is that banks really do have to go the extra mile, because many customers simply do not believe that offering their view will lead to improvements, but in general terms, we need to recognise that if the Americans could get a man on the moon, UK banks should be able to get more than 20% of customers to provide feedback.

Let's look at what's holding back this tide of customer opinion. First of all, how do banks ask us for feedback? Maybe the first question should be: why don't they ask us for feedback? I ask this because many people I know never hear from their financial services providers. But to revert to the first question: we usually receive a paper survey through the post. To be honest, I've probably subconsciously welcomed the form, but rarely filled it in. I routinely fill in my Premier Inn email survey when that arrives, but that's because I'm likely to be sat at the laptop when it beeps in to my in-tray. If I only switched the laptop on once a day to pick up emails, I might not click on the survey and give them my ten minutes.

I receive at least three telephone calls a day as I sit here sharing my thoughts with you. They all want to sell me something, even if the chat starts with some fairly see-through attempts at feedback. In reality it's never anything more than a 'how are things with your Sky subscription?' before they sink their teeth in with a 'did you realise how much it could cost if your Sky+ box needed repairing?'

Increasingly I'm receiving recorded telephone calls. That's right. You lift the receiver and a financial services company's pre-programmed automaton describes in a kind of Asimov-like alienated neutrality the benefits of their new consolidation loan.

This, my friends, represents the highest form of contempt I have ever come across. If you can't even be bothered to have a human ring me, then that highlights just how important you consider the 'customer', in spite of your fur-lined, 'leading edge' customer service sessions.

No one ever rings for feedback. I'd give it wholeheartedly, but no one ever rings. The reason I don't hear from them isn't because banks don't do it. It's because the sample they choose is so small, the chances of their long, evil fingers pointing at me are so remote, I'd be better off putting my pension on the characters of *Shameless* winning the Queen's Award for Industry. You see, the need to get just 20% of us to provide feedback even influences their planning. Just *that* sample, just *this* amount, etc. It's not ambitious thinking by any standards, unless your standards are very low indeed.

How about it if I could show banks how to get the other 80% of their customers to give feedback? Well, this may come across like cheating, but I'd start by asking customers what we'd have to do to get them to provide feedback. I'd wager my next pie and chips dinner that most would reply with either 'by actually changing things as a result of my feedback' or 'make it easier for me to give you feedback'.

Making it easy to give feedback should start with an assessment of when and how we Brits like to communicate. We're renowned as a taciturn race. Any time spent on the Tube readily evidences this. You speak and you're regarded as some kind of anthropological anomaly. Keep quiet. Keep your opinions to yourself. This is Britain. The fact is that the British do not pro-actively communicate. We are prone to silence and introspection at the best of times, so some considerable effort has to be made to overcome our shyness. And yet, recent news confirms what we've all feared. We are the nation who most enjoys texting!

Regardless of whether your preferred personal form of communication is texting or email, it raises an interesting point. How many of us would happily provide feedback by text if we were asked for it? I rest my case. My bank has never texted me, but if the request came I'm sure we could address that 20% response-rate ceiling, so invisible and risible. The problem with the lack of customer feedback is that it has not been made easy for us, so we choose the easy option and don't give it. Perhaps they know that texting, for example, would open the feedback floodgates. The problem is, most of us would probably be inclined to text in as we stand in a queue in a branch where there are six tills, but only three cashiers serving. The advent of texting feedback may quickly expose some of the darker elements of banking strategy, so maybe that explains its slow emergence.

Leaving the method of collecting feedback to the side for a moment, let's consider what companies do with the feedback they receive. Well, it's all shrouded in mist. Actually, it isn't. I've argued previously that most feedback is 'managed' internally, usually via a trip through the Market Research department, via several internal recommendations, but almost always ending up leading nowhere. Where fortune smiles on the customer and the feedback does actually lead to change, this is more likely to take the form of something 'imposed' on front-line colleagues, rather than something resulting from cross-functional engagement and brainstorming.

What is needed is a process that quickly identifies the flavour of feedback and presents it in an undiluted, transparent fashion. It seems we are also a nation renowned for its self-deprecation. And yet, as banks, we cannot seem to take criticism. I suspect that the first bank to take this point seriously will experience an outbreak of nervousness at senior levels, so maybe we should leave it to some enterprising regional building society to recognise the need and fill the gap.

I've also been making the assumption in this argument that banks would want our unedited, verbatim, free-form, individual feedback, as this would most effectively convey our individual experience with their service – our emotional highs and lows – and a true indication of which 'hot buttons' would set off our rampant advocacy. The fact is, however, that banks remain constrained by a question set which better reflects their view of the world than the external perspective provided by the customer.

In actual fact, most surveys, as I have argued earlier, seem to reflect the subconscious mind of the survey designer, in that they seem to contain questions to which the bank already knows the answer, rather than an invitation to introduce something new to improvement discussions. This ushers in the distinct impression that banks are going through the motions: that customer satisfaction surveys are required, otherwise they wouldn't get our quality mark maintained for a further uninspiring 12 months – not because there's a distinct chance that they might uncover a real opportunity for differentiation.

It's frustrating, because the lack of honest advancements in banking transparency tends to blind us all to some of the positive initiatives out there. Among those who contribute the most to the UK exchequer are the banks and our football industry (specifically, the Premier League and its members). And which organisations receive the most media criticism? The very same.

As I sit squinting into the late-afternoon glare of a young February sun, some green shoots of (service) recovery are beginning to be visible, but while the internally-fixated, audit-crazed tyrants of the near past may have retired to the hills, their ghosts still clearly hold sway in boardrooms up and down the country.

4
Sorted?
August 2006

It's difficult enough trying to get into my bathing shorts (you could start by taking me out for a drink) without making me feel bad about my weight, but that's not stopped the Royal Mail. Today, they're introducing a new pricing structure that will see the cost of my mail based on the weight of my items (as well as their size and thickness). Put simply (and believe me, that's not easy) the cost of your mail will depend on whether you're posting a small letter, a large letter or a packet.

For me, the comic potential of this big change outweighs any sensible benefit, as I'll be queuing up to hear my local postmaster ask about the size and thickness of my packet and preparing a number of inappropriate responses. But, having said that, this is apparently the greatest change to our postal system since the introduction of the penny black, so we owe the Royal Mail some careful scrutiny.

For customers, we'll have two further sizes to think about when contemplating sending something. This is going to be particularly important when sending birthday cards, as the ones carrying badges or containing that little musical device will cost more to send. The changes may lead to initially longer queues in Post Offices, but it may well prove easier than the current approach. Take me for example.

I usually buy books of six first-class stamps and then, to my horror, discover that I have an envelope a little heavier than the rest. Rather than trot along to the Post Office, I simply estimate the additional cost in terms of multiples of first-class stamps. This probably costs me money in the long run.

Businesses, on the other hand, face all of the above, plus possible investment in new equipment, new designs for their direct mail, etc, extra labour costs in the post room and even changes to the way they frank post. No exceptions have been made for small businesses, other than to tell us that we're likely to save money in the long run. But a major change such as this should have some clear user benefits and as I've received my measuring template through the post, perhaps they'll be explained there. Er, no. Unless the measuring template is the benefit.

But the Royal Mail say that 'Pricing in Proportion' (to unveil its wonderful sobriquet) will introduce a 'fairer and simpler pricing system which more accurately reflects the cost of handling mail.'

Apparently, the size and shape of most items of mail are the key factors in determining the cost of sorting and delivery. If you send an 'outsize' envelope, it has to be sorted manually. I see. So it's an attempt to pass on savings to the consumer, one presumes. Royal Mail says '85% of stamped mail will stay the same price or be cheaper.' That sounds a bit oblique to me. What percentage of that 85% will be cheaper? And will 15% of mail be more expensive?

But I'm being a little disingenuous here, since as a business owner, two-thirds of my mail should be cheaper and I can understand why a business needs to be in control not only of its costs, but of its future revenue too. And Postwatch, the industry watchdog, is mainly concerned that the Royal Mail mitigates the impact of the changes and communicates effectively to groups such as the elderly, isolated and disabled, rather than challenging the principles behind the changes. So let's examine the bigger picture (as long as it's not wider than 165mm, as that's going to cost you). The Royal Mail has been at a disadvantage for some years, for a variety of reasons. From dreadful industrial relations, via TV exposés of pilfering, to admissions that the infrastructure was insufficient to meet current needs and increasing competition, the organisation is in need of modernisation, in the widest sense of the word.

It needs to re-build employee relations, create clarity going forward and establish a competitive edge that will see it survive and prosper into the future. But given the unique place the Royal Mail occupies in this country, the change must be evolutionary rather than revolutionary, so as not to lose us all along the way. I see this as just one small part of that immense journey, but understand why the nature of this particular change makes it initially uncomfortable for UK consumers.

Like Chip and PIN, it's a change that will be scary at first. But let me assure you that it will soon slip alongside all those other unconscious daily routines, like encountering a queue at the Post Office, finding your local shop has run out of stamps and wondering what happened to all of that postal competition we were promised.

5

Still Not Sorted

September 2007

Believe it or not, it's now almost two years since it was announced that Royal Mail would face competition for both its business and residential services. From January 1st 2006 any licensed operator could choose to compete head on with one of the longest-established public services in this or any other country. Customers could cheerfully anticipate a new age of choice and improved service without, it was implied, losing the country's proud postal USP: one price anywhere. Business owners could look forward to a new competitive era where a poor-performing postal services provider could be swiftly replaced with a new one.

So, in the two years since then, what has happened? Not a lot, it has to be said. From a personal viewpoint, I have to admit some misplaced optimism. I'd envisaged the traditional red post box being joined by some little orange TNT post boxes and some tasteful gold and brown UPS ones. DHL's corporate livery would adorn many of the remaining boxes, while independent locally-based services would establish a local niche (Ackroyd and Son: fast, cheap and reliable – but only to Todmorden).

Our garden path would be crowded with postmen, as if a subbuteo pitch had appeared in Land of the Giants – elbowing each other out of the way and competing for the affections of the divorcee at number 42. Life would be a lot more colourful – and still one price anywhere. So, unless you've mistaken your porridge for hallucigens (again), this scene has not yet materialised – and, to those with a less limited intellectual capacity than your author, was never likely to.

The fact is that competition has had an impact on business services, but its impact has been to the detriment of residential services – the likes of you and me. Put yourself in the expensive shoes of the MD of a large parcel distribution service, from any of those mentioned above. Like us, he or she will have applauded the Royal Mail's sophisticated network, their one price anywhere basic philosophy and their redolence of everything British.

But will the MD jump into the residential marketplace? Could they offer something to eat into the Royal Mail's monopoly (when last counted, they had 97% of the letters market)? Could they partner with the Royal Mail and provide competition for sections of the process (for example, final end delivery, mass transit of mail, etc)? Once you consider these questions their unwillingness to get involved becomes plainly understandable.

Take paying a single price (admittedly first or second class) regardless of the UK destination, for example. This is exactly the sort of social obligation that private companies tend to 'avoid like the plague', as one commentator put it. Private companies are motivated by profit, regardless of any recent carefully timed philanthropic conversions in the boardroom.

The reality is that most of us will not be offered competitive choice for several years, or probably even longer. But business customers? That's another story altogether – and that's currently at the top of the MD's list of priorities.

Of the couple of dozen organisations who have successfully obtained licences to deliver mail, all have focused on business services (as far as I can see). TNT and DHL are the most recognisable new players on the scene, but anyone who ever worked in a solicitors' office or a building society will recognise the natural extension into this market of the former exchange service company DX.

Some have stepped forward to milk the opportunity, most appropriately Express Dairies (my profound apologies). Deciding that it could use its existing distribution network to deliver packages to customers initially seemed like a good idea, but ultimately failed to trouble the company accountant, so they soon went off the idea. When the history of this company is written (Express Diaries, anyone?), the punning potential will start a bidding war among ghost writers. The losers will be well cheesed off.

But business customers still have their gripes – and in this they are joined by residential customers like me and my confused tomcat, who, like my mobile phone, has limited memory capacity and thinks we get a new postie every day. The fact is prices have risen way beyond the quality of service provided.

A recent poll in Scotland highlighted that only 28% of respondents believed that their post was always on time and always arrived. Aside from prompting an obvious question – how do you know post you weren't expecting hasn't arrived? – it strikes me as a low figure. To reinforce my point a further 64% of customers valued the service, but would not call it reliable or efficient. 8% said they had switched to other modes of communication, mostly to the ether of modern technology.

What further galls these respondents is the fact that post prices are rising faster than Postcomm promised us. Who? Postcomm is the organisation charged by government to regulate the postal services industry. When the Royal Mail wants to put up prices, they ask Postcomm which, in turn, examines the company's cost, efficiency and service performance, before deciding on whether any proposed increases can be allowed. The fact that it has been announced that second class mail is to rise to 29p (i.e. by 20% in 2009) and that the Royal Mail has announced that there will be no more Sunday or Bank Holiday collections from October 28th this year, means that the public is generally more aware of the organisation Postwatch, than Postcomm.

Postwatch defends consumers and businesses in this competitive age, arguing recently that Postcomm should not have allowed the second-class price hike. The latter says it's cost-reflective. In effect, they have to do that to maintain the service. Postwatch points out that the Royal Mail has failed to meet efficiency targets and cost-reduction targets, allegedly ignoring its own criteria for price increases.

And while these arguments are played out in the newspapers, a series of wildcat strikes continues to blight the image of the Royal Mail, while the CWU planned more industrial action this summer in response to, among other things, lower-paid foreign workers coming on board, presumably to help address the Royal Mail's cost-reduction targets. Some allege that this further compromises postal security, which has featured in a number of shocking TV documentaries.

For residential customers though, the new dawn promised by the opening up of the postal market is as far away as ever. Prices are rising, service is not what is used to be and if I'm not happy with my postal provider, I don't seem to have an alternative. I wish the post would get itself sorted.

6

The Green Family
January 2007

There's never a good time to introduce the notion of an 'environmental audit' to your household right now. You may be sitting amid the debris of the post-Christmas comedown, the 37-inch LCD screen just visible behind an Everest of discarded battery packets and the sparkle of a thousand sweetie wrappers. The dishwasher, microwave, fridge and cooker may all be going at full blast and the nightly family teeth-cleaning ritual visibly empties Scammonden reservoir. Suddenly it strikes you that maybe, only maybe, you could be doing more for the environment.

The first feeling is an overwhelming sense of guilt. But a quick calculation produces some notable positives. We pick up our veg from a local organic farm in Norwood Green and we buy our meat from the farm shop in Southowram. We recycle our bottles (thanks to the good folk at Bradford Council who installed a mini glass-recycling box in our special paper-only wheelie bin).

My wife Ana got us a composter this year and a clean-up of the guinea pig hutch is swiftly followed by a new consignment of poo, shavings and paper. 'But that's not enough!' scream the sort of people who harangued the *Guardian*'s Leo Hickman, author of *A Life Stripped Bare*, as he tried to purify his lifestyle. 'Why aren't you running your toilet from a rain harvester?' Guilt returns. You've been waving your arms around so frenetically, you wish you'd been powering a mill, rather than playing with your Wii. I dare not even say what Sarah Miles does with hers.

But if I'm honest, there's so much more on the other side of the ethical scales. We know water is scarce (in spite of having to wade through floods on an increasingly regular basis) but we don't collect and use rainwater and haven't abandoned baths as the favoured self-cleaning process. We know packaging is environmentally questionable but we have more plastic bags in the airing cupboard than you could shake a stick at. At least the stick is biodegradable.

We don't use public transport as much as we should (although readers will be aware of the nightmare journeys we made – so you don't have to – in 2006) and I power my car with diesel – hurtling down the motorways with the sound system at full tilt, mobile phone on hands-free and more flashing lights than Piccadilly Circus.

The fact is, we should do more. But where do you start? What do we mean by a commitment to the environment? Is it about living ethically? Are we supposed to be green? Is it all about recycling? We figured the best response was to audit a typical day in the Bradley household. It begins with a shower. No, not that cricketing shower whose latest antics in Australia have us up at 4 a.m., but the electric shower that propels Father into action. It's a very old electric shower, so ancient that the odd coelacanth has washed through the pipes. It uses less water than a bath, maybe, but is difficult to envisage without electricity, short of persuading several neighbours to fire water pistols at me simultaneously. Rainwater? Don't even go there.

Breakfast consists of cereals, sometimes even organic ones, but all purchased from the supermarket. A microwave is used to heat the milk while the kettle fires up and the toaster is regularly called upon. I say 'toaster', but we use the grill. Oh dear.

A fleet of vehicles then exits the drive like the starting line at the Indianapolis 500. Ana's little Polo takes the kids the 3 miles to school while my diesel saloon lumbers down the road to destinations unreachable by public transport (or at least not in a way that allows three meetings in three places in one day).

Our meals are always home made, always eaten together and, wherever possible, bought from local suppliers who (in this part of the world at least) seem to offer better quality and value than the supermarkets. What can be composted generally is – and when someone hasn't cleaned their plate, our tomcat Dini is usually on hand to process the remains.

Our audit shows that we do our best for the home environment during the day – when we're out! Only the reassuring click of the central heating kicking in would tell you the house was inhabited.

And we've just installed an energy-saving combi boiler. It may seem a lot to you, but to the likes of Donnachadh McCarthy, the London-based environmentalist, this is but (organic) chicken feed. He was the first in the capital to export solar electricity from the roof of his home to the local electricity board. His hot water is produced by a solar heating system and his toilet runs on rainwater. I hear he's now installed a wind turbine on the roof and has become London Energy's first ever domestic wind electricity supplier. Donnachadh probably doesn't regard us as hell bent on planetary destruction, but he probably doesn't have school-age kids, a mortgage and a haddock addiction either.

So, on balance, we could do a lot more. Our problem is that we don't know what's possible, affordable and practical. Our 'audit' was nothing more than measuring our lives against a set of imagined 'green' principles. We feel we fall short but we don't know by how much. Therefore, we calculate our household's carbon footprint (my granddad was a miner – how he would have enjoyed that phrase) just to measure the destruction we're innocently causing. Amazingly, we come in way lower than the average UK household (check it out for yourself via www.carbonfootprint.com).

Not only that, but we finally have a set of priorities to focus on: buying energy from a renewable source, making more use of public transport, saving energy in the home and taking fewer flights. You know, maybe we're not so far behind Donnachadh.

We are, however, miles behind Arthur Boyt. For it is he who has decided that the best way to combine his twin loves of wildlife and ethical conservation is to eat road kill. Arthur's household menus have in recent weeks contained fox, deer, otter, dog and greater horseshoe bat. Moreover, he calculates that being run over is more ethical than being farmed. Now there's a level of environmental commitment to aspire to in the future.

7

A Chance to Score with your Employees
June 2006

In 1981 I had a dilemma. We'd turned up in a gloomy frame of mind, not only because Miss Arthurs was about to march us through another rehearsal of *Joseph and his Amazing Technicolor Dreamcoat*, but also because England was about to lose a test match against Australia. As the more aged of you may recall, Australia had posted 401 and England's miserable total of 174 meant we'd have to follow on. This hadn't gone to plan either and we were soon 135-7, still 92 runs behind.

As reports of England's demise somehow made their way to us in the assembly hall, the embattled figure of Ian Botham had marched to the crease, issued a cheerful 'Right, let's have bit of fun,' and the rest is history. Well actually, the rest of the day was double Latin, but Botham's 149 not out gave England a lead of 129.

Cue the dilemma, the following morning. Could we possibly see England bowl out the Aussies and become only the second side in test match history to win a match after following on? Or would we be endlessly repeating the Hairy Ishmaelite routine from *Joseph* until we got it right and end up missing the last day's action?

Being the epitome of Catholicism, riddled with guilt, but innocent of everything, I decided the best course of action was to attend. Several other members of our ragged troupe, however, were mysteriously afflicted with an unidentifiable virus so Joseph's first team squad of brothers were quickly reduced to a 5-a-side team, armed with carefully secreted wirelesses, as Bob Willis ploughed through the Aussies and won us the test.

That dilemma is with us again as the World Cup Finals hove into view. Business magazines are full of employment lawyers' advice to businesses, while the now adult members of St Bede's thespians are praying for a sniffle.

Unsurprisingly, the general tone of employers' advice to staff is stark and vaguely threatening. Firms are advising employees to make holiday requests well in advance of the World Cup (as if none of your colleagues had thought of that!) and also appending a warning that any sickness during this period will be closely monitored. Fair enough, but does that generate any goodwill – or would it be sufficient to persuade Benjamin and his absent brothers to throw back the multicoloured duvet and clock in?

The general rule of thumb appears to be a recommendation that organisations reach a fair consensus with their employees. Asda, for example, has introduced up to 2 weeks' unpaid leave for employees who may want to watch the World Cup.

Others are finding that a little flexibility here (say, allowing people a chance to make up time later) achieves the right balance, while others are entering into the global spirit by hoisting flags, decorating the office and temporarily adding portable TVs to the office indent.

But most organisations, in my view, are missing the point. This impending feast of football is an opportunity to engage with the workforce, show them they're valued and, in a low unemployment era, attract and retain the best people. And if you think hiring a few TV sets and negotiating a little give and take is all there is to it, think again.

Rackspace Managed Hosting won the overall UK Service Excellence Award[4], primarily for demonstrating that successful businesses are built on great employee relations. Let me illustrate what it means in an organisation that's deadly serious about it.

Rackspace offer their employees subsidised massages, an extra day off when it's your birthday, a free half day so you can go Christmas shopping, free Starbucks coffee, tea, soft drinks, breakfast and fruit, season ticket loans, a monthly free lunch with the MD for every new recruit for their first six months, free parking, free food day (on the last Friday before pay day, since people are generally short of cash and a free lunch is most welcome then), a games room and a birthday cake day (a big cake is made and eaten on the first day of the month to celebrate everyone who has an impending birthday).

Oh yes, and Hawaiian shirt days (most employers dress down once in a while – this one dresses up!) and house teams for inter-company

---

[4] In 2005

competitions and events. And all of this is before you land one of the best personal development packages around.

Funnily enough, this organisation is able to attract and retain some of the brightest talent the UK has ever seen – and all they have to do is make sure your server doesn't go down. They're also one of the only organisations of its type (in managed hosting) that's turning a profit. I wonder if these things are related. That was rhetorical musing, by the way.

The World Cup offers us all a chance to see fantastic athletes at the top of their game, but it offers an even better opportunity for right-thinking businesses to show some goodwill to the traditionally embattled UK employee.

I was brilliant as Pharaoh, by the way. Absolutely faultless, with my Elvis lip so pronounced it was slapping against my chest. But I didn't get to see RGD Willis perform his heroics. So let's hope that we can work it out so that as many people as possible get the chance to see our boys reach the heights this summer.

8

A Winter's Sale
December 2005

I used to think the most frustrating job in the world must be a price checker in a pound store (How much is this, Derek? ... It's a pound!). But the news that retailers' tills are positively ringing in the New Year reminds me of an occupation even more misery-inducing – yes, it's the researcher who counted the 150,000 cars in Bluewater Shopping Centre today. I imagine the anoraked unfortunate urging God to send him a Fiat Multipla to break the monotony of people carriers and 4x4s. But perhaps I do him an injustice. It may well be that he knows that there have only been 15 shoppers who've had to return 10,000 times to have their new Hi Def TV explained to them again.

But for someone who holds a fervent belief in the link between great service and successful retailers, experiencing our beloved winter sales is sometimes like being persuaded that the world is flat. Where else would you queue for hours in driving snow to fight over a juicer, a neon kettle and some luminous ambient colour-change lights? Where else would you struggle to the till to be met by a face icier than Briggate at 6 a.m? Er ... Leeds.

But my family and I venture forth regardless (presumably, you're thinking, so you don't have to). We've spent several days pre- and post-Christmas, in downtown Leeds, experiencing the quality of service, celebrating the Good King Wenceslases and tutting at the Herods.

We've witnessed a fascinating *tableau vivant*, a vivid, entertaining and often deeply unsettling insight into what makes businesses work and what makes us humans tick. We're not all the same. We all have different needs and expectations – and while common courtesies are a necessary foundation for a great shopping experience, the grief accumulated during several fracas over the crockery is liable to be unleashed on an unsuspecting young shop girl further down the line.

There were some marvellous moments. There were the two young lads, presumably disorientated by sharing the same brain cell, who pushed into the baker's queue and provoked a chorus of muttered dissatisfaction from further down the queue.

There was the young girl who, no doubt weighed down by her extravagant 2-kilo eyelashes, held up the queue at another fast food eatery. Unable to compute the value of having one's change ready, she took the words 'two pounds ninety' as an invitation to empty the contents of her handbag over the counter to the chagrin of a disbelieving throng.

Or my favourite one, where my beloved had her perfect top snatched away at the last minute by another shopper. Fortunately, by narrowing her eyes at her foe across the shop floor, my wife wove a magic and malevolent spell of self-doubt (am I really a 10?). The top was ours!

They say that great service emerges when a business gets both the basics and the human elements right. The basics, in this case, would be some recognisable flexibility and creativity in the face of large crowds of shoppers.

Our best example was at Lush, where the pre-Christmas queue of anxious shoppers was assuaged by the handing-out of free bath bombs. A lovely touch (and one that explains the seasonal glitter in my receding hair). I'd seen this approach practised before at Prêt à Manger, where I'd been given a free coffee 'because we saw how long you had to queue.' Businesses who can practise this sort of well-intentioned creativity at busy times are businesses that truly understand the importance of service.

Elsewhere, many of the shop assistants reacted to the crowds by imitating the startled demeanour of my tomcat the moment the remote control Dalek started threatening him on Christmas morning.

There was no better example of this complete lack of focus than at my enforced pre-Christmas bank visits. I say 'visits' as the queue outnumbered the cashiers by five to one as I entered on the first occasion. On the second, upon seeing that we were all too old to represent good 'visa card' leads, the sales-fixated employees chose, instead, to look miserable.

'Never mind,' I thought to myself. 'There's a poster behind the cashier offering a higher rate of interest on children's savings accounts. She's sure to mention it to me.' Guess what? Neither a smile, a welcome nor any words at all. Order-taking of the most miserable type and another nail in the heart of UK retail banking. Incidentally, we're almost all on line now (and looking for a suitable children's account).

But there was warmth among the snow in post-Christmas Leeds, with evidence of organisations whose processes are designed to get the basics right and who have the nous to inject warmth into each transaction. Companies like Prêt and Lush, who presumably look for recruits with a natural flair for empathy and a glint in the eye.

To this list must be added the girls at Hobbs, who managed to maintain business as usual, in spite of the increased crowds, by helping us with our wet umbrella, engaging our kids in conversation and nodding encouragingly at every woman who, after the eating frenzy of the past two days, still believed she was a size 10.

As Leeds continues its development as a leading European destination, the value of service, as a clear point of differentiation, will become clear. As Internet communities spread the word and dissatisfied shoppers start to vote with their feet, and as enlightened businesses recruit the right people, listen to customers and build the right processes, my travails as Yorkshire's own service detective might abate. And, you know what? I might not even have the most frustrating job in the world any more. A fact demonstrated by the items in our bags from Lush and Hobbs.

9
Parenting Problems
March 2007

When Henry Kissinger coined the phrase 'a riddle wrapped in a mystery inside an enigma,' he may have been describing schools' admission procedures, rather than attempting to evoke the inscrutability of the former Soviet Union.

As Hannah's parents in last year's Channel Four documentary *Admission Impossible* discovered, when one school is popular and the local option is failing, the odds of securing a place in your chosen senior school increase to the point that putting money on Leeds United escaping relegation seems a safer bet. In Hannah's case 700 pupils were vying for 100 places. The vast majority of com-plaints received by the Ombudsman last year were related to admissions procedures – and these complaints are on the increase. Parents complain that some faith schools were trying to identify which families had shown the most evidence of their religious commitment before offering their children places. And yes, ITV didn't miss the opportunity, producing a drama in which Christopher Eccleston pretends to be a Catholic in order to get his child into a good school, mocking up on the rituals and ending up in a predictable bloodbath.

Regardless of the ethos of the preferred school, the reality is that it's sometimes difficult for the families themselves to understand the decision-making process or to know why they have been unsuccessful. So Ministers have rushed to ensure that, in the state sector at least, schools should not be deciding admissions on the basis of interviews. This has led to education managers in Hove deciding that they will, in future, adopt a lottery system to populate their most over-subscribed schools, arguing, quite reasonably, that randomness negates any notion of unfairness.

Others, again reasonably, have argued that this approach may produce a scenario where a child, living at the gates of his preferred school, loses out to someone several miles away. Neither has the media missed the opportunity to depict a number of nightmare scenarios, with one commentator speculating that a child's future may soon depend on a scratch card.

So what is it like for a family in this position? In our case, our son is the first to experience the big move. Academically, he's done very well at his Primary School, to the extent that we're worried he might soon try to deselect his own parents, on the basis that we're not bright enough to support him any further. In fact, once we'd embarked on the admissions process, we came to the conclusion that we might not be bright enough now. But, following advice from other parents, we consulted widely, speaking to teachers, friends and neighbours and entered the labyrinth feeling suitably equipped to survive it.

The first step: open evenings – events that perfectly illustrated the parents' nervous mental state. Nervous looks, worried expressions, polite handshakes and their kids with eyes as big as saucers taking in the enormity of their expanding world.

We liked all of those we visited and our son soon had a favourite (which we suspect was a direct result of him participating in the creation of several small explosions in the chemistry lab). Dutifully, we decided to support his emerging abilities by submitting him to the entrance examinations at this and the two other West Yorkshire Grammar schools whose open days he'd enjoyed.

To us the exams appeared very daunting, filling the darkening days between autumn and winter and producing untold levels of stress in the hundreds of parents, all of whom were arranged in silent family groupings at the schools' exit gates.

It's a big step – being, for most kids, their first experience of sitting an exam – but we were impressed at the help each school provided. In one case, the head explained that he'd sat a GCSE with his pupils the previous year, to understand the experience better. That school's evident care for the child was a testimony to this.

Back at the school gates, upon completion of the first admissions test, we noticed an interesting contrast between the tormented disposition of the parents and the laid-back adolescent cool of the kids. 'How did it go?' 'Yeah, fine.'

But for us, the long wait for March 1st began, made even more stressful by the tone of the correspondence from the administrators.

It implied a degree of worrying risk: put us first choice or risk losing out. The mind races ahead. Would any of them make an offer? Had he actually answered any questions in the first place? Had he had a Mr Bean moment and forgotten to turn the page over?

Like all parents, we want the best for our children. We voted for a government who promised to focus on 'education, education and education'. We ushered in league tables to extend choice and improve performance and, naturally, we expect all schools to improve at the same speed exponentially over time, offering top-quality education everywhere, to everyone.

No system can easily resolve this supply-and-demand puzzle, and parents and children alike are destined for more complication ahead. From our experience we offer this counsel: be aware of the choices, talk to teachers, experience all of the options (preferably a year before the process begins), listen to your kids – and keep a rabbit's foot handy.

As a postscript: our son has a place at the school of his choice. For others, however, the picture is less clear, as appeals procedures kick in. The unwelcome side-effects of improving educational standards will keep the stress levels high for some time yet.

10

The Other Great Yorkshire Show
August 2007

We weren't able to get to the Great Yorkshire Show. A combination of factors, including parents' meetings, the impending arrival of garden furniture, the erecting of a guinea pig run and preparing for the Brighouse St Joseph's Great Beanie Bear raffle, had all conspired to keep us housebound and well away from the essence of Yorkshire on show in Crimple Valley.

'What's the essence of Yorkshire, Dad?' my 8-year-old daughter enquired. A tough question perhaps, but nowhere near as difficult as some of her other ones (What are gay rights? What's a transsexual?). So, inspired by the image of the bottle of Yorkshire Relish spinning in my head, I took the gastronomic path. 'All of the experiences we have here in Yorkshire are like ingredients in one wonderful dish. They may all be different, but they're *Yorkshire*-flavoured.' I'm not sure she was convinced by my answer, as moments later, I heard her quietly repeating the question to her mother.

I had an idea. 'Remember that walk we did before the rains came?' I announced to the family, as if I were some wizened elder emerging from a teepee. 'The one where you got us lost?' the family responded together, as if they'd been practising. Undaunted, I continued. 'That walk had a lot of essence of Yorkshire.'

The walk in question began with an intriguing ascent, up beyond West Vale, through Greetland, along the Calderdale Way and then down through Norland to Sowerby Bridge and back along the canal to Clay House. But more than offering some exercise and some wonderful scenery, it was the abundance of unique experiences that made the day so memorable – and so characteristic of the Yorkshire our family has come to love.

My wife and I are economic migrants, having moved to Yorkshire to be able to afford a pint. In fact we got so emotionally charged during the joyous leaving celebration that by the time we got to Bradford, there would soon be three of us. But fast forward to a taste of Yorkshire, where the (now) four of us were trying to make sense of the map kindly provided by Messrs Brook and Hinchliffe, authors of the *Alternative Pennine Way*.

The car park at West Vale wasn't hard to find, but within minutes an argument had broken out. In one corner, my wife and daughter, skilled enough to interpret the directions and make some sense of them. In the other, Mr Pedant and Son, whingeing about the lack of clarity and questioning the cartographical accuracy of terms such as 'zig-zag up the bank'.

Striding upwards through Greetland, we passed a buddleia bush, ringed with Red Admirals and Small Tortoiseshells on our way up to the Methodist Chapel at the side of the Calderdale Way. A lone whippet wandered by as the heat began to rise. We conjectured that he might have been completing the walk in reverse. In which case he'd just passed the 6-mile point, something of an impressive achievement, given that he wasn't carrying either a water bottle or any Kendal Mint Cake. The heat was growing intense. My choice of a dark top was not a good one. I was attracting more heat than Lord Levy.

As the Calder Valley appeared below to our right, we skirted the escarpment above the woods, as the kids imagined Isengard (Halifax's Wainhouse Tower) and the Forest of Fangorn (North Dean Wood). A robin danced in front of us, remaining close enough to show off, but just short of tame.

A small hatchback appeared from the left. 'Have you seen a brown and white cow?' the young driver asked us. Not an easy thing to lose, you might imagine. 'It's jumped the fence,' the youngster explained. Moments later, as we continued towards Norland Moor, we thought we heard a rustling at our side. We couldn't be sure but we thought we glimpsed two shifty bovine eyes blinking from behind a dry stone wall.

'Am I on the right road for Norland School?' asked a lady in a car, as we departed from the Calderdale Way. I made a series of unconvincing pointing movements and sent her the wrong way up Norland Road. The kids traversed Norland village and Sowerby Bridge rose from the valley below us, the sun catching the convergence of the Ryburn and Calder, as tiny people splashed along the kayak courses.

With water levels running low and 3.5 miles on the clock, the kids began to flag, suggesting that some snacks might be a good idea. So, following a progressive lecture from Dad on the value of fresh fruit, whole foods and their energy-giving properties, we stopped at a café for four sausage and egg teacakes and a bottle of Dr Pepper. At this point the decision was taken to return to West Vale by the considerably less exhausting mode of taxi, so we collapsed into the car, straining our necks upwards to see the beauty of North Dean Wood.

When we finally emerged back into the car park at West Vale, the kids were talking of adventurous whippets, missing cows, tasty tea-cakes, the talking trees of Fangorn Forest and Meadow Browns, as my wife and I continued to debate the quality of the map and directions. In the end we decided that it was best not to complain. After all, a friend of mine who made a series of complaints to his local GP found himself being prescribed a barium enema the next time he visited. Best keep cartographers on your side, most likely. You don't want them hacking into your sat nav and sending you up Norland Road the wrong way.

We may have missed the main event in Harrogate last week, but we've learned that in our little part of the world, with its small but affecting details, the Great Yorkshire Show is an everyday occurrence.

11

A Winter's Sale (Part 2)

December 2006

I still remember that episode of *Monty Python* vividly. Terry Jones, as Mrs Non-Smoker, is asked why she's bought a piston engine. 'It was a bargain,' she screeches helpfully.

35 years ago, the idea of purchasing something completely useless truthfully reflected the surrealist bent of the Pythons. But now the sketch has something of a satirical air, as material accumulation has us all in frenzy.

In the weeks approaching Christmas we fought over Nintendo Wiis, overran designer outlets and scoured the virtual shelves of eBay, like delinquent locusts. We found new and exciting ways to part with our cash, from e-vouchers and reward-card points to collect-in-store and buy now, pay later (and regret permanently). Now, as the fairy dust settles, the dog finishes off the turkey and the chocolate wrappers flutter down around us, we survey our credit-card balances with a deep sense of guilt, take a deep breath and, er, hit the Sales.

Back in the days of the Pythons, the Winter Sales occupied a logical place in the calendar. With businesses eager to maximise income by clearing out old stock at a time when money was scarce, the sales became a vital destiny for people who, only ten years earlier, were experiencing rationing. Bargains were scrutinised meticulously. Fundamental basics like winter clothes and household items were Mum's priority, as mine set off down Northumberland Street in Newcastle with a clear list of objectives, like a crack SAS operative in a headscarf.

Even in the 70s and 80s, quiet news days focused in on the sales, usually featuring hand-to-hand combat over the crockery at Selfridges or a collection of parka-clad shoppers, flasks and packed lunches lined up outside, banging their hands together for warmth and lighting up the freezing winter morning with their breath. The Winter Sales were an institution – a welcome one – for a nation too closely acquainted with scarcity.

But now, in the noughties – an expression uncomfortably conveying the emptiness of our times – the sales are everywhere, all of the time and, as the evidence makes clear, not even proving effective for the businesses behind them. As early as November, analysts were predicting a dire performance from retailers. 'It could be the worst Christmas for us in 25 years!' one expert announced (to universal indifference from consumers). Discounting had already begun before December was even with us and, in an unprecedented move, London's Oxford Street and Regent Street both went traffic-free in a desperate attempt to generate spending.

The Winter Sales, a once proud institution, will be as indistinct as the eponymous hero of the Where's Wally posters, now that retailers have removed the sanctity from January. But are their fears justified? Not to my eyes, at least. And a bird's eye view of Meadowhall in the weeks before Christmas looked uncannily like the speeded-up sequence from TV's *Planet Earth* where an ugly fleet of ocean-floor creatures cruelly stripped the carcass of a dead whale in a matter of seconds.

So we have something of a dichotomy here. There seems to be no end to our appetite for 'bargains' here in Consumer World. And yet, conversely, our retailers are bemoaning the lack of profit and finding that their annual winter cash cow has become less the fatted calf and more the anaemic antelope. The result is that sales have become a habitual feature of our lives. Whatever we want, we can get it 'cheaply'. Someone can 'do us a deal', whether by using price comparison websites, visiting auction sites or eBaying it. And if we don't have the money, we can borrow it.

But my take on all of this is shaped by the historical proximity of subsistence. Fewer than 50 years have passed since rations put food on the table. Career advice from your parents was limited to 'get a good job so you can feed and clothe your family' and just enough was preferable to a surplus. Indeed, the generation before mine is characterised by its relentless interest in hoarding ('don't throw away the piston engine, it could come in useful').

And, as befits this season of reflection, there's a nagging feeling that the convenience of modern lives has created a moral void. Where once our houses were a home, they've now become a commodity, whose increasing value is required to support our frenetic pursuit of 'more things'.

I'm indebted to Roger Steare, whose book *Ethicability* is a compelling assessment of our generation's moral compass. He not only highlights the 'accumulate and throw-away' nature of our modern lives, but also describes the shattering contradictions this creates. We abandon the previous model for the new one, whether it's our hi-fi, our cooker, our car or, increasingly, our partner. The social implications of this are worrying, as our kids survey our curiously contradictory values and draw their own conclusions on the gaps between what we say is important and what we actually do.

The January Sales may have surveyed this scene and slunk back into the crowds, indistinguishable from every other bargain bonanza. But it is what this tells us about our modern lives that's feeding my guilt. As Confucius once put it: The superior man understands what is right; the inferior man understands what will sell.

12

To Switch or Not to Switch

March 2007

Champion of the embattled consumer, crusading customer 'cage-rattler' and, curiously, the Carrie Bradshaw of UK service, I've been called many things. Personally, I prefer the latter, mainly because I like to coil myself around my duvet and type questions like 'why does my queue take the longest, even if I change queues?'

But lately, I've been feeling pangs of guilt. Perpetually in rant mode and railing at the low profile customer service has in the UK, I'm constantly advocating that consumers should vote with their feet, especially when they're not receiving the service, the quality or the deal that they're paying for. The fact is there's something close to home that I've been wilfully neglecting. My gas and electricity supply.

We've been loyal customers of British Gas since moving into our semi-detached home 12 years ago. While the likes of Powergen and N-Power emerged to lure friends and family away with cheaper packages, we cemented our relationship with the old faithful by opting to have them supply our electricity too. What loyal customers. Loyal or just lazy? A recent visit to one of the utility price comparison sites revealed that we were currently paying nearly £300 a year more than if we were to opt for a dual fuel, fully Direct Debit automated, online meter reading, sexy power package (not actual name). £300 a year? I know fuel bills have shot up lately, but that means we might have saved ourselves a thousand quid, had we acted earlier. My finger trembles on the mouse pad.

OK, so let's analyse this loyalty. What have we had from British Gas over the past few years, in return for our blind allegiance? The answer is: nothing. Just like football season-ticket-holders invest hundreds every close-season to renew – and then often hear nothing until they're asked for more money a year later – there's been no attempt to 'earn' our loyalty.

Other than the regular home-appliance-servicing offers and the recently launched monthly draws (smacking of closing the stable door so long after the horse has bolted that the once proud stallion is now occupying several glue pots), we've received no recognition of our 12 years' service.

A call would have been nice. Perhaps some vouchers at Christmas or discounted entry to leisure attractions. In fact, just one letter thanking us for supporting them through the hard times, would have conveyed enough warmth to keep me away from the competing courtiers. But not once during our 12 years have we ever been asked to provide feedback on the service we've received.

So, practising what I preach, I conduct a frenzy of mouse clicks and conjure up an attractive dual fuel package. Without having to speak to a human (always preferable when dealing with matters of the conscience), we begin the process of signing up with Scottish Power.

The formative stages of our new relationship are quite coy, being wholly based on a series of emails, confirming our progress through the various stages of the change of supplier. It might have been nice to meet over a *Cosmopolitan*, as our Carrie might do, but this'll do.

However, back at British Gas HQ, it's come to their attention that one of the inmates has vaulted the security perimeter and is heading to the woods, laughing hysterically. The metaphorical searchlights pick him up and our phone rings.

'Hello, can I speak to Mrs Bradley?' a voice stirs.

It's British Gas! They want to speak to my wife, but we're jointly responsible for paying the bills. Interesting. Unsurprisingly, what follows is an attempt to attract us back, sadly only begun following our decision to leave. Without going into the details, we are immediately offered a considerable one-off discount on our next bill, plus a revised monthly payment that would come in under the Scottish Power offer. They will also take care of reversing the switch.

The sad thing is, this is happening everywhere, whether it's your mortgage, your car insurance or, in our case, your fuel. Whole industries exist to poach business from competitors, while competitors pull that tempting ace from their pack and fight back, often with horrifying revelations of what the new supplier might do to us. Software companies flourish on the production of new and exciting ways of spotting potential defectors, and budgets increasingly contain sweeteners to appeal to the departing customer.

It strikes me that there are two forms of customer loyalty. Firstly, there's the loyalty that the provider 'buys' through discounts, purchase points or 'cash back' (although, as we've seen, most of these ideas only seem to occur when you've decided to leave). This type of loyalty seems a little facile, by nature of the filthy lucre underpinning it.

However, some companies are learning that loyalty is best 'earned' – largely by remaining a pleasure to do business with, being easy to contact and brilliant at solving problems. A big part of this is making customers feel that their patronage is welcomed – and not only at times when your money is required. John Lewis's success at the top of *Which* magazine's recent retail customer satisfaction league table is no doubt down to this customer-led ethos.

I accept that we're partly to blame for falling for these injury-time changes of heart, but it's a shame that British businesses cannot bring themselves to earn our loyalty throughout the relationship, rather than hurriedly buying it at the last minute.

13

Customers are Stupid
July 2007

Last year the National Consumer Council condemned levels of UK customer service in a direct and uncompromising report entitled *Stupid Company*. While this was hardly news to your relentless service chronicler, I have a revelation of my own to make, based on a qualitative assessment of multiple user / provider interfaces (I always find you can soften the greatest of blows with some pointless business babble).

The revelation will be old news to anyone in a customer-facing role, but one perhaps less understood by service strategists and senior management. It's a revelation that is crucial to understanding and leveraging the customer base – and fundamental to releasing the potential of employees everywhere. It's key to appreciating the cultural barriers to great service in the UK and, as I wrote in *Inconvenience Stores*, it lies at the heart of my contention that 'we get the service we deserve'. The fact is: customers are stupid.

OK, maybe not all customers are stupid, but I can prove that a significant number are – and this is a segment that is much greater than the percentage of customers who regularly fill in feedback forms, for example, or (from my own research) than those who believe customer service in the UK is excellent.

Let me expound my theory. Last month I travelled on a flight from Belfast to Leeds Bradford. Just as the last passenger had taken his seat, a series of brief security announcements were made, including the not unexpected or surprising 'please switch off all mobile phones as they may interfere with aircraft equipment.' Some moments later, the stewardess's safety briefing was missed by the lady in seat 9E. Reason why? She was making a call on her mobile. I think that was flight 328 from Belfast on 21 June, leaving at 1910 hours (in the unlikely event that the idiot concerned can configure her brain cells sufficiently to identify herself here).

My sister called yesterday. Her house was surrounded by water, living as she does in South Yorkshire, one of the areas worst affected by the recent floods. Sarah and her husband run a landscape gardening business, with customers in Barnsley, Rotherham, Sheffield and surrounding areas. One customer, who'd just had a water feature installed, woke yesterday to find it far more active than described in the brochure, complaining that their garden was flooding and that Sarah should dispatch someone to resolve the problem. Managing to stifle a comment about Moses being elsewhere occupied, she explained that persistent heavy rain often does lead to floods, a fact apparently hitherto unknown to the caller.

She might have gone on to mention that several people had to be rescued by helicopter from a nearby rooftop, that cracks had appeared in Ulley Dam, that the M1 and Meadowhall had both been shut as a result of the unprecedented downpour and a poor man had been drowned in Hull after getting his foot caught in a drain cover. She's now considering updating her website to alert people to the following curious meteorological phenomena: it gets wet when it rains; it gets warm when the sun comes out and things move about the lawn when it's windy. I have to say that the latter never ceases to surprise my tomcat who, as I write this, is narrowing his eyes at a recalcitrant leaf.

I recall Terry Wogan reading a letter from a supermarket employee recounting a visit he'd received from an angry customer. The lady concerned was complaining that the instant barbecue she'd bought did not contain any hamburgers or sausages. While the assistant attempted to stifle his laughter, he noticed that the box was extremely cold. The lady explained that she'd kept it in the freezer for several weeks so the meat wouldn't go off.

Last night I visited Marks and Spencer's in Oxford Street and watched as every other customer attempted to queue at the wrong end of the queuing-rail in front of the pay desk, in spite of a large sign trumpeting the correct queuing direction. Just like the bewildered old *Fast Show* character, one man said to me: 'So I queue over there, do I?' while I resisted attempts to explain that he also had to place his underpants over his head and emphasise every second syllable if he wanted to be served.

So many of these thoughts have been buzzing around my head like the large mosquito that kept me awake at my other sister's in

Cambridge last night. It appeared to be operating a high-pitched pneumatic drill between the window and the blind and resisted several of my attempts to stun it with a sock (which never fails to subdue any other living thing). This is relevant, because the recent floods in Yorkshire led to me abandoning a rail journey home and diverting via Peterborough, Cambridge, Ely, Waterbeach, back to Ely and Peterborough and then home via York.

As the breakdown repair man re-charged the flat battery I discovered upon returning to Leeds Station car park, he told me of a woman who had called him out the previous day. She'd explained that the car was damp and the engine wouldn't start. When he turned up the car was 60% submerged. Unbowed, the lady requested that he attempt to fix it anyway. He declined her request, explaining the futility of the exercise, reinforcing his argument by opening one of the doors and watching as several hundred gallons of water swept her and her garden gnomes away down the drive.

So if my anecdotal assessment of levels of customer stupidity is anywhere near accurate, it does stress the need for understanding, resilience and tolerance in customer-facing staff elsewhere. Perhaps we ought to provide another outlet for employees to rid themselves of the frustration caused by stupid customers – maybe by launching a national award scheme? But then again, who's to say we wouldn't all be caught out at some time?

The reason my battery was flat? I'd left the lights on when I parked there three days earlier.

14

Fish, Chips and PINs

February 2006

I wasn't present to witness my family become European, as I was away at college. But one day, without warning, in submission to the subliminal waves of continental influence, my mother made the decisive leap. She retired the white pepper and introduced black pepper to our dinner table. In a moment, fish and chips, corned beef pie and jam roly-poly would begin to contemplate extinction, as broccoli became enhanced with coriander seeds, balsamic vinegar out-muscled brown sauce and garlic lay siege to our landscape like a particularly peckish Chinese Mitten crab.

My musings on this during a Valentine's Day seafood meal with the family were interrupted by the appearance of the waiter, approaching us with what looked like a Star Trek phaser in his hands. Fearing it was set to stun, I arched back in my seat. But no, this was the remote Chip and PIN machine and payment was about to be taken.

Like the black pepper mill in 1984, the Chip and PIN phenomenon, borne out of sound European success, has arrived to make us all more modern. We will no longer need to sign for transactions, using our personal PINs (personal identification numbers) instead. Security experts argue that fraud will decrease, thereby the industry will save money (money that, incidentally, never seems to be passed on to customers, though that is always the implied outcome).

Businesses without chip and PIN will now become liable for credit card fraud carried out on their premises and, perhaps unsurprisingly, APACs, the body that represents banks and credit card companies, has confirmed that some 90% of UK tills have converted. Many of the remaining organisations have decided against the move, either because their particular enterprise is not generally attractive to fraudsters (restaurants are a good example) or because they find the cost of installing the equipment too much of a security investment.

Some reports have confirmed that B&Q, the DIY store, have not yet completed their upgrade, for technical reasons. One imagines that our Police will be trailing a number of people carrying hardwood, kitchen tiles and artex in a suspicious manner.

So the last day is St Valentine's Day. Thereafter, where Chip and PIN is the method of payment, signatures can no longer be accepted, so if you're planning a romantic meal on the big day, you've no need to worry that a technical glitch may put an end to your evening's entertainment. Just as the responsibility for fraud passes to the business owner, so our responsibility as consumers increases. Recent research has highlighted the fact that 50% of British people forget their PIN numbers, while around 25% of people will divulge their secret digits to their partners. Men, it seems, are partial to keeping a copy of their PIN in their wallet while woman tend to write it in a diary. Some people, by their nature, are number-averse and a four-digit number is akin to calculating pi to its fiftieth decimal place.

We're advised to think of sequences that are meaningful to us, but the problem here is that the familiar is more easily guessed at than the random. And the random is much less easy to remember than the familiar. Pass the aspirin. Many argue that insufficient information has been provided to consumers, and it remains to be seen how and if cashiers will apply flexibility when an elderly shopper struggles to come to terms with the changes.

But while we wrestle with these possibilities, our businesses have begun to understand the consequences of Chip and PIN. 'Card not present' fraud, when we purchase items through the mail, over the internet or by telephone, has increased since the introduction of the new scheme, by some 6% over the last twelve months, particularly for items such as iPods and laptops.

Security experts fear that organized crime will turn its attention to other areas, just as many businesses believe that the sudden interest in card fraud is misplaced, pointing out that it represents a drop in the ocean compared to stock theft, either through shoplifting or break-in. And that's not to mention the need to become more vigilant at ATMs, as the PIN we use to authorize a card transaction is the very same one we use to withdraw cash from the machine.

Chip and PIN is undeniably a step forward for card security, but it ushers in a new age of change by placing increased responsibility on the business and the user. And at a time when UK customer service lags so far behind its European and American counterparts, my fear is that businesses quite rightly embracing Chip and PIN may manifest this increased responsibility through less flexibility in their dealings with consumers (if you've not got your PIN, you've, er, had your chips). And consumers, rattled by the pace of change, may need some TLC at the crucial moment.

With the UK retail experience characterised by indifference, it's a challenge that may be beyond all bar a few shining organisations. But good businesses will rise to this challenge and reasonable consumers will accept the changes with grace. Pass the black pepper, Mum.

15

Parenting Problems (Part 2)

May 2006

For many of us, the Government's Respect Agenda conjures up an array of preventative measures, restrictions and curfews. From the much-maligned ASBO to on-the-spot fines, we could be forgiven for equating respect with obedience. But it's my passionate belief that another, less heralded and controversial element of Government policy offers a much more secure and natural path to restoring the ailing profile of respect. Put simply, by 2010 every child in primary education should have access to foreign language tuition.

The UK is alone in Europe is propelling its youngsters into adolescence without any appreciation of foreign tongues (with the possible exception of a furtive snog in a phone box in Lloret de Mar). And yet, as we know, children's instinct for learning is never stronger than in their formative years. The preferred interpretation of my own academic career, which peaked in nursery and declined steadily thereafter, provides testimony to this theory.

But it isn't a question of academic rigour either. It's about sharing and enjoying the culture, the traditions and the passions of the country being studied. It's especially about revelling in those customs that fly in the face of our own conventions. We may regard erecting a tree and filling socks with satsumas as perfectly seasonal, but in Barcelona households kids are hitting logs with sticks and urging them to defecate a present for them.

For a youngster, such studies open up the world for what it is: a myriad of colours, some recognisable and some meriting further investigation. It encourages a world view and when we draw our kids' attention to the importance of Holocaust Day in stressing our essential similarities, it's the differences that inspire the imagination of the very young.

An interest in languages is the next coherent step to breaking down the fear that characterises the uncomprehending. The media understand that the sound of spoken Arabic to an English-speaking audience feeds misconception and fear, through implied and imagined links to anti-western sentiments. In actual fact, Arabic, in its many forms, lies at the root of many European languages, its definitive article al (the) still present in Spain's remnants of its Moorish past, such as Granada's mesmerising Alhambra. We should be exploring the influence of historic Arabia on the modern world. We should know what it sounds like when parents read their kids bedtime stories.

But when our kids reach adolescence, it's often too late to introduce these ideas, as other elements such as peer pressure, media and life experience have got there first. We're then left with a group of people whose only response to diversity is indifference, fear or rejection. It's then but a short step to the frankly ignorant performances of many holidaymakers who, like Lord Melchett of *Blackadder* fame, believe that if people don't understand you at first, then a round of shouting should do the trick.

It's the old guard, spread along Spain's southern coast, grouping together under the Union Jack, scowling at the greasiness of a Mediterranean diet (pure myth: it's olive oil and it's better for you) while forcing down fry-ups and passing on the tapas in favour of chips. Had they been exposed to Andalusian culture in their early years, maybe, just maybe, someone would have dared to try the kidneys in sherry or the gazpacho. Perhaps Easter week would have involved witnessing the spectacle of Semana Santa in Seville, rather than a donkey ride on the beach.

My interest in languages came at the point at which I was asked to consider my future career. I figured back then that a university degree in Modern Languages might entail some time spent abroad, hopefully at the expense of the local education authority. I chose Spanish, as my County Durham tones were more similar to the flat vowels of Iberia and my long-term romance had begun.

In 1983, instead of arriving at the University of Barcelona, fate took me to Girona, where I combined study of Spanish and Catalan with a year in a small restaurant. Working with a close-knit group of Catalans on a daily basis obliged me to take on the language and the effort taken (and the many hilarious mistakes made) soon brought benefits. Doors opened, friends were made and my first few forays into spoken Catalan were greeted with astonishment, just as the new master race reacted to Charlton Heston's first few words in *Planet of the Apes*.

Subsequent adventures in spoken Spanish and Catalan were often as disastrous as they were entertaining. I recall my sister asking for a mind-flavoured ice cream, instead of mint – *mente* instead of *menta* – and my beloved wife announcing to the fourth floor of a department store in Barcelona that I was too big for my bathing shorts. She was trying to say that they didn't fit me (but I do not recall rushing to correct her).

My own contribution to linguistic chaos occurred a couple of years ago when, with a nonchalant confidence, I ordered a series of German-themed tapas at the famous Alt Heidelberg bar in Barcelona. After several frankfurts, sauerkraut-laden hamburguesas and accompanying drinks, I muttered our requirement for the bill. Not fully understanding me, the waiter muttered back. 'Sí,' I responded and proceeded to list the items consumed, believing he was making up the bill. Some moments later, the waiter approached us again. Not with the bill, I recall painfully, but with the entire afternoon's order, repeated at my request. Having briefly contemplated eating it all again to avoid embarrassment, I swallowed my pride and explained my error ('I'm sorry, I'm English'). Episodes like this have kept family and friends entertained for weeks, but also, and more significantly, keen to try using the language themselves.

I returned to Catalonia in 1985 after graduation and taught English in an industrial town called Manlleu, at a school owned by Terry Parris (mother of Matthew – see his book *A Castle in Spain* for a real insight into that part of the world). I developed a bond with the town that persists to this day and which, I fervently hope, has helped me open up my children's eyes to the beauty of difference.

I've learned that fear is compounded by an inability to communicate, to share values and opinions and I'm reassured that our Government appears to understand this. So, if we can provide the resources to build this basic appreciation of other languages into primary education, then we will bequeath an appreciation of difference that will help our children grow up with an understanding of the word 'respect'.

16

Fish, Chips and PINs (Part 2)

June 2006

Picture the scene. You return from the supermarket laden with shopping. You put the milk down on the kitchen table and go to check your emails. Among the emails is one from your carton of milk. It says, 'put me in the fridge now or I'll go off.' Couldn't happen, surely? But it has. One of the world's largest retail organisations has recently ordered 10 million small chips called 'radio frequency identify devices' so the talkative milk carton is more than a possibility.

So if supermarkets are actively progressing such technological advances, you know the initial skirmish is over and the real battle for our patronage has begun. They're desperate to understand how to secure our loyalty – and the prospect of being able to 'eavesdrop' on the way we use our products was not going to sit on their shelf for long, as it were.

The fact is, our loyalty is worth millions to them. Consider how much you spend a week at your local supermarket. £100? £150? Now calculate how much you're worth to that supermarket over a year. £5200? £7800? See what I mean? If it's true that, on average, we stay in the same house for six years then 'bingo!' you're worth up to £50,000 to your local supermarket. Now you know why they'd want to send their little devices into our fridge to see where all the other nanobots have come from.

Only a few years ago supermarkets traded on our inertia, just like the majority of banks do now. We'd shop at the closest one that met our economic requirements. Take me, for example, as a man of irregular means. I'd regularly start the month courting the asparagus at Waitrose. Week two would involve a clash of the trolleys at Morrison's, while the end of the month (especially prior to pay day) would feature a desperate sortie into Aldi, armed with loose change retrieved from behind the sofa (and from my children's savings accounts). Now if someone were bright enough to launch a supermarket called Penury and place it on the corner of Down and Out, you'd find me in there, browsing the end-of-line offers.

Then, in the early 90s, a man called Clive Humby marched up to Tesco and presented his idea for a reward card. At first this development was derided by Tesco's main competitor Sainsbury's. It took a while for them to perform a volte-face, take their turn and unleash the Nectar card on an indifferent world.

Tesco got to know its customers better. It learned to keep its shelves stocked through using the reward card to anticipate the buying habits of customers. Its marketing focused on things the individual shopper really wanted and it further upped the ante by promising to honour competitors' vouchers and began to occupy the business pages as its profits shot into the stratosphere.

Sainsbury's, on the other hand, struggled to fill its shelves with the right products, failed to connect with shoppers on a 'human' level and couldn't get its pricing right.

This was never better illustrated than on an occasion where my wife was told that the act of giving an unweighed grape to our 2-year-old daughter was 'shoplifting', or the time when I couldn't find any fresh bread, as I stood in the shadow cast by Madagascan vanilla pods and brioche. Elsewhere, Tesco was calculating that the loss of a grape was preferable to the loss of our lifetime value to them. But things have changed. And I'll tell you how, but give me a minute, as my turkey has just texted me asking to be basted.

The intervening years have seen Tesco reach that unsettling position in the UK where success becomes a bad thing. The National Consumer Council has just revealed survey results that show that UK shoppers regard the Co-operative Group as our most trusted organisation. Tesco, on the other hand, generated the most extreme of reactions, with people either extremely trusting or extremely suspicious of it.

Sainsbury's, by comparison, is finally getting some reward for re-engaging with its customers, as last week's figures revealed. Justin King, the recently arrived and appropriately youthful CEO, has gone back to basics, asking customers what's most important to them. Availability, pricing and good old-fashioned customer service have unsurprisingly emerged as the customers' main requirements and the gap between Tesco and Sainsbury's has begun to narrow again.

So the battle for shoppers' hearts and wallets goes on unabated, with both of the above protagonists now looking awkwardly over their shoulders at Walmart's Asda, with its Abramovich-sized wallets and North American customer nous. Morrison's won't always be distracted by the Safeway acquisition either.

Things will continue to change. Technological innovation is only in its infancy and nanobots in your shallots might just be the start. But console yourself with this thought. If your fridge is anything like ours, you'll soon be inundated with emails from your broccoli, longing to be loved. You might even get spam.

17

Uncomfortably Screwed

January 2007

My son has discovered a talent for cocktail making. At 11 years old you'd expect him to opt for the family viewing of the *Pirates of the Caribbean* DVD, but he preferred to mix a Bourbonnaise for his father (bourbon, extra dry vermouth, lemon juice and crème de cassis) while the rest of us wondered if the creators of this latest swashbuckling epic had ever concerned themselves with devising a plot. Nevertheless, the effect of the cocktail was to cushion the blow of another 12 months of excruciatingly poor UK service.

It was our Christmas Eve trip to Haworth that once again high-lighted the uniquely British approach to consumers. Parking at the infamous car park above the village, where an infamous welcome party sits waiting for someone to wander off for change so that they can leap out and clamp them, we descended the streets to an evocative scene. A man, dressed as a demob-happy 40s gent, crooned old standards to an orchestral accompaniment as his white scarf fluttered in the breeze. The gentle soothing perfumes of the Apothecary refreshed the senses while families enjoyed the day.

With lunchtime approaching we decided to stop at a pub. Upon approaching the bar I was told that we'd have a very long wait if we wanted food. We did, so we left, wondering if it was our fault for being hungry at lunchtime. Never mind. We next happened upon a small eatery with two rooms. The first was full, so we stepped downstairs to the second and spotted a spare table. Having sat there untroubled by any waitress for several minutes we spotted a sign. Only tea and cof-fee in the downstairs room!

We found another café. This time the proprietor was clearly in some difficulty. Apparently his water machine was malfunctioning. We ordered toasties and mine arrived untoasted. Fortunately, enough heat had passed by to melt the contents of the sandwich, but sadly not enough to brown the bread. An effect, my wife pointed out, that I could have matched by breathing frenetically on a cold sandwich. A customer returned his toastie. 'I ordered cheese and onion, not cheese and tomato.' Any self-respecting café owner would immediately bin the article and start again. Not here in Haworth. The sandwich was simply tidied up and handed to another customer. Presumably the one who had ordered it in the first place?

There are many vibrant businesses in Haworth that are deserving of our patronage and many that perfectly evoke the historical and literary uniqueness of the place. However, for Haworth to continue to thrive as the essential Yorkshire tourist destination, some basic service lessons must be learned. The grandparents are coming this weekend and they want to go to Haworth. Son, mix me a Mai Tai!

18

Supertram Reaches End of Line
December 2006

The news that the Government has pulled the plug on the Leeds Supertram produced a surprising reaction in my household. My 10-year-old son looked up in dismay and announced the true cost of this decision: 'That's a pity, Daddy. Leeds would have been in the Metro Maps of the World book[5]. But it won't be now.' Not a comment one would expect from local government politicos, lobbyists and the like, but one from the heart and, it has to be said, from someone to whom we'll bequeath this city in the years to come.

I can recite all of the arguments in favour of the Supertram – all of the ones you know (the positive cost-balance benefits, the environmental argument, the need to support an expanding city and the improved links to major conurbations) as well as some you don't (the fact that it's been calculated that 25% of Sheffield's tram users also have access to a car but choose not to use it). The opportunity to bring local people and tourists right into the heart of the city in a convenient and unobtrusive fashion may have been ignored, as well as the chance to produce a great reduction in city-centre traffic, but my son sees a different picture.

The book was a birthday present. Like many kids his age he is fascinated with public transport systems. Hour upon hour is devoted to producing the most detailed of maps, intricate and integrated, intersecting lines of bold intent, arteries serving his invented city, crisscrossing rail systems and tunnels delivering workers to their destinations. It seems futuristic – and that's the point. We're buffeted by so many conventional and constraining arguments that we fail to see the bigger picture. It's not a question of simply improving the City's transport system; it's about putting Leeds onto the global map and securing its citizens' pride and advocacy. And here's where it hurts my son.

---

[5] *Metro Maps of the World*, Mark Ovenden, Capital Transport (revised 2005), depicts and describes of all the existing and planned light rail networks around the world

'Even Sheffield is in the Metro Maps book,' he tells me. And, in case you're wondering, so are Shenzhen (China), Volgograd (Russia), Seattle (USA) and Yerevan (Armenia). If insight has not deserted you, you'll have noticed the immense, undiminished confidence in the future shared by these vibrant cities. These are principles that transcend simple arguments of cost and logistics. It's a question of civic self-esteem.

Behind the front-runners with their Olympic bids, Expo dreams and international business conference pretensions, there is a cadre of progressive, visionary cities which see both the logistical benefits of a properly integrated transport system and the power of the message to its citizens and visitors.

Some years ago Leeds was being talked about as a Barcelona of the north, with the will, passion and bursting creativity of its striking and unsettlingly brave mentor. In the years to come however, some other upstart northern metropolis will have assumed the mantle and will be planning its own light railways and tram systems (and advising on the correct wording to accompany its entry in Metro Maps of the World). Maybe my son has a point.

I vainly trot out the counter arguments. 'Experts say there'll be 32,000 new workers in Leeds by 2015. They reckon at least 70% of them will have to travel into the City from the suburbs and beyond. Maybe 300 extra buses is really all we need.'

But buses speak of yesterday. Even supporters of London's soon-to-be-extinct Routemaster buses accept their argument is 'retro' in the face of the new extended bendy coaches. Buses snarl up traffic, add to pollution and, as experience tells us, are subject to delays (see the 'wait half an hour for one and three come at once' scenario). Buses are thoroughly unprepared for the modern world, as anyone who dares to take a child in a wheelchair on a single-manned vehicle will attest. Health and safety reasons prevent the driver from carrying the wheelchair on board, while security reasons are cited when not leaving the cabin to help you.

You think I'm exaggerating? Ask my sister and her disabled son what happened when they tried to use Stagecoach's 'service' in Cambridgeshire last year.

Buses do not represent the brave new world envisioned by the founding fathers of Leeds; neither does a city full of buses (and nothing else) deserve the label 'integrated transport system' so beloved of government.

Not a problem with a light rail service since it's designed to reflect our more humane principles – our more respecting world. This intent is signalled by the thoughtful, low-threshold design and interior seating arrangements. I see no light railways or tram systems in court arguing against claims made under 2004's new additions to the Disability Discrimination Act.

We may argue that the Government is being selective in its transport policy. Indeed West Yorkshire appears to have achieved a double whammy by having the weakest public transport infrastructure and the least investment (warning: they may be linked). I should know. In my native County Durham we don't even have a road that starts with the letter M! But Leeds' existing reach and future potential easily match those of major European cities such as The Hague, Lyon and Valencia.

It's difficult to convey the power of finding a place in the world for Leeds in cost / benefit tables and in the meticulous science of engineering project plans, but my son has no difficulty overcoming all of this urban myopia. For him, there's been a chance to get Leeds into his favourite book. The fact that it's been passed by makes all of us poorer.

19

Family Goes on Holiday
July 2007

One week to go before the schools break up for summer and families all over Yorkshire are making last-minute preparations for their holidays. Mum scans the supermarket shelves for Moroccan market-trader repellent while Dad arrives at the opticians and announces his intention to purchase some prescription sunglasses. 'Excuse me, sir,' the assistant chirps, 'this is Greggs. The optician is next door.'

But this is the great British summer and the tourism industry can't lose. If it warms up over here, we'll be all over the Dales, the Lake District and the South West like a particularly badly dressed rash, but if the inclemency continues, we'll be off to the Mediterranean to dive headlong into the sea (the rest of the family) or into a bucket of *calamares a la romana* (Dad).

When you consider how easy it is to hop on a plane these days – whether to fly to Newquay from Leeds-Bradford Airport, or to flash a twenty and séjour as far as Venice – the opportunities for our tourism industry are enormous and exponentially expanding. You would think, quite naturally, that our industry would exploit this to ensure an invigorating (or relaxing) hassle-free family holiday experience.

So, as Yorkshire's very own caped customer service crusader, let me assess the situation and begin with flights. I remember 20 years ago when I worked in Barcelona. Flights home were so expensive I didn't bother, until my bank threatened to extradite me were I to continue my carefree attitude to the unofficial overdraft I was operating. Even then it cost over £200 to fly from Barcelona to Heathrow.

Now, for £250 I can fly my entire family to Girona and back. The flights themselves are between £20 and £30 per person each way. However once taxes, booking charges and baggage fees are added in we reach the aforementioned sum.

So, having secured passage I breathlessly briefed the family on our itinerary. 'We're flying from Newcastle on Ryanair,' I announced to general dismay. You'd think I'd signed them all up on a 'learn to smoke with David Hockney' workshop, such was the lack of enthusiasm for this particular provider. The reality is, of course, that society has made a compromise, along the lines of 'if it's a cheap flight, don't expect an easy ride'; an opinion hardened by some of our budget airlines' recent attempts to contain costs and boost revenue.

I drove a friend to Leeds-Bradford Airport the other day. He found the experience quaintly unique. 'It's like driving through the Dales and finding an international airport at the end of a small village.' He was, of course, highlighting the desperately poor transport links. There's no dual carriageway (unless you count the tunnel under the runway), no direct train line, no easy bus route and the taxis drop you off in Otley and make you walk (OK, so I'm exaggerating). The fact that this chimes with UK families as an entirely typical scenario high-lights the challenge our tourism industry faces.

When we arrive in Girona, we'll be spending the evenings walking the streets of the town, stopping for a reviving coffee, smiling at other families as kids circle their parents. Perhaps we'll dine at some relaxed late hour. In the UK (with London as the one notable exception), most families, whether British or tourists, know that there's no point staying out beyond 6pm. Few family-friendly coffee bars open beyond that hour – and who would want to take their kids around our town centres after that time anyway? Imagine the commentary from the tourist bus: here we have another sick-gilded doorway and two drunk-en women beating each other senseless. Hurrah for British tourism!

The UK does have a lot to offer the family group, but in certain parts of these sceptred isles, the concept of welcoming families is still as alien as transparency is to Leeds United's administrators. The Yorkshire Dales still has much to learn on this front, as it seems their family-friendly strategy is based on the assumption that anyone bring-ing a child into a restaurant or pub is intent on havoc, where, for the most part, children have better table manners than grown-ups these days.

I remember a particular visit to Dentdale a couple of years ago where the level of practised indifference displayed to our children led me to suggest that the barmaid should audition for the part of Herod, next time the Nativity comes up.

On the West Coast of Scotland, some tourist destinations could save us all time by erecting 'families not welcome here' signs, such is the disdain the experience conveys.

And back to the airlines, where, unless you have your wits about you, you may end up boarding a flight and having your family members seated miles apart from each other. Which family hasn't had that unnerving experience of seeing their pram, destined for the hold, lying alone on the tarmac just as the engines spark up? Which family hasn't been crushed by the rush of halfwits trying to board before their seats are called? Who has been offered priority boarding, but then got on a bus and stood by helplessly as the aforementioned halfwits storm the aeroplane steps?

The challenge is evidentially a cultural one, as it seems that neither our tourist industry nor our inhabitants recognise the damage they're doing to our country's prosperity by failing to cater for the family. Our tourism industry has not done enough to engage family groups, with their considerable spending power, and our selfish, individualist culture demeans us further.

Perhaps we ought to bring in the experts. Let's have Disney operating our airports. Imagine the fun in the queues, with kids' entertainers. Let's have TGI Friday take over Dentdale; you might get a smile at the bar. Then we would really be seeing things. Which reminds me. I need to call the optician.

20

Not an Omnibus Special
October 2006

As an economically challenged youth growing up in the North East of England, my use of buses extended beyond the usual first proper job and well into my mid-twenties. Most of my pals were cruising the frosted roads of County Durham in their Capris and Datsuns well before my raucous yet reliable Morris Ital made its maiden voyage. Prior to that the bus was king. For a few pence, the old Northern shakily negotiated Lanchester Bank on a school day and supported my sorties to Virgin Records in Newcastle every Saturday. Mechanical setbacks, small delays and fading livery were but an inconsequential backdrop to price and service.

Even the bumpy rides have helped me explain away my balding pate. I've always claimed that the repeated banging of my head against the roof led to my current glabrous state. In actual fact, I share Clive James' observation that my baldness is due to the intense pressure of rampant testosterone forcing the remaining fluff out through the top of my skull.

Buses provided a reliable anchor to life growing up. Concessionary fares made it possible for this eternal student to reach such impenetrable places as Pickering Nook, to attend matches at Roker Park regularly and to cavort with girlfriends in windswept moorland outposts.

But somehow, 20 years of de-regulation have relegated the bus to the unenviable position of transport pariah. Where the railway network fell into decay in the 60s and 70s, the bus rode out proudly. Now, the railways are experiencing a boom in passengers (which, incidentally, has yet to be matched by an appropriate increase in carriages) and buses occupy the slow lane of public conscience. Never better is this sad scenario explained than by reflecting on passenger reaction to the phrase 'and the section between Grantham and Peterborough will be replaced by a bus service.' 20 years ago we would have whooped our excitement. Now we slink back into our seats, anticipating hassle. So what's caused this decline in the fortune of the omnibus?

The authors of a recent report point to a number of contributory factors, including poor reliability, shabby, inaccessible, uncomfortable vehicles and rude drivers (and I won't tempt a repeat of the correspondence that followed my last comments on this area). To underline the failure of de-regulation, they point to an almost doubling of fares in the last 20 years and a halving in the number of passengers

For West Yorkshire, the failure of central government to support an integrated vision of transport only serves to highlight the malaise. The proposed Supertram should be replaced by an increased number of buses, they declared. So that would be an increased number of ecologically unsound, uncomfortable, expensive and unreliable buses, then? The requirements of a service that is fit for the future are best articulated by future users, and yet surveys of bus-users – and, more importantly, non-bus-users – have been conspicuous by their absence (as if to mirror the service they describe).

People I speak to talk of the need for a more ecologically sound service, perhaps electrical, citing Florence's impressive ecological minibus city centre service, as a shining example of a future redemption for our buses. They contrast rail services' increasing focus on customer service with the characteristic lack of flexibility shown by some bus drivers. Everyone has a story of a young student being ejected from a bus in some remote location simply for having left behind his or her school pass. They regret (but understand) the impact of increasing prices on those who decide the car is a better alternative and, like me, they bemoan the lack of class of a country whose cities fail to see their transport links as a statement of urban pride.

A first step should be an investment in widespread public consultation, so that we have a strong representative basis for change. This may herald a new age of regulated transport, but will at least project a vision to work towards. We then need greater co-ordination across the country so that journeys, concessions and reliability are joined up rather than discordant.

We need bus services to make a case for themselves, by investing in service, training their staff to recover problems in a more customer-focused style, and showing more creativity with pricing (I don't think I'm alone in finding National Express's maximum journey price guarantees very persuasive). Do this and we might just redeem the chariot of our youth. Fail to act and we'll consign buses to museums and fading memories.

21

An Inconvenient Tooth
April 2006

Back in the summer of 1980 I joined my fellow lower-sixth-formers on a retreat to Minsteracres, a Passionist monastery on the Northumberland-Durham border. I wouldn't recall this with such blinding clarity had it not been for the incident that jolted me out of my meditational calm.

On the penultimate day, a game of rounders had been arranged. While I waited to step up to the plate (and wondered why I was americanising at such a young age) Janet Rogan lost her grip on the bat as she attempted to bisect a monk and a nun at long-off, and watched helplessly as it span viciously into my face, knocking me and several teeth sideways.

Later, when I walked into the kitchen, everybody screamed. Due to my slight concussion, I'd gone to the wrong house. But when I finally did make it home, everyone screamed again, thereby adding a headache to the facial pain.

The next day, with my teeth hanging by the proverbial thread, I was carted off to the local dentist, who pronounced my teeth dead and proposed to remove them immediately. 'I demand a second opinion,' interrupted my mother. 'I think they're dead too,' shouted the nurse from the back of the room. But maternal persuasion prevailed and thus began my adventures with UK dentistry.

I was referred to the dental hospital in Newcastle upon Tyne where I became a guinea pig. I was placed in a box in the waiting room and fed celery stalks. Actually no. The nature of my injury meant that I was a perfect case study for the rescue of seriously damaged teeth. Over the months that followed, armed with a transparent plastic mouth guard to keep my teeth in place, I made several return visits, where I'd reciprocate the care and attention supplied, by removing the guard and releasing the odour of several weeks' worth of trapped food to an unappreciative group of second-year students.

That period of intense dentistry (surely a good name for a heavy metal band) gave me a fascinating insight into a part of the NHS that we rarely call upon, but which, with the arrival of the April 1 deadline for dentists to sign up to the government's new system for remuneration and for extending NHS treatment to more citizens, is suddenly in the news. Anyone throwing no more than a cursory glance at the press will have seen the headlines: greedy dentists, months for treatment, can't sign my kids up, cheaper to go to the Philippines (£11 for a check-up, a clean, a polish and two fillings for a party of two, incidentally).

But if you speak to dentists, there is real frustration that this smoke-screen of media outcry is preventing people from looking at their situation objectively. However, their baulking at the contract – which was meant to make things fairer but has been conspicuous by its lack of flexibility and sufficient consultation with dentists – has been presented as an appalling statement of greed.

An example that reached me highlights the reality of the issue. One Midlands-based dentist, tired of accusations of greed, signed up to the new scheme under protest (it's claimed by senior dentists that 60% of dentists only signed up because the alternative was no budget at all for performing NHS work) and has taken on 2500 new NHS patients since December. To meet the rising demand, he's had his case for four dentists approved by his local Primary Care Trust, but has only been offered two contracts by the Department of Health. He could make £30k a year more if he were to sack one dentist and lose 1200 NHS patients, but he refuses to do this on a moral and professional basis.

The new remuneration package brackets root canal treatment, which can take up to 90 minutes, with a 20-minute tooth extraction. Treatments such as periodontal work are not viable in surgeries any more but many dentists don't want to add to hospital waiting lists. Granted, there may be some dentists who have used this as an excuse to find rich private pastures new, but to introduce such an apparently unworkable contract without sufficient dentist input, and sit back and watch dentists being accused of greed up and down the land, doesn't strike me as the actions of a wise government and doesn't appear to address the crucial aim of increasing NHS dental treatment availability.

It seems inevitable that the only reasonable solution for patients will be to sign up for a dental care plan, thus guaranteeing access to a dentist and preventative care but hammering another nail into the NHS.

Thanks to the skill of those students in Newcastle, my teeth were saved and remained in situ for a further 23 years before finally being declared 'dead' and removed. And the Department of Health? Maybe they just need some wisdom teeth putting in.

22

Really Green Grocers?

March 2007

Today I discovered that I have the 118th most common surname in the UK. Helpfully, the magazine bearing this information also included a reference to my predominant social category. As a Bradley, I am 'welfare borderline'. As if that wasn't dispiriting enough, there is a further explanation: 'often in minimum wage jobs and living in council accommodation. Transient family formations.' I immediately recall a politically incorrect *Viz* cartoon, featuring another transient family whom the magazine more brutally categorised.

And so it often is the case that certain positive impressions can be removed once one digs beyond the apparently reassuring initial picture. Take the supermarkets' current commitment to all things green. From a check of all of the major *megagrocers'* websites, it's clear that something of a revolution is underway.

Tesco's Terry Leahy has recently announced a 'green revolution' at Britain's largest supermarket. Their commitments range from helping to establish a Sustainable Consumption Institute to work on calculating a universally accepted and commonly understood measure of the carbon footprint of the products Tesco sells, to promoting and incentivising energy-efficient products through the new Green Clubcard scheme. And even though we don't yet have an accepted carbon footprint baseline, Tesco is confident that it can reduce it – by 50% by 2020. One way they will achieve this is by ensuring that only one per cent of their products will be air-freighted. There will even be a tiny aeroplane symbol on the packaging, so you'll know if your thyme has flown.

Sainsbury's hasn't been idle either. Today I popped into my local store to find that the plastic bags were made from 33% recycled material. A quick check of their website obligingly provides a lengthening list of 'green' commitments and achievements, from a new emphasis on renewable resources and plastic recycling to greater efforts to help customers recycle, compostable packaging, fewer road miles travelled by their distributors and the ubiquitous re-usable shopping bags.

Marks and Spencer's weighs in with a promise to triple its organic food range – and to include organic linen and clothes. Ethical shopping website www.newconsumer.com reports that M&S also plans to use bio-diesel in all of its lorries, reduce energy and run its stores on renewable power, while Walmart (owners of Asda), Waitrose and Morrison's are all going public with their commitment to eco-business.

We can neatly summarise these efforts under three headings: carbon neutral progress, a commitment to renewable energy resources and an increase in organic / free-trade products. So, while one commentator hails Marks and Spencer's as the leading eco-supermarket, principally on account of their commitment to avoiding offsetting and becoming totally carbon neutral, we consumers should be aware of some of the basic contradictions at work here.

Take recycling and the re-use of packaging, for example. By law supermarkets have to take measures in these areas – they are not just philanthropic, environmental gestures. Even biodegradable packaging will not solve the waste issue. Biodegradable packaging needs to be composted – and there are simply too few of us with a composter for this to make any difference.

Perhaps I'm a cynic, but isn't it true that the best way supermarkets could make a contribution would be to supply their stores locally, so the miles generated by a central distribution system would be wiped out completely? It's fine and dandy for Sainsbury's to tell us that all of their Taste the Difference meat is British. It's not necessarily local – and usually not inexpensive either. And why are our suspicions aroused by an 'own brand' fair trade product?

Perceptions of the all-encompassing greed of our grocery behemoths have led us to believe that somehow the poor producer at the sharp end of the supply chain doesn't benefit from this arrangement as well as they would from a company like Café Direct or AMT Coffee Bars. In fact the latter's continual consultation with consumers has just led to their ousting of kitkats from their railway station kiosks – they just don't fit their 'fair trade' principles.

And isn't it true that the best place to go to see the failure of public transport in this country is any 'out of town' supermarket – with cars packed like sardines (and probably not even line-caught) as far as the eye can see? That's not very eco-friendly, is it?

It's fair to say that this whole environmental issue can throw up some surprising contradictions, and it would be easy for any of us to speculate on what is really driving the supermarkets' green crusade. Are they really committed to the environment – or committed to appearing to be committed? And before I'm committed, maybe I ought to acknowledge the riotous contradictions thrown up by our own environmental family audit. We're equally guilty of half-hearted measures, as any interview with our guinea pigs would reveal. Some days Daddy composts their waste. Other days the composter is just 'too far away'.

Perhaps there's a lesson here. Making shopping 'green' needs to be a partnership between the supermarkets and their customers. So let's work at finding out how we can both make a difference together. Tell me less about your medium-term carbon-neutral strategy and help make it easy for this transient family formation to go green!

What's this? Tesco is halving the price of energy-efficient light bulbs. Now that's a start.

23

No Transports of Delight

August 2006

A couple of weeks ago my wife and I learned that there were companies who would buy your old mobile phones. You could make as much as £80. What's more, you can do it on line and they'll pay money straight into your bank account. Our eyes lit up, like a football agent on transfer deadline day. Within seconds we had gone on line to complete the sale. However, the website stubbornly refused to spring into action and, instead, presented me with several blank screens. As this had happened shortly after I had keyed in my bank details, panic welled in my stomach like one kebab too many. I'd been had.

Or so I thought. The next morning a delightful assistant helped me out over the phone. The website faults would be looked into and she'd process my transaction manually as we spoke. She listened, took responsibility for the problem, put me at ease and my panic subsided.

You see, we UK customers expect reliability, but that alone doesn't guarantee our continued loyalty. What does, however, is a really well handled problem, just like my experience above. Research shows that if you get this right, even when you ultimately can't give the customer what they want, you can really lift your customers' perceptions.

Cut to London where a friend was travelling north by train. The train was full, so he wandered into the empty dining car and sat down. As the waiter approached him, he asked for a drink, as he'd already eaten. You've guessed it. He was told in a very direct style that he'd have to leave the dining car if he didn't intend to dine. 'Well, once you've announced that the dining car is open, I'll wait to see if anyone comes along to dine. If they do, I'll leave,' he responded, expecting a reasoned response. 'You'll have to leave now,' he was told again, in a tone suggesting any further discussion was unwelcome and in a manner suggesting Roy Keane's first team talk at Sunderland.

A similar experience awaits anyone who fails to book ahead and turns up to a busy train. You may have paid the full fare, but you're only guaranteed to 'travel', not to sit in comfort. No, you may not freely upgrade to First Class or sit in the dining car, unless you're about to take on today's specials.

So are these companies right to take such stances? Take GNER, for example, and the 'overcrowded trains' issue. They would argue that you should book in advance, as that guarantees you a seat. And if they offered a free upgrade to passengers who'd turned up on the off-chance, wouldn't that discriminate against those who had booked ahead? Perhaps GNER could introduce a limit to travelling passengers. That would also address some of the safety issues of overcrowding, to which anyone travelling back from London on the day of the airport security problems would bear witness.

But there are, as far as I'm aware, no regulatory limits to the number of people travelling on trains and, to make matters worse, you'd also face the prospect of turning up at the station well ahead of your train, but being told there are no seats left. Naturally, they're attempting the most practical solution of introducing more trains on the east coast route, but this is by no means a simple process, complicated by negotiations with Network Rail, the Office of the Rail Regulator and the emergence of new competitors such as Grand Central Trains, with their proposed services from Sunderland to London.

If GNER, like any other transport company, want to reconcile these difficulties with a need to generate goodwill and loyalty among their customers, they need to build a team who are skilled at dealing with problems. Their people need to be able to welcome problems, apologise, listen, explain the background and offer flexibility and common-sense solutions. There are no easy answers to some of the problems they encounter, but the benefits of presenting a human, understanding front are far-reaching and will go a long way to demonstrating that our public transport companies do indeed have the passengers' best interests at heart.

To do this, public transport employees need clarity and support from their employers. They need to have a clear understanding of the value of each individual customer and the impact that a bad experience has upon them. They need a tool bag of practical responses to some of the problems we've explored and their best efforts should be recognised, as a failure to do so only confirms the low priority for service in the transport industry. Most of all, they need to show a human face and a positive attitude, recognising the need to consign any 'jobsworth' characteristics to the past.

The mobile phone company were understanding and flexible in arriving at a solution. Perhaps a renewed focus on the 'human' side would help UK public transport balance its challenges and help us all reach a similarly happy destination.

24

Suffer a Jet?

July 2006

I certainly had a sheltered youth. Discounting my first tin of Heinz spaghetti, my first genuine pasta meal was celebrated at university in Sheffield when I was 19. I had lasagne and, it is claimed by those present, I asked if anyone wanted my 'skin'. This first gastronomic gamble was closely followed by my first curry, a moment of courage largely inspired by several cans of the alcoholic drink bearing the same name.

But a year later, I made my first manned flight. I flew with Air Canada to Montreal to work at a French Canadian supermarket as part of a student exchange. I was now a member of the 'jet set'. As I celebrated the miraculous arrival of my luggage, I remember reflecting on how lucky I had been to fly across the Atlantic – and then seeing the smug faces of the ground staff, reflecting on how lucky I had been to play a small part in their ego trip.

On the return journey, as I nonchalantly secreted sugar sachets into my pockets, as evidence of my pioneering exploits, the well-practised, prison-camp glare of the intolerant air hostess was already upon me. 'Please put your seat back, sir.' I suppose she had a point. I had managed to remove it entirely and was about to take it home with me.

You see, for those of us born in the 60s when air travel was still out of the reach of the working-class family, flying represented a small window into the world of the rich and famous. I just didn't quite fit the role. Now, with the emergence of the 'no frills' carriers and the dawning of mass-market air travel, it seems none of us fit the role.

How different it is now. We calculated the other day that my daughter had flown abroad three times before she was 3 years old. Rising standards of living and the arrival of the concept of the 'cheap flight' have put towns as alluring as Brno, Bydgoszcz and Friedrichshafen within easy and affordable reach. But our wide-eyed wonder at the magic of flight has been spoiled by the airlines' failure to realise that their continued prosperity will depend on the quality of service they provide – not on us prostrating ourselves before the majesty of their technological wizardry.

The Air Transport Users Council reports that in the first quarter of 2006 their most frequently received complaints related to cancellations, delays, mishandled baggage and overbooking. Europe has helped with its 2005 regulations on Denied Boarding, Cancellations and Delays, but anyone with the misfortune to have experienced one of these problems will attest to the lack of responsiveness and humanity displayed by many airlines.

Take the example of a traveller who arrived in London while his luggage took a ten-day trip around Mexico. Not only was the luggage a mobile phone lighter than it was when it originally set off, but even though they'd known all along, the airline concerned only let the passenger know his bags were missing after he'd spent 90 fruitless minutes in the baggage hall.

Following the customer's complaint, the baggage services team, while claiming a commitment to customer service, promised that they would 'endeavour to respond' to the passenger within 28 days. Unacceptable, especially when their 'preferred method' of communication is email. Had this been a parcel, a freight company would have a tracking service to let you know exactly where your item was, at any given moment. Airlines, it appears, see customers as having a much lower inherent value than this, as they fail to invest any of their profits into this widely available technology.

A friend emailed the provider of his frequent-flyer card to ask for some help with a problem. They emailed back: 'As you are a blue card member we can only deal with written queries. You have to be a silver or gold card holder to be able to enjoy our email help service.' As it turned out, midway through the correspondence, many more points accrued and he was upgraded to the silver level. His letters were now rejected because 'your silver card membership means you must correspond with us by email.'

And with our cheap flights, the message appears to be 'you get what you pay for.' But, as modern consumers, we want more. We want added value from our service providers. So when Ryanair asked 12 disabled passengers to leave a flight 'for their own safety' last year, consumer bile rose. The company had for many years maintained a limit of four disabled passengers, agreed with UK and Irish disability associations, to ensure that the 90-second evacuation requirement could be met and disabled passengers were asked to alert the airline to their disability at the time of booking. The unfortunate 12 failed to do so and, whether this was an oversight or a protest for equal treatment, the perceived parsimony of Ryanair's 'no frills' pricing strategy influenced public opinion negatively then and now. And yet Ryanair is one of the main reasons my children have a much wider appreciation of the world around them than I ever did at their age.

We do want flights to Lodz, Linz and Limoges and we do understand the trade-off between 'no frills' and cheap prices. But when things go wrong we just want airlines to treat us as people rather than human cargo. There's a massive premium to be earned by the airline that consistently balances 'no frills' with good service. And good service is not about avoiding mistakes. It's about resolving them with skill, ownership and humanity. So whether you need rescuing from Rzeszów or you're late at the check-in at Szczecin, 'no frills' shouldn't mean 'no service'.

25

In Defence of Football
July 2006

It was inevitable, wasn't it? Our national team's demise in Gelsen-kirchen is immediately followed by the predictable outpourings of football's detractors. Overpaid players, isolated and protected from true fans, clubs increasing season-ticket prices to cover extortionate wages and incredible tales of horrific late-night behaviour in London hotel suites. All of these stories combine to give the beautiful game a stamp in the groin, just when it was contemplating glory.

To the cursory reader it would appear that football is a self-indulgent and selfish sport, characterised by a lack of transparency and an unwillingness to consult with its supporters. It's all too ready to implement the 'easy' solution of ticket price increases, even when the fare on offer is more 'economy' than 'taste the difference' (to pinch a supermarket device).

It's certainly true that the pressure on clubs to perform on the pitch is more powerful than ever and it's also true that clubs will throw millions at team development while resisting a request to invest a few thousand pounds in collecting feedback from fans. But there is a counterbalance – and it's one that merits closer inspection.

The hawk may attract the headlines, but it's a lesser-heard and sel-dom-spotted creature that deserves recognition. The football industry – the clubs, their administrative bodies and the players themselves – constitute one of the UK's largest corporate charitable donors. Football does give back what it takes.

Much of this unheralded work is co-ordinated by the Football Foundation. Funded by the FA Premier League, The FA, Sport England and Government, they've invested £425 million since 2000 in national and local schemes to support 'grass roots' initiatives. But their remit goes beyond the physical and tangible to encompass social inclusion and education. Schools, clubs and community centres across Yorkshire have benefited from their direct support, which has includ-ed kit, equipment, safer goalposts, upgraded dressing-rooms and showers and a much-needed focus for some of our more troubled neighbourhoods.

And beyond this, our clubs are doing their bit too. Bradford City's family fun days added 1000 extra people to the gate, while the much-derided Leeds United have been addressing social inclusion in Beeston through their Football in the Community and Learning Centre initiatives.

In South Yorkshire, Doncaster Rovers have been working with Active Doncaster and the Royal National Institute for the Blind to bring football to the blind and partially-sighted, while the Football Foundation and leading football figures helped Scunthorpe United celebrate the success of their Study Support Centre – where 2000 engaged and enthusiastic youngsters receive 'out of hours' personal tuition and support from talented and caring mentors.

Towards the west of the region, in Huddersfield a £600,000 grant from the Football Foundation will help the Sikh Youth Sports Foundation to restore the Warrenside Sports Complex. They'll be able to build a new changing pavilion and seven new pitches – reaching out to hundreds of young kids, dreaming of emulating their heroes on TV.

And while it's often those very heroes who receive the most vitriolic criticism in the press, there are many among them who deserve our respect – or at least our acknowledgement that the tilted media snapshot of their glamorous lives may not be a true reflection of their need to 'give it back', a need to acknowledge the people upon whom the game relies.

Niall Quinn did a lot for his fellow pros when he split the proceeds of his testimonial game between children's hospitals in Dublin and Sunderland, to the tune of £1 million. And our much-vilified and departing captain, David Beckham, regarded by those who have met him as one of the most compassionate and caring of his profession, does not absolve himself through massive donations of cash. He actually cares too.

A few years ago a friend had co-ordinated a press shoot where some local kids would receive some new kit from the Football Foundation. As the kids posed for pictures on the edge of Manchester United's

Carrington training ground, my pal noticed Beckham leaving a distant changing-room in his suit. Upon seeing the kids gathered in the distance, he quickly retreated to the dressing-room and emerged a few minutes later, resplendent in his kit. As the kids focused on the cameras in front of them, Beckham sneaked up. 'Does anyone fancy a kick around?' he shouted to the amazed and excited group. I'm not a gambling man, but I suspect that particular memory will be passed down the generations in Salford.

A sport that rewards its top players so ludicrously well, deserves close scrutiny. But we should reserve judgement on football until we've a better understanding of its role for good in the community. Lazy hacks and detractors do us all a disservice by only reporting one side of the story.

Football can be a powerful force for good. Recently, the Derby-based Walbrook Group rewarded the efforts of six young filmmakers with a trip to Chelsea FC – an experience, according to Scheme Manager Mike Umphray, that will stay with them for the rest of their lives. And the title of their winning film? *The Loneliness of a Spot Kick Penalty Taker*. Tell me about it.

26

Details of the Unexpected

May 2007

'But how easily we forget ...' a friend wistfully counselled the other day, while I hysterically celebrated Sunderland's promotion to the Premier League. Naturally, he was keen to restrain my rampant optimism with a spoonful of reality. 'Even if you combined the points your team got in your last two stays in the top division, you still would have been relegated last year.'

It served its purpose. I started to remember the misery. Depressing details, such as the time we scored three own goals in ten minutes at home to Charlton – and going 1-0 up at home to arch-rivals Newcastle, before folding like a pack of cheap cards and losing 1-4 – flooded my mind, pushing images of Niall Quinn and Roy Keane to the side, replacing them with the dark, foreboding figure of Howard Wilkinson.

Football fans do have selective memories – and we choose to manage this according to our prevailing emotional state. But with customer service?

Any expert will tell you that exceptionally good experiences lead to a life of advocacy, where one skips down the high street randomly confronting nervous strangers and telling them about Innocent Drinks' good works. They'll tell you that negative experiences will lead you to write epistles to several hundred acquaintances explaining how you are praying for a pox upon your PC repair company. Well, I may be exaggerating, but you get the point.

Now, as a consequence of this, you'd expect organisations to be set up to obtain feedback from customers on their specific experiences, so as to capture these relevant little moments, analyse them and make the necessary improvements. But when you submit yourself to a probing assessment of a typical 'customer experience' I'm not so sure we have enough data to be making such profound pronouncements. In fact, I'm beginning to wonder if we're missing the point altogether.

Let me take you through our experience at a hotel in the Midlands last weekend. Two families arrive, having spent the afternoon at the zoo with their four kids. We have a youngster in a wheelchair with us, and we're keen to check in and book a table for dinner, preferably one around which the family could sit and at which our disabled nephew Jack could feel comfortable.

Initially, the receptionist phoned the restaurant manager who confirmed all of the larger tables were already booked, but that they could put us on adjacent separate tables. While not ideal, we agreed to this and met at the restaurant an hour later. At this point any cursory glance at our emotional 'dashboard' would have found a mix of readings. Nice welcome from the receptionist, who became a little hassled as the queue lengthened behind us. We're not getting our needs met from the restaurant, in spite of agreeing to eat as soon as.

Upon entering the restaurant the manager presents himself with a broad smile and explains that they have been able to create a table for us, by putting two together in an area that Jack could access via the chair lift, which the man himself then operated on our behalf. Dials start to whirr, readings positive, emotions calmed.

Seconds later we receive one of the warmest welcomes I can recall from the young waitress. A few of our group remark on this. 'The manager was lovely. Do you think all of this warmth is planned?' It seemed so. There was a level of pro-activity aimed at making all of the experience excellent, especially at those times where tensions can emerge (e.g. choosing food for the kids, dealing with bored 8-year-old daughter, numerous toilet trips, using the chair lift, asking for split bills, etc). Our internal 'emotional' dashboards rattled with positive information. We have so much to share …

At the end of the meal we presented the waitress with a large tip and explained how we thought the service had been outstanding. I'm sure we'll do the same when we get the feedback email from the hotel itself, if one arrives. But I wondered. Are our processes all set up to record this level of detail from customers? I think not.

Ten years ago we got by on an annual customer satisfaction survey (opinions and ratings, no detail). Five years ago we were collecting generic monthly feedback (higher profile, still no detail). Then came the event driven feedback, giving us time to put things right, or so we thought – and now that we're into the 21st century, real-time customer feedback is bringing the data in the second that it's available.

Now I've no doubt that this latter development has really helped our cause, especially as it's considerably raised the profile of service inside our organisations, but does it convey the multiple 'emotional' readings we register during our customer experiences? We reckon we received outstanding service on Saturday evening. Our waitress knows that – and we do too. But if I weren't able to share this with you here, I'm not sure anyone else would get to hear all of this rich detail at all.

27

No Transports of Delight (Part 2)

June 2007

There was a point during my travels this week when delirium began to set in. After I had been asked to remove my shoes at the security scanner, the stress created by a week that would make Steve Martin's *Planes, Trains and Automobiles* look like an uneventful commute, finally began to take its toll.

'Your belt please, sir?' asked the assistant and as madness gripped my brain cells, I started to unbutton my trousers, undo my tie and continue undressing. His concerned voice brought me quickly back to reality: 'Sir?'

My week began innocuously enough, although I did think that it might not have been a good idea to arrange meetings on Monday morning in London and Tuesday afternoon in High Wycombe, as well as in Crawley on Thursday.

I decided to take my wife's reliable little Polo to Leeds Station early on Monday morning and catch the 7.20 to King's Cross. Had we been told of the trouble ahead, I might have alighted immediately, but we set off on time and only began to suspect problems when a fellow passenger pointed out that the train was now apparently an amphibious vehicle. The track had turned into a river and we were struggling along at 2 knots.

When we reached Newark the truth emerged. There were floods ahead and we would be proceeding at 5 miles an hour. This, together with several impromptu stops, led to a delay of 2 hours, with the only consolation being free tea and coffee, most of which was consumed by delighted passengers getting on at Peterborough, thinking this was all part of the service.

I missed my morning meeting in London, putting it all down to experience and clutching my compensation form guiltily. I've missed my meeting, but it's hardly GNER's fault. However, inspecting the schedules revealed the full tragedy hitting Yorkshire and Humberside, so it was with some humility that I decided to remain in London and return after my Tuesday meeting. I checked with my wife and she told me trains were running as far as Doncaster, but when I arrived at King's Cross at 4.55pm I was told that the 5.00pm would be the last train leaving.

The man sitting next to me was making his second attempt in two days to travel north and we agreed that if we only got as far as Doncaster, we'd share a taxi to Leeds. Then my wife called. Things were looking bad, she explained, so she would set off with the kids to pick me up. Then the train announcer explained (and I'm paraphrasing) that they'd really rather we all got off as there was little chance of onward travel from Doncaster, other than by gondola.

As the train headed north each successive announcement grew more grave in tone, with the result that by the time we reached Peterborough we were all biting our nails, like characters in a particularly scary episode of *Scooby Doo*.

By the time I got to Peterborough (that other Jimmy Webb classic) fear gripped me and I decided to abandon ship (an ironic turn of phrase in the circumstances, as such a vessel would have been welcome), once I had established that my family shouldn't attempt to drive anywhere at all. I managed to track down one of my sisters, who offered to put me up for the night, but this involved travelling to Ely and then onward to Waterbeach, near Cambridge. Strange name for a village – for when I first rang to ask for her stop, I thought she'd said 'what a bitch!' in sympathy with my predicament.

Two further train journeys later, I was watching the situation unravelling in Yorkshire. So, by the next morning, sobered by the human tragedy involved, I attempted to travel home again. This time, I made it, albeit via York, returning to find that the Polo had a flat battery and wouldn't start. 'Waterbeach!' I cried.

Within hours I was headed to Crawley, this time via Leeds-Bradford Airport and Heathrow (given that all my alternative modes of transport were unavailable still). I attempted to check in on line and discovered that, as a result of a gas leak at Hatton Cross, flights to Heathrow were severely delayed. This was important, as someone was going to pick me up there and needed to know my time of arrival. Yes, I know I could have lessened my carbon footprint by taking the train, but I would have needed my carbon wellies too.

I approached the check-in desk and enquired. 'No problem,' I was assured, 'everything is back to normal and your flight will not be delayed.' As I boarded (having had my deodorant and shaving gel helpfully confiscated) I sent a quick text confirming no delay to my colleague in London.

As I listened to the security briefing, switched off my phone and settled back into my *Yorkshire Post*, one further announcement was made. 'I'm not sure if you've been told this' said the pilot casually, 'but there's at least a 40-minute delay on this flight.' Thankfully no children were on board to hear the volley of obscenities from seat 9C.

The driver picked me up and swiftly deposited me at the luxury of the Crawley Ibis (which sounds like a particularly unpleasant insect), just in time for me to check in and consume a welcome beer.

The next day, I arrived back at Heathrow to join the security crew and to be overwhelmed with a need to disrobe. What a week!

When I look back at how our transport systems coped with the unprecedented weather conditions, I have fond memories of the Customer Service Manager on the 7.20 from Leeds last Monday. He took the time to speak to us all, in small groups, as he made his way down the train and we watched startled sheep floating by. Announcements were regular and having abandoned the chance of making my meeting, I could at least be sure that I'd reach London safely.

Travelling back, however, there were no announcements at all, and I only discovered that a journey to Leeds via York by train was possible by texting my wife and sister (two different people, I assure you).

Back at Leeds Station car park the breakdown man explained how he'd been called out to Wetherby earlier to start a 'damp' car that turned out to be submerged in three feet of water.

Up in the skies, however, the service was less helpful. Security was, as always, a priority, but announcements were few and far between, with the eventual information given being so evidently wrong as to constitute a dereliction of duty. Heathrow Airport was as disappointing as ever. Terminal One was dated, scruffy, crowded and disorganised.

There were huge queues through security at lunchtime (when

you'd expect it to be quiet) and yet several scanning machines were not being used. Again, we boarded on time, but the pilot threw us another curve ball by announcing we were in a queue. Ultimately we spent more time taxiing on Heathrow runway than we spent in the air to Leeds.

When I finally landed, having aged several years since the Monday, I was whisked off by my family to Murgatroyds for some therapeutic carbohydrates. It was there that I assessed the balance of my woeful week of wandering. You'd think the question 'which mode of transport coped best with the floods?' would be an unfair one, as trains can't fly, but it was they who managed best.

The traveller's lot doesn't look any better in the weeks ahead: last week floods and this week an increase in terrorist activity. Pack an extra shirt.

28

Justin Time
April 2005

Justin King is the latest in the new breed of very young chief executives. Of both a fresh complexion and fresh ideas, he's the man who's been brought in to revive Sainsbury's. There could not have been a greater contrast with previous incumbents, the last of whom left under the shadow of an unsightly bonus controversy. But Justin's appointment and his openness and honesty about the challenge at Sainsbury's puts business leadership back under the spotlight – and in the sights of your customer service correspondent.

What characterises great leadership in business today? Can one individual make a difference to a business with huge, complex distribution structures or is leadership more to do with action than personality?

A recent experience highlights the power of a truly effective business leader. On my way back from running a workshop with matchday employees at Leicester City FC (given their current performances, I don't regard that as name-dropping), I happened by the local supermarket to purchase a bottle of wine. As the conveyor belt lurched into action and my bottle slid by me, the cashier looked up at me, smiled and said 'I assume you are over 18, sir ....'

'That's the nicest thing anyone's ever said to me at a supermarket,' I retorted. Sadly, there is no possible chance that she could have been serious. As anyone passing more than a casual glance at the mug shot on the back cover would attest: rather than approaching the legal limit for the purchase of alcohol, I am a multiple of it.

Happily, the lady was reassuringly in control of all her faculties. She told me she was simply following the encouragement she got when she met her new Chief Executive earlier that week – try to build a rapport with the customers; try to put them at ease and make them feel special.

Last month I recorded several disturbing examples of retail déjà vu. This month, there's evidence that someone has recognised these issues and is doing something about them, and that man would appear to be Justin King at Sainsbury's, for it was there that I experienced the sweet little cameo I've described above.

Justin King knows that for people to believe in an organisation, they've got to believe in its leaders. So that means that an approach characterised by remote detachment (at which many UK leaders excel, incidentally) needs to be replaced by a highly visible and collaborative approach. Justin, like Terry Leahy at Tesco and Richard Kimber at First Direct, believes in making himself available to his employees. Getting a one-on-one opportunity with your new CEO means you can cut straight through the 'spin' to the real man, offer your own opinion and pin him down on the detail.

And it's not just the symbolic reality of the 'back to the floor' initiative. Accessibility is equally achievable whether the CEO is helping you drive your bus today or whether he's 200 miles away. Many are now abandoning some of the more conventional approaches and giving employees the opportunity to ring them on their mobile, to email them personally or to meet them in small groups, socially, to discuss what the business needs to succeed. Each conversation shortens the distance from the leader to the team and every phone call makes the message clearer.

In the past the UK has suffered because of its unwillingness to shake off some of the lazy habits of the traditional hierarchy. So, ladies and gentlemen, hats off to Mr King for visiting his people and helping me feel like a valued customer.

No Transports of Delight (Part 3)

April 2007

I had an interesting conversation with the lady at the rail company the other day. She was warmth personified as she processed my telephone request for a return advance first-class ticket to London. And before you start making assumptions about my vast fortune, let me tell you that the advance first-class ticket works out cheaper than the standard equivalent. As I congratulated myself for negotiating the complexities of modern-day rail ticket purchase, I smiled at the sweet incongruity of the outcome. First-class travel cheaper than standard.

What followed nudged me closer to a paroxysm of mirth. The lady explained the restrictions. 'You can enjoy all of the benefits of first-class travel but you do not have access to the first-class lounge.' Fair enough, I thought, so I gave my credit card details, completed the purchase and opted to collect my tickets. 'That's fine, sir. You can collect them from the ticket machines or from the first-class lounge.' I'd actually put the phone down before I remembered she'd told me I wasn't allowed in there. Perhaps you stand outside and shout.

The incident provokes recollections of other recent customer service 'double takes'. My friend John once queued at the M6 Toll Road late into a Sunday evening. Inexplicably there was only one gate open, and the young lady was vainly trying to process a long line of grumbling drivers. As he passed through he asked why there weren't more open. 'We don't have enough people to man the automated barriers,' came the straight-faced reply.

It's customer service, Scotty, but not as we know it.

Unconvention
August 2007

Like both of my readers, I occasionally get invited to business conventions. Organisers panic as the data projector fails to project and each presenter shares his or her take on the *look after your people and they'll look after your customers* line while delegates reflect on those nice bacon bagels in the reception area.

In fact, I find that a complicated-looking pyramid slide usually impresses sufficiently. It need not matter that it makes no sense or cannot be explained – it's usually enough to provoke a gasp from the strategic marketing director at ACME industries or some such. Not that I'm a sceptic, of course, but it only takes a cursory glance at the word convention to reveal one of the greatest challenges to UK customer service. We're too conventional. We lack new perspectives, we fear change and we even call our meetings 'conventions'.

I include myself in this group of traditionalists, as it took a long time for my particular penny to drop, but when it did, it came down like a bin lid. What began as an everyday conversation with a colleague ended in uproar, as my colleague said: 'we spend all our time trying to get suggestions out of our experienced staff, when the truth is, it's only the new starters who can see the wood for the trees.'

I quickly recalled a time in a previous life where I had the joy of inspecting a batch of staff suggestions. 'Put a metal ring outside our branch so people can attach their dogs to it' was one memorable contribution. Having worked at that particular branch, I can't recall a single canine companion over a three-year period. Or perhaps the staff member had a dog.

So, on the basis that our new recruits have, as a minimum, the least blinkered view of our organisations, how should we harness that new perspective? Why not begin by turning some conventions on their heads?

At one organisation, their Damascene moment occurred when they observed that new starters were often hurried away into a corner to co-pilot a PC and enjoy a thrilling first-week schedule, which included a trip to the IT department and a chance to open the post.

At a second organisation, every new starter receives a welcome card on their first day and at a third, new starters have lunch with the MD on their first day and go away with a little black book to collect their initial impressions, meeting a few weeks later to share these perspectives with the boss.

At another, some wise guy commented that the main reason for a celebration in British work time is when someone is leaving (which, in itself sends out a strangely persuasive message about why service might be so poor in these isles). Cue the bin lid. Just why should we hide the new starters and expect lateral thinking from the rest?

So how do we create a swelling tide of lateral thinking without commandeering the moon? The simple solution is to learn from those lateral-thinking exercises that used to drive us mad at management development courses and start creating a 3-dimensional view within our 2-dimensional organisations.

How, for example, do we institutionalise objectivity in our organisations, if that's not a contradiction in terms? As an awards assessor a few years ago, I noticed that very few managers divided their time equally between peers, employees and customers. Most, unsurprisingly, spend 90% of their time with fellow managers, choosing to relegate employee- and customer-contact to superficial (and Young Mr Grace-like) expressions of goodwill at key message times. Those organisations with a clear competence for learning and progression saw that it was important for their managers to spread their time in this way, even stretching the definition to include peers in other organisations.

Among customer-facing employees, some of the most pioneering progress has emerged where external and reciprocal visits have pride of place in the work schedule. Whether it's arranging a swap with a local business or sneaking a walk in the customer's shoes around your local supermarket, there's much to be learnt, as well as the added richness of the external perspective.

At performance management level, let's go beyond having team-, departmental- and company-wide measures and include an external performance measure for comparison and mind-stretching.

A colleague explained that in one Japanese manufacturing organisation each team works towards internal company-values targets. Nothing surprising there. However, they also have an external values measure based on the performance of an aspirational organisation (which for their purposes was Disney). In practical terms, each improvement discussion is not restrained by internal, conventional thinking, but by an external boundary that's bound to take them further.

And with the word 'convention' our language doesn't help either. *Front line* implies hand-to-hand combat, while *at the coalface* suggests the imminent arrival of emphysema or pneumoconiosis.

The solution, as I've indicated, needs to be company-wide, not a question of individual ability. And while I pray for an invite to the very first business unconvention, let me leave you with a thought. Imagine horse racing without blinkers. They'd probably cut across the course to save time, order sugar cubes on the internet, opt for champagne in the winners tent and punch anyone attempting the *why the long face?* joke. I'd be more inclined to tune in, believe me.

31

Couldn't Care Less about Apathy
June 2006

Not for the first time, a recent conversation turned to the fact that people get better customer service in the USA. Shop assistants are more charming and responsive, children are welcomed almost everywhere without the slightest hint of awkwardness and problems are resolved without fuss or delay – all rare experiences in the UK. Travellers talk about remarkable holiday experiences in Florida, where they are recognised by a waiter who last served them 10 years ago and every visitor to a theme park recounts the touching exploits of a hotel employee who'd gone that extra mile for them. Here companies run a mile in the opposite direction.

So why does the USA have such a great reputation for customer service? Perhaps the comedian Reginald D Hunter is right when he says it's because most Americans carry weapons. As much as that opinion amuses me, the fact is that Americans not only know how to complain, but they do it better and more frequently than the taciturn Brits. They don't stand for poor service.

But here in the UK, it's no laughing matter. The more we resist the urge to tell it like it is, the worse the service we will receive. There is a real fear that organisations will see 'trading on apathy' as a sustainable business strategy. So where does this apathy have its roots? And can I be bothered to find out?

To begin with, customer service has a low profile in this country. Customer interaction is an ancillary concept, between office cleaning and mass catering, a career hazard, most usually hurdled in the pursuit of the 'desk job' – that tidy, anodyne vision of security, projected as desirable upon the masses from the post-war years.

The concept of deriving professional satisfaction from serving well is rigorously established in many Western societies, but not in ours. For us, it's too reminiscent of the old Albion and its submissive subjects. The sixties, we're told, saw the ousting of deference, but in the era's revolutionary haste, the concept of good old-fashioned customer service was thrown away, like the proverbial baby with the bathwater.

Anyone embarking on a career in the services industry (which now dominates globally and which is expected to be the main long-term focus of economic stability) can expect to be dropped straight in front of a customer. Little surprise service has such a low profile when you don't even have to earn your stripes behind the scenes first. But in our world, if you perform well you're rewarded by being removed further and further away from customers and closer to the warm isolation of the office with your name on the door.

Customer service departments have become one of the greatest misnomers since the phrase 'military intelligence' was first coined. In recent years, they've become no more than a 'catch all' for tasks and problems not easily accommodated elsewhere.

Complaints departments are set up as 'cost centres' and the now well-proven concept of generating profitable customer relationships through excellent complaint-handling is regarded with deep suspicion, as if a presenter on *Most Haunted Live* had just revealed this pioneering strategy.

Customer feedback is treated with the same thick veneer of 'lip service'. Suggestion cards and survey forms abound, but the amount of effort expended in craving our feedback is seldom matched by any visible improvement in service afterwards.

The fundamental structures of our largest organisations hint at this nascent strategy of trading on our indifference. For example, whereas £millions of retail resources are invested in the 'look and feel' – the TV displays promoting the latest offer, the ubiquitous 'branded' in-store radio, kidnapping chart music to generate lucre, etc – the absence of shop-floor staff and their general inability to engage betrays the real intent. But we don't care enough to make them care.

If we want our service providers to improve, we have to recognise the impact (or lack of impact) that our inertia has. I'd like to beseech us all to overcome our British reserve and start to demand better service, but at the same time I recognise the fact that responding to the enquiry 'is everything all right with your food?' with the statement 'no, my steak is overcooked' would represent something of a Bastille Day for the restrained Brits.

But we can take every opportunity to express our dissatisfaction when presented with surveys, we can surf the web to see whether our complacent service-provider has generated any customer action groups and we can blog our feedback to the masses.

We are not a nation renowned for recalcitrance but we'll need a little of that old American revolutionary vigour if we are to stand up for customer service in the Old country. As my inaccurate though well-meaning friend points out, when he had difficulty getting some service from a PC retailer, we're still a long way from The Night They Drove Old Dixons Down.

32

Déjà Vu (All Over Again)
March 2005

As the Welsh goalkeeper Danny Coyne let that late Austrian attempt trundle underneath him and into the net, it struck me that one of David James' last acts for the England football team was to do roughly the same thing against the same team in the same stadium last October. You might have been tempted, as a famous football pundit once was, to shout 'it's just like déjà vu all over again.' But just recently this unsettling sense of life repeating itself has been haunting me too.

It seemed to start in January when I visited my local supermarket for petrol. Being a bear of very little brain, as A A Milne once put it, I'd parked with the petrol pump on the wrong side of the car. So, having almost disemboweled myself trying to stretch the dispenser over the boot and being bewildered by the multiple choices already on offer (pay at pump, pay in kiosk, etc), I was a little disheveled as I entered the kiosk.

'Number 3, please,' I offered.

'That'll be £20, please' came the reply. 'Do you want a VAT receipt?'

'Yes, please,' I stated, as I handed over my card.

'Do you collect the school vouchers?' she asked.

'Yes, please,' I replied, trying to look alert.

'Do you have your reward card?' she asked.

'Yes, here it is,' I retorted, the will to live diminishing by the second.

There was a pause while the lady processed my payment. She looked up again.

'Do you want a VAT receipt?' she asked.

'Er, yes,' I replied, feeling that a response along the lines of 'I've already told you once' might accidentally reawaken the latent 'prison guard' tendencies that she's been repressing all these years.

Strange. And not three days later it happened again. This time I was asked 'Do you want a VAT receipt?' as I began my transaction. After

I'd answered in the affirmative, the assistant failed to produce said receipt. 'Can I have a VAT receipt, please?' I continued. 'Oh, sorry, I didn't know you wanted a VAT receipt,' came the predictable reply. Déjà vu is obviously very contagious as it's now spread to the checkout at the supermarket.

Last Thursday I piled up my shopping and watched as the person behind me tried to profile me from the assorted items on the belt. As this included guinea pig food, some bin bags, some Chinese dry white rice wine and a tub of margarine, I was almost tempted to join in the speculation myself.

'Would you like some help with your packing?' the young girl asked me.

'No, thank you, I'll manage,' was my reply. I proffered my card.

'Would you like some help with your packing?' came the question again.

'Er, no. I'll be OK.'

It strikes me that the one reliable bit of human contact you have when filling up or doing the weekly shop is when you're paying at the end of the transaction. And given that we know that the human element is what really causes people to spread the word about our businesses, it's disconcerting to know that the repetitive nature of many of today's jobs is effectively stifling the unpredictable and riotous complexities of human interaction. The smile replaced by the grunt, the opportunity to strike a conversation replaced by repeated phrases, so much so that every customer gets 'processed' twice, in case the cashier isn't sure they've asked the question in the first place.

There are a number of contributory factors to this unsettling state of play, which could be addressed through applying the most basic principles of service excellence. Find out what customers think, most importantly, and work with your front-line people to create an environment in which this can be delivered consistently. This may lead to deciding that more variety is needed in front-line roles to counteract the boredom of repetition. It may lead to increased 'job swaps' within the store to keep everyone energised. It may even lead to supermarket managers focusing on observation, giving feedback and coaching.

With growing interest in non-supermarket food suppliers and locally sourced family shopping, there's talk that the 'boom years' of the big supermarkets may be at an end. Keep up this tendency to 'automate' service and the end will be quicker than expected. And, as if to make my point, I'll be repeating this article in my next book.

33

Underground
July 2007

Tom Waits once rasped, 'There's a lot going on underground.' Judging by a series of recent visits to our vibrant capital city, I think he's right.

As a resident of Yorkshire with his origins even further north, I envy Londoners and the quality of their transport infrastructure. Here in West Yorkshire, we've been sternly rapped on the knuckles for asking for Government support for a Supertram and told we must get by with a few more buses. The result of all of this is that even though I live 6 miles from Valley Parade, 12 miles from Elland Road, 7 miles from the Galpharm Stadium and 25 miles from Hillsborough, I couldn't attend a midweek football match at any of those stadia and expect to get home before midnight on public transport.

In London, however, I can get anywhere, anytime. I'll soon be able to take a tube until 1 a.m and if things get really desperate, there's even a vessel that I can pick up at Waterloo that's capable of driving off the roads and into the Thames!

Looking at Harry Beck's famous Tube map I can go up and down at my leisure, at most times of the day and at a reasonable price. Oh no, I've just missed a Victoria Line train. But look, another one in 60 seconds! And if I do want to fly around (defying the ground), I can catch Carsten Höller's slides in the Tate Modern's Turbine Hall. It's public transport, Jim, but not as we know it.

But it's the Underground that draws me in. David Bradley, of Cragrats fame, once told me how he'd recently visited London and joined the silent despair of the queue for tube tickets at the pre-modernisation King's Cross station. Shuffling forward like execution fodder, he found himself in front of the till. 'Can I have a travel card, please?' he asked. 'No,' came the reply. As David was shaken out of his moribund state, the ticket seller smiled back at him. 'Just kidding, here you go!' The result was a reinvigorated Mr. Cragrats, an extra joyous leap in every step thereafter.

There's even more evidence of the Underground's twinkling eye on www.goingunderground.net, a site which joyously corrals a multitude of subterranean opinions, stories and, to lighten the heart of any traveller, a selection of unorthodox tube driver announcements.

When some halfwit insists on trying to board a train when it's clearly too late, you just pray for a driver who will announce: 'To the gentleman wearing the long grey coat trying to get on the second carriage, what part of *stand clear of the doors* don't you understand?' You just wish you'd been travelling with the driver who announced Knightsbridge's obvious tourist attraction as *Mr Al Fayed's little corner shop*. And you yearn for a Jubilee Line journey into town with a driver who does birthday requests, encourages singalongs with the busker in carriage 4 and insists that people give up their seats for Mums on Mothers' Day (all for the price of a one-day travel card).

Paul Weller may not have had so much fun down in the tube station (it didn't do him any harm in the long run, though, as my wife observes) and the *Evening Standard* now has a regular feature where its readers share their transport rants, but these Londoners don't know they're born. Each time I visit London I witness enough smiley cameos and helpful staff that I sometimes fear that customer service may have broken out. I've seen employees engage with my kids, help me with bags, point me in the right direction and help me with the new technology (Oyster Cards).

I find a website that's incredibly useful. I find ticket machines take any method of payment with instructions in all the major languages. I find ticket machines that work. In fact the only improvement request I've seen from a London Underground customer recently was a request to have the trains painted the same colour as their lines on the map (blue trains for the Piccadilly Line and brown for the Bakerloo, etc).

Elsewhere, transport executives throughout the land, au courant as ever, are blaming all of our transport ills on central government, Network Rail, the RMT, leaves on the line and, in some cases, passengers, who all insist on travelling into work in the morning and home again in the afternoon.

In the capital, however, transport management and rail unions have just shaken hands on a new pay agreement, based on the need to improve service and respect the people who deliver it. London Underground employees are expected to accept a three-year above inflation deal, spiced up with the promise of £250–£500 annual customer satisfaction bonuses.

So when you next hear the soaring sax of Gerry Rafferty's 'Baker Street' or when you next emerge blinking into Ray Davies' 'Waterloo Sunset', take your hat off to the wonderful people underground.

34

No Transports of Delight (Part 4)

November 2006

My family, more than any other one I know, deserves the adjective 'long-suffering'. Having shared the bleak trek around the UK that led to the publication of *Inconvenience Stores*, they've had to travel by train over each of the last three weekends.

My reasons for choosing to travel by train were twofold: firstly, my unstinting commitment to the environment, whereby I only use my car when absolutely essential; and secondly, the fact that I've reached the annual mileage limit on my lease car two months early. While you wait for the smell of hypocrisy to escape the room, let me describe our adventures.

Our first trip involved a weekend stay in Norwich, occasioning the interaction of GNER and Central Trains. As I nonchalantly printed off my tickets at the machine, our excitement was curtailed. 'These reserved seats aren't together,' my wife pointed out. 'The whole point of reserving was so we could be with the kids.'

'I could have sworn that the lady I called promised we'd have a table seat.' I say 'could have sworn' but I actually did cuss audibly, when we discovered how randomly the four seats were spread around coach C.

Following a quick chat with an assistant, we were told nothing could be done, other than paying for a first-class upgrade. 'It's £15 for adults and I'm not sure how much for kids.' Five minutes later I could have helped him. 'That'll be £60,' concluded the train manager as we took our only option. The family looked at me darkly, suspecting that my general telephonic incompetence had led to the mix-up.

So, with me feeling smug at the free biscuits and tea our £60 had bought us, we settled into our journey. At Peterborough, we alighted. I like this verb 'alight'. It evokes a soft landing, as if on compressed air. It suggests comfort, warmth and safe arrival. However, on this occasion, we joined a Central train to discover two people in our reserved seats. We did the usual British performance of raising eyebrows, coughing politely and making helpful gestures, but to no avail. It wasn't until they got off at Ely that we realised they didn't speak English.

A week later we took a Virgin Train to Birmingham for the day, with Father confidently announcing that we'd be waltzing around the Bullring in approximately one hour and forty minutes. I had reckoned without weekend engineering work, which extended the outward journey by an hour and the return journey by an hour and twenty minutes. During the outward journey, we found an elderly couple in our kids' reserved seats. Again, my conscience raged. But, having balancing all of the stresses of the moment, the fact that they spoke English justified our ultimate decision to turf them out. They were only going to Sheffield, after all.

Last week, with a recklessness bordering on the psychopathic, we decided to visit Torquay by train. This involved crossing London, and picking up the GWR train at Paddington, our minds full of dreams of Laurie Lee, clotted cream and dodgy cider.

In order to contain the entire trip within the weekend, we'd left our luggage at Paddington on the outward journey, intending to pick it up at 9.30 later that evening, when our return train from Exeter would arrive.

Our task in Torquay having been completed (I feel justified in inserting the Herculean reference), we set off back to Paddington, only to be told minutes into the journey that because of a failing train 'behind us' we would have to wait at Taunton for an hour to pick up the passengers. My deep-seated philanthropy finally snapped. 'Let them wait for the next one. Left Luggage at Paddington closes at 11.' Although understandable, my prayers were unanswered.

The kids were hungry – and their appetite had been fanned by some glossy brochures announcing a range of hot sandwiches. Father set off, only to return empty handed. 'All sold out,' I was told. But, with a swiftness of thought hitherto unwitnessed in our household, I took advantage of the hour's delay at Taunton, to sprint across the platform to the café bar, where three other demented passengers and I fought over a tuna sandwich and some pasties.

To add to our joy, the drunken family in the next seats had reached the performing-flatulence-and-overt-smoking phase. While I smugly anticipated their swift removal, the opposite happened. Having decided that the day couldn't get any worse, the train employees decided to 'give up', retire to the buffet car, and play out the journey by announcing just how far we were away from Paddington. Later, as I sprinted down platform 12 towards our luggage at 10.45 pm, I dreamed of my car.

35

Bradford's Market Forces

February 2005

When the *Bradford Telegraph & Argus* asked me to report on my family's experiences of shopping in the city as part of the 'Buy it in Bradford' campaign, I did wonder if they'd read my first book. My criticisms of UK retail businesses and their failure to recognise the 'bottom line' benefits of customer service are well known. Added to that, my family's experiences of service up and down the land hardly augured well for a city apparently not even regarded as a half-decent shopping destination.

But appearances can be deceptive, especially when service is the objective. It's people who make the difference, and it's the warmth, reassurance and ownership of the best people that makes their businesses stand out from the pack. It's the readiness to engage and the ability to take every opportunity to care that draws the hyperbole, that spreads the word, that converts what, on the face of it, is a dowdy establishment into a 'must visit' locale. It's this that we're assessing.

Then again, with half of the east side boarded up, the rain thundering in horizontally and the wind so strong the city elders were reviving the old joke about the chicken laying the same egg twice, I did think twice before leaving the house. It occurs to me that service in this town is going to have to be superlative to compensate for this weight of dissuasion.

We abandon the car for the day and take the bus into town, alighting at the main bus station whereupon a Southern Electricity sales person immediately sets upon us with a discounted dual-fuel package. We spy the Bakers' Oven shop across the concourse and I'm reminded of my upbringing in County Durham where a searingly hot Greggs pasty was the best 'dual fuel' option: filling your stomach and keeping your hands warm at the same time.

Perceptions are everything to customers and, not being locally born, I link Bradford to a colourful array of figures, from the German settlers, to Titus Salt, from Hockney's honest reality to Andrea

Dunbar and her controversial *Rita, Sue and Bob Too* (especially the adjectives attributed by one of the main characters to 'Mavis').

But, even with two kids (courtesy of the Bradford Royal Infirmary, of course – and my wife, who was also seriously implicated in the act) my perceptions of Bradford are less formed than those I have of its neighbours. Today is an opportunity to take an objective perspective.

Bradford's topography is another challenge. Hills lurch everywhere from the centre and even this has no river, no greenery (or piazza). Anyone got Sherpa Tensing's mobile number?

In New Market Place shoppers file past a 'fire and brimstone' evangelist, who's being circled by a distressed-looking man carrying an empty Starbucks coffee cup. Hmmm.

As we ascend, the town becomes busier and we make our first stop at Renata's delicatessen on James Street. Tempted in by the sight of so much alluring charcuturie, father approaches the counter and a wonderful exchange ensues, during which the proprietor and her assistant hand out selections for my kids to taste. What could have been a quick-fire visit for a bag of pasta evolves into a ten-minute stay with little change from a tenner. Sopocka, gypsy ham, cabanos, kolska and brawn all make their way into our shopping bag and put us over-budget already.

Having decided to start at the highest point we cross the road to the Oastler Shopping Centre. I recall a previous visit characterised by a lot of cheap clothes stalls and mentally prepare to be underwhelmed. But it's here that our expectations really begin to be confounded.

To make service impact the bottom line, you can't just get the basics right: the right produce at the right time and the right price. You have to generate warmth – and that only comes from the human touch. Service quality only thrives in locales where both these factors are consistently delivered but, as my previous book shows, finding this consistency in the UK is about as likely as a TV ad without a Tom Baker voiceover.

The aroma from J & I Beaumont's fruit and vegetable stall attracts us first. In addition to the traditional offerings, there are self-serve boxes of an array of spices, including gems such as sugar-coated fennel seeds. Seeing my kids' intrigue, but without the facility of fluency in English, one of the assistants uses the international language of kindness, smiles at my kids and gives them some to taste.

Parents impressed and kids well and truly engaged, we continue onwards, picking up some pudding rice, sugar cane, a rabbit, some mutton and the ingredients to make a steak and kidney pudding for Sunday lunch ('put some gristle in it' was the advice from J Holland's).

And on to Roswitha's. 'How much are your Italian sausages?' I ask – and this leads to an engaging exchange with the proprietor who not only points out the improved taste and better price of the nearby Bratwurst, but also has an even more persuasive diamond up his sleeve: 'I made them, by the way.' There's variety here, for sure, but there's also more than the fair share of warmth, engagement and perspective. These people know that a smile, some advice and a freebie for the kids are more than the UK shopper usually expects.

There is also a little of the 'inconvenience stores' in one or two establishments, where assistants are clearly striving for the West Yorkshire Indifference award, but, in contrast to my wider UK experiences, these people were in the minority.

Oastler Shopping Centre? This is a market, not a shopping centre. That title produces a different picture altogether and, for me, not one that engenders affection. It's a place, I'm ashamed to say, that I was completely unaware of before, but which I'm in awe of now.

We take leave of the man at Solly's, grab a tray of reviving pakora from the unlikely-named Papa Carlos Kebab Centre and start to descend.

We enter the Kirkgate Centre. Here, there is a range of mall-type establishments, from the well known, like WH Smiths and Argos, to the less fêted, like some of the myriad of special-interest stalls secreted about the adjacent market – which is where its true heart lies. But the overall impression is of a lack of distinctiveness. The Kirkgate Centre is no different from its cousins in other towns. Service in WH Smiths is fine and a jocular exchange around the offer of half-price chocolate and the size of my midriff keeps the warmth (although the inevitable failure to stock my book doesn't help).

Further downhill, physically and metaphorically, is the 'bottom end' of town. Waterstones, with its Starbucks Coffee Shop, is a haven from the wind and rain. A beautiful home that, for me at least, is a benchmark for superb renovation and a tempting glimpse of the Bradford to come. Service is warm and helpful here, advice offered and assistance given. The whole package and kids' books at 2 for 1 into the bargain.

Beyond Waterstones, we return to the pre-demolition zone. Dreary it may be, but there are bargains to be had, especially in BHS. The challenge for this zone, however, and more than for any other part of Bradford, is to keep people's interest through the changes ahead and present a unique and different experience.

I may not be from Bradford, but my kids are, so my pride in the city is automatic and my instinct to defend it from criticism is heartfelt. As we take the bus home I ask my kids what was best. 'We got to taste new things,' they concur. And the worst? 'The rain.'

If we are to 'buy it in Bradford' we need to encourage and reward those businesses who are trying to forge distinction. Our patronage of places like Roswitha's, Beaumont's and Renata's can propel them to wider regional recognition. As a community, we should seek to promote and educate the benefits of service and its links to economic regeneration. Why not encourage our pupils to develop an interest, by placing service excellence squarely on their curriculum? After all, they're the future.

Why not hold an event to celebrate and learn from Bradford's best, as organisations like Customer Service Network do? Why not bring Bradford business owners together to debate the issues and feature case studies from people who've made a difference?

Our Saturday has shown that Bradford's future market share of customers could be linked to its increasing share of markets. But we've got to make people see beyond the present and the tawdry 'look and feel' into a future of distinction and real, genuine difference. Oh yes … and make sure my kids have cabanos in their school lunch box from now on!

36

Service Calls
November 2006

A strange thing happened when I went to pick up my car after a service the other day. It was the first scheduled one for my new car and it took place at a dealership I'd never visited before. As I slipped into depression at the size of the mounting bill, the curious event took place. The assistant said, 'Would you like a follow-up service call?'

With my previous car, I'd get these post-service calls routinely, without me being offered the chance to opt out. They weren't the most engaging calls I ever received (personally I prefer it when the phone rings, I pick up and an automated voice tells me they can't speak to me right now) but they struck a chord of reassurance as I sped around the country with rampant abandon.

Why would I *not* want a follow-up service call? Perhaps I don't have a phone or don't know how to use one. You may laugh, but North West Durham was one of the last places reached by answering machines and my forebears are still capable of having 5-minute conversations with unresponsive recorded messages before noticing the lack of engagement.

Perhaps I'm too busy to spare the time to share my reflections on the service itself. For the record this included the dealership not being open when I turned up to leave the car. Someone had forgotten the keys. It also included a failure to call me to tell me when it was ready, the failure of the card-swipe machine to work and the assistant implying this was my problem and asking me if I could settle the £340 bill any other way (livestock? Some sheaves of wheat?). Plus their failure to re-set the 'service due' warning light or, indeed, to enter any details at all about the service in the service history manual, nor to be able to tell me whether VAT was included in the bill or if it was extra.

At this point I'd half expected Jeremy Beadle to hove into view and proclaim that I'd been framed, but at least I was beginning to understand why they would want me only to have an 'option' of a follow-up service call. Or maybe, they're cleverer than I thought. Perhaps they want to give me the option because they know how hard it is for

British people to give honest feedback. Think about it. When was the last time you chimed 'very nice, thank you,' to a waiter enquiring after your opinion on the medium-rare steak you ordered, as its charred remnants stain your cheeks black. Why can't we bring ourselves to be honest?

How about that manager you had who was happy to give feedback but who took it very badly himself? Why didn't we respond to the question 'what could you do to perform better?' with the honest, but nevertheless justified response of 'have a better manager'? Perhaps it's our stiff-upper-lipped politeness that is offended by the prospect of hurting someone's feelings. Or perhaps it's the implication that the British, genetically pre-disposed to coldness, would baulk at such openness.

Just look at the distances between us in formal situations. There's never less than 3 feet between a UK customer and a bank clerk, but in Mediterranean countries, the distance is so close you could lick the assistant's face without stepping forward (I don't recommend this, incidentally, as it didn't help me secure a personal loan in Barcelona in 1987).

But back in Blighty, why is it that millions of feedback cards flutter around uncompleted when the restaurant in question is going down-hill as a result of customer alienation? Businesses know that great experiences create recommendation and recommendation drives the bottom line, but somehow they can't get us to play ball with the, frankly crucial, customer feedback process.

So what's gone wrong? My view, based on relentless monitoring of UK Service PLC, is that feedback has to be earned. You earn our participation by transparently sharing other customers' feedback with us. You earn feedback by transparently acting on findings and actually changing elements of the customer experience.

You earn feedback by applying the above philosophy internally, both in terms of encouraging and acting upon employee input and also in terms of having leaders in the business who speak up for the customer and raise the profile of informal feedback. You reward employees who pass on customer feedback and you develop systems capable of making this easy, for both your team and your customers.

Do this and the resultant profile of service lets customers know that there's value in responding honestly. Currently, however, there's so little physical evidence that organisations take feedback seriously, that we've grown weary of the requests.

Did I get my chosen follow-up service call from the car company? No. But I'll be adopting the 'close up and personal' approach to my feedback later today.

37

The Tourist
May 2007

I was brought up in Stanley, County Durham, very close to Beamish Museum, where visitors can experience life as it was in 1825 and 1913. Folk from further afield used to tell me that the reason they built the museum next door to Stanley was to give us all a glimpse of the future. I'd been quite prepared to put that cheap jibe aside until my Dad and I made our first visit to the museum in the early 70s.

We headed for the Sun Inn, an early-20th-century drinking establishment and took the weight off our feet. Only moments later, as I sat in the shadow cast by Dad's peaked cap, upturned donkey jacket collar and sideburns, two Japanese tourists started taking photographs of him. They thought he was an exhibit. Now that I'm in a similar state of decrepitude, I fear the return journey.

Cut forward to May 2007 and I'm speaking at a tourist conference in the North West, where the audience's main concern is no longer a shadow, but the glare from my balding pate. The message from the other speakers, who included travel journalist Simon Calder, X-Leisure's PY Gerbeau and David Falk from Visit Britain, was that the UK is beginning to understand the importance of tourism, the need to invest in it and the need to provide outstanding experiences, so as to benefit both the local and the national economy. Experiences are improving, but in a nation where customer service still has a profile lower than a dachshund's delicate bits, there's still some work to do.

At the conference we heard from some encouragingly progressive attractions, from Liverpool's Tate to Number One Blackpool (the UK's leading B&B) to the Chester Grosvenor, all of whom had built their success on understanding what visitors want and providing excellent experiences and perceived value for money.

So how do we fare in the UK and in Yorkshire specifically? To start with, let's examine the potential. In 2006, 31.2 million visitors came to the UK and spent £15.4 billion. This was a record year for the UK. In terms of the origin of visitors, 3.4 million are from the USA, followed closely by 3.3 million French (and a similar number of

Germans), with 2.8 million from Ireland and 1.8 million from Spain. It's estimated that 2 million people work in the UK tourist industry, so this upward trend is good news.

But how about Yorkshire? Our goal, according to Yorkshire & Humber's Tourism Marketing Strategy, is to achieve an increase in the value of tourism earnings in Yorkshire and Humber of 5% per annum to £5.9bn by 2010. Sure, high-profile events like the International Indian Film Academy Awards weekend in early June will help keep the flag flying and attract plenty of interest and attention from the media as well as from international visits, but is there evidence that Yorkshire tourist attractions offer quality and value for money?

First, put yourselves in the shoes of our overseas visitors and ask the obvious question: what's going to be most important to these different groups of people? Americans have the highest expectations when it comes to customer service. Here, it's still a way for one business to stand out from another, but over there, excellent customer service is a 'given'. As a minimum, visitors from the US expect friendliness and flexibility as standard. Attractions shouldn't make the tourist work – and problems should be solved with the minimum of fuss and the maximum of warmth.

As I go about my day composing my customer service travelogues, I've yet to see widespread evidence of this. There's still a sense that customer service is a rare 'add-on', and not something many attractions appear to consider important. Sentences beginning with 'we only do ...' and 'you can't do ...' still proliferate and it appears that many visitor-facing employees still stick rigidly to processes rather than flexing according to customer need. Several years ago an American friend visited a town in Calderdale and asked for a cappuccino. 'You'll have to go to Leeds if you want one of those,' he was told.

Elsewhere, working farms and museums, in spite of being perfect family destinations, still persist in making some elements of their experience 'not suitable for children'. In recent years, experiences at places such as Dent and Haworth have had our overseas guests in wonderment at the UK's well developed 'sales prevention techniques'.

The French and the Spanish expect to find families catered for and our archaic licensing laws sometimes make it difficult for Mediterranean families to feel welcome. Signs such as 'kids only allowed in at lunchtime and only if consuming a substantial meal,' etc, hardly offer the hand of friendship and understanding, but they are legion in our region.

We also need to start to address the binge-drinking culture of our major towns and cities if we want to see the true potential of tourism realised in this part of the world. While any visitor to Barcelona will appreciate an evening promenade down Las Ramblas (admittedly clutching one's handbag to one's chest), the equivalent Yorkshire offering – a nervous dash past the sick-gilded doorways of city centre pubs – is a less pleasing option.

But underpinning all of my doubt is a stark reality. Tourism suffers from a low profile. Employment in tourism is not the attractive career option it should be and not enough is invested in understanding the needs of our visitors and addressing the associated training needs. Tourism is capable of sustaining the economic development of the region for many years into the future, but only when effort and investment match the undeniable beauty of our immediate surroundings.

38

Patients Are a Virtue
June 2005

My friend Bob knows his local hospital really well. But before you idly speculate, it's not because he's some kind of malingering hypochondriac. Bob's a field hockey player and being locally based, he's often called upon to accompany injured colleagues to the accident and emergency wing.

Picture then, if you will, this gruesome scene. His captain had stopped a flailing hockey stick with his mouth, a manoeuvre which had completely removed four front teeth and left several others hanging by a thread. He was not a pretty sight, quite literally spitting blood and unable to issue any protest stronger than a muffled grunt.

When they approached the front desk the nurse asked 'Name?' and Bob, being a good citizen, offered the patient's name. 'Are you the patient?' retorted the nurse, who appeared to have recently graduated from anti-septic to anti-service.

'No, it's him,' Bob added helpfully. The nurse once again turned to her unwillingly taciturn patient and asked 'Name?'

Bob's friend tried to splutter a few letters, unintelligibly, before the dark mist settled around Bob's usually benign countenance and the nurse was told in no uncertain terms that her ability to interact successfully with her customers fell short of the acceptable standard. These were not the actual words used by Bob, but my tenure as resident business commentator in several newspapers may be shortened, were I to repeat them here.

This is not a criticism of our beloved National Health Service but an impassioned attempt to get organisations to recognise that their systems and processes may suit their own needs, but often fail to appreciate the impact they have on their customers (and patients).

A recent survey showed that 92% of leading UK business figures believe that the 'customer experience' will be the next great business battleground. Now, I'm a sceptic when it comes to statistics of this nature, because if that were true, we'd be experiencing many more positive emotional connections than we currently do. But even more alarmingly, experiences like the one my pal Bob encountered tell me that, as often as not, the basics aren't even up to standard. If a nurse can't recognise that a man with a serious mouth injury cannot speak, what hope have we of an emotional connection?

The next time you're thinking about improving your business, put yourself in the customer's shoes and try to create a register of the outcomes and emotions that your current processes cause. Follow the advice of one bank, which recognised that the way they dealt with bereaved customers only created anxiety, anger and helplessness. One small change to the way the conversation opened shifted the entire experience up a gear. 'How would you feel if we could transfer your late aunt's funds into your account?' they will ask. 'Well, let me explain exactly what we'll need to do to achieve that.' For me, this is evidence that the bank truly understands great customer service. At Bob's hospital, however, the only connection being made was the one between the hockey stick and his friend's face.

39

Forty-tude
June 2006

Many men believe that women approaching 40 do not want their impending milestone celebrated. In fact, rather like my Dad who paid £100 to have his family tree unearthed, and then another £200 to have it hushed up, it's perhaps understandable that one's partner would want such a milestone treated in the same way.

A friend believed that his partner shared this view and decided to be pro-active in his inactivity, whereas in reality his wife had been looking forward to being swept off her feet to some dreamy far-off location. When we visited them recently, the silence that engulfed the room announced just how wrong he'd been. So, with my wife's big birthday approaching, a surprise party was accordingly organised.

You see, I've never been bothered about turning 40. In fact, when it happened to me three years ago, I shared Madonna's opinion that 40 was the new 20, although I don't think she had my decrepit, balding profile in mind when she dropped that particular bombshell. Neither did I see it as a life-changing event. These days, unless you live in that part of Glasgow where the sweet factory used to be and where life expectancy is 53 (make the connection yourselves), it hopefully represents a halfway mark. But for this Mark, it's ushered in some new perspectives on life.

Most unexpectedly, I've discovered Country music. Yes, you heard me. You may be hanging on to your youth in your late 30s, exposing your kids to extended 12" versions of Soft Cell's 'Tainted Love' and the Associates' 'Party Fears Two' while meekly acknowledging that Girls Aloud's 'Biology' is quite a decent power pop song and appearing to understand hip hop. But nothing quite prepares you for the moment where you find yourself strangely drawn towards the Emmylou Harris and Hank Williams sections, as if hypnotised by some pied banjo-player.

Now before I expand on this theory, let me immediately exclude the likes of Leanne Rimes and Shania Twain from this inspiring canon of artistes. By Country music, I mean, rootsy, soulful, pared down, three chord heartache. 'The Blue Moon of Kentucky' lighting up the 'Lost Highway', not 'K'Ching' or 'Man, I Feel Like a Woman', which both sound like lingerie adverts to a man who senses that this whole subject should hold something of an allure, but who is far too old to remember why. I'm now exploring Boxcar Willie, which until recently I'd taken to be an ailment suffered by male show jumpers. But the connection with Country Music is somehow much more logical when you reflect on its key themes of yearning for the old ways and the importance of the journey, rather than the destination. And this was all eminently clear at the surprise party we organised for my beloved last Saturday.

Whereas many of our aged friends had endured the treadmill, saddled themselves to scary mortgages and accepted the dehumanising conventions of the modern 'career path', such as the earlier starts and later finishes, their post-40 years are characterised by a rejection of the superficial in favour of something more substantial. Hands up readers who've suddenly conjured up an image of Dolly Parton! And yet my friends' altering values are indicative of a greater sea change, since attitudes to work are indeed changing. Work psychologists tell me that youngsters entering work for the first time have rejected loyalty to an employer, for example, since they spent their youth watching their parents give their everything for industries that subsequently found it convenient to dump them shortly before their pensionable age.

And at the other end of the scale, my tattered 40-plus friends have similarly distanced themselves from conventional work attitudes, opting for downsizing, in lifestyles and in job status, seeking a better work / life balance and re-engaging with old friends and the passions that stirred their youth. All of my musing was somehow crystallised by the appearance of Martin Stephenson, the special surprise guest for my wife's celebration.

For those with long memories, Martin and his famous Daintees were the darlings of the Indie scene in the early- to mid-80s. Through until 1992 his band embraced commercialism with gusto as his familiar pork pie hat appeared at venues around the country. But then Martin had his road to Damascus moment, divesting himself of the trappings of the music industry, rejecting the schedules that left no time to engage more fully with people.

So this finger-pickin', travelling minstrel was to appear at my wife's special day, lighting up the room with everything from Scott Joplin to Doc Watson and Chet Atkins, imitating the rain with his guitar and invoking shooting stars with a twinkling harmonic, before the rapt and silent children at his feet. 'I'm giving awareness of the power of the small,' he said. Obtuse? No. We all understood exactly where he was coming from.

We've all got a gene that kicks in at 40 and focuses us back on what matters. Yours may be Gene Clark, mine may be Gram Parsons, but as we watched all our guests stroll back down the hill to Holmfirth with their kids circling them with laughter, we both felt good to be older.

40

The Computer Still Says 'No'

October 2007

The books we read as children left a lasting imprint on us. Some were sad but uplifting (*The Diary of Anne Frank*), some were magical and fantastic (*The Hobbit*) and some were probably illegal (I'm sure I had the *Boy's Guide to Collecting Birds' Eggs*). But of all of them, the science fiction ones with their apocalyptic visions of a world run by computers and robots, were the most enduringly scary. And what frightened me most was the inhuman reaction of so many automatons, devoid of humanity and emotion. Well, hide behind that pillow, my friends, because I've got some news for you. They're back – and in the most unlikely places.

A friend bought a cooker and the accompanying hood in a sale recently. Only the cooker was in stock, he was told, so he arranged for its delivery the following Wednesday. Some days later the phone rang. It was the cooker company. 'We've got your hood in stock now, sir. We're calling to arrange delivery.' Joy coursed through his veins.

'Can you arrange for it to come on Wednesday with the cooker?' he asked confidently. 'I'm afraid not, sir,' came the unexpected reply. 'You see, sir, Wednesday's already finished.'

Shaking his head in disbelief, my friend continued, 'But Wednesday's not finished. It's only Monday now. There's still two days to go.' Then the awful truth was revealed by the embarrassed caller: 'I'm afraid the computer won't let me.'

So, having been initially separated at birth, the cooker and hood were not to be re-united just yet. Wednesday came and the cooker turned up almost apologetically, accompanied by a driver who looked like he had an A level in indifference.

'Have you booked the fitting too?' asked the van driver. 'I wasn't aware it wasn't part of the original service,' responded my friend. 'I can't fit it if it isn't on the computer schedule,' announced the driver. 'But I wasn't even given the opportunity,' protested my friend, to no avail.

Admittedly, the bayonet fitting in his cooker-less kitchen didn't look that difficult to connect to the new cooker. Perhaps he could do it himself. 'Or is it such a highly skilled and specialised piece of work that the Gas Police will come and cart me away if I don't do it properly?' he mused audibly.

The cooker could not be installed, so a further phone call was required. Having established that the computer would not let the hood and cooker travel together and learned that a qualified driver needed to be present to connect the cooker, my friend shared his unhappiness over the telephone. 'Tell you what,' the assistant helpfully explained, 'we'll cancel both orders and set up a new one. I can credit your money back to you and then take payment again. I can't organise delivery today – and I'm afraid the cooker and hood will come separately. Oh, and there's another thing,' she continued, my friend's hopes and mental health fading by the second. 'Since you ordered the cooker and hood, the price has gone up.'

'Why can't you honour the original price?' my friend argued reasonably. All together now: *the computer won't let me!*

Little Britain's cruelly accurate lampooning of the UK's renowned lack of customer service might raise a smile, if it weren't so true. Not a day passes without someone getting in touch with me to describe a wonderful Walliams moment. There is the motorway toll assistant who told a driver that they only had one booth open 'because we don't have enough people to man the automated barriers' and then there's the other friend who had to have two side portions with his fish and chips 'because the button on my till for one side order is broken.'

Another friend wished to complain to the Head Office of a department store who had let him down. He asked for the telephone number of the Customer Service department and was told, 'I'm afraid they don't take calls.' I had difficulty with a software security provider who repeatedly failed to deliver the goods. When I finally got to speak to someone, I asked them to pass on my negative feedback to the senior management team at her organisation. Her reply? 'I'm afraid you'll have to do that yourself sir. We're not allowed to speak to the management.'

I recently bought some rail tickets over the phone, saving a packet by booking First Advance. According to the lady I spoke to, the reduced price still provided all of the benefits of first-class rail travel, apart from granting access to the first-class lounge. Moments later, having completed my transaction, she asked me if I wanted to receive the tickets by post or collect them in the station. My collection options? Either the fast ticket machine or in the first-class lounge.

Everyone has the story of going to a famous burger restaurant and only asking for fries – and then being asked do you want fries with that? But this state of affairs has gone beyond mere humorous anecdote to reveal a huge cultural problem in our organisations today – a rigid adherence to process for fear of upsetting that age old precept: we do what we've always done.

The business that prioritises time spent in the 'customer's shoes' ultimately develops the best perspective. The business that sees the new starter as a real source of objectivity, rather than someone to hide behind a PC for several weeks, visibly ups the tempo. The business that learns from other organisations, within and outside of its own industry, amasses a mountain of ideas for improvement and prosperity.

And the rest? Lurching from one farcical comedy sketch to another, until their circuits melt and their screws fall out. Panic over, ladies and gentlemen. I think the world's safe for now.

41

Parenting Problems (Part 3)

I have an inability to be honest with people, especially when this involves passing on bad news. I don't know whether it's a psychological scar from a Catholic education, because I showed the other cheek so often I soon ran out of cheeks to show and ended up being held in detention for resorting to a third cheek and displaying this from the school bus window.

In work, which I've creatively resisted over the years, this weakness no doubt lowered my particular glass ceiling and restricted my career options. People told me to invest in a 'life coach', but I've found a better learning opportunity: my kids.

As we all know, the younger the child, the more honest their observations. As experts will tell you, the foetus represents the epitome of selfishness, draining the mother of nutrients (and a sense of humour too, in my experience), totally focused on its own needs and unlikely to assent to a bout of unpasteurised cheese-eating as a reward for Mum's selfless sacrifice. So it's natural that in their early years, some single-mindedness might manifest itself.

I'm away for a few days, so I call home from the hotel. My daughter answers.

'Hello, sweetheart,' I respond. 'What are you doing?'

'I'm on the phone, talking to you.'

'So what have you been doing at school today?'

'Studying and stuff. It's what we do there.'

She's seven years old and, thanks to having worked her way through eight series of *The Simpsons* on DVD, has mastered the art of irony. So much so that I won't share her response to my question: is your Dad still handsome, now that he's 44?

More family research has shown that a child's initial acquisition of language also reveals remarkable levels of perception. Our three-year-old niece draws faces and calls them 'maskies'. Could it be that she's implying some precocious understanding of how faces can hide our true feelings?

On the other hand, any time my brother-in-law has a brief naked moment, she takes great pride in pointing at his 'squashies' and laughing hysterically, so maybe we're stretching the contention a little.

If our kids are so single-minded when it comes to having their particular requirements met, perhaps we parents should open up when it comes to discussing those delicate issues – the ones that our own parents failed so abjectly to broach.

There have been plenty of opportunities for us to test this out, the most recent of which was prompted by a short piece on the car radio about health awareness. The feature began innocuously enough with a reference to good hygiene, before it unexpectedly veered off in the direction of sexual health.

'What's a condom?' our 7-year-old asked before we even had a chance to draw breath and formulate a cryptic explanation.

Dad played a blinder though. 'It's something people use to prevent the spread of disease,' I announced nonchalantly to my rapt audience, while Mum's eyebrows arched upwards.

'What? Like antiseptic?' came the reply.

'Yes,' I continued, without considering the hastily assembled helter-skelter of associations that my children were now working into a logical conclusion.

Through the mirror we could see the kids eying each other knowingly, as they computed the available evidence. But before they could share this, the same radio programme that caused the problem in the first place swiftly redeemed itself. Daughter pipes up again:

'What's Al Qaeda?' she asked.

Before I can even begin to verbalise my response, a follow-up question was being prepared.

'What are gay rights?'

The moment was apposite. A chance to divest myself of the cotton wool I'd been wrapped in as a kid. A chance to re-invigorate our family values with a strong and well-intentioned dose of honesty. A chance to emulate my kids' searing frankness. I drew breath, held one more internal rehearsal of my response and prepared to sail into unchartered waters.

'Shall we stop here for a cup of tea?'

The fact is, children know who they are, what they want and how they like it. They represent an interesting constituency among customer groups, displaying a vivid set of contradictions, where the residue of parental values often seems at odds with their new world view.

I recognise the respect shown to elders and the resigned commitment to 'clean my plate' but I'm often left speechless at those moments where the inheritors of the future begin to roll out their own independent Magna Carta. 'How dare you ask for a plastic bag, Dad! Do you realise how much damage you're doing to the environment?' or 'Do we really need two cars, Dad? Couldn't you run to work?'

So, it's been with some trepidation that I've upped the ante, the uncle and many distant relatives and invited my kids to take a more prominent role in our travels. What this reveals often shocks traditionalists as much as it soothes them. But what it emphasises is that children represent a knowing and strongly opinionated group. Such precocity can influence the strategies of successful future businesses, but it all begins with finding out what matters to them (just like other customers) and delivering it well.

Just today, we enjoy a family meal at a restaurant close to where we live. At the end of what has been a very pleasant meal, we find some feedback cards. Given that children plainly made up a great percentage of the customer base, my son asked if he could go on line to complete his feedback. A little later, when we did, we noticed that respondents had to be over 18 (even though one of the questions asked for the respondent's age and gave an option of '15-18'). Disappointed, my son left the laptop to me and I completed the feedback alone.

Football is another industry where clubs' futures reside in their ability to engage through the generations. And yet, most supporter panels are made up of what might be termed 'core' supporters, who are more likely to be interested in performance on the pitch and team investment than in the antics of the mascot or the pre-match entertainment.

The emergence of websites like www.stardoll.com reflect the large number of young communities who are making judgements about the business they will interact with when they are older.

My daughter could probably put it more plainly, as she has no trouble being honest, but at least we will soon usher in an age of more assertive consumers. I sense that the age-old non-confrontation might be replaced by a more 'interesting' consumer generation. One that we treat with indifference at our peril.

42

On line versus Retail
December 2006

Monday 10th December probably isn't a date etched into your memory, but it is possible that you made a purchase on line during that day. If you did so at 1309 hrs precisely, you may be surprised that the total amount spent by you and your fellow surfers at that particular moment in time was £767,500. It's estimated that in the course of those record-breaking 60 seconds, some 30-50,000 British customers made an online purchase. Over the day as a whole we spent £370m on line, preferring the comfort of our desks to a lunchtime sacrificed to our gilded malls.

Research shows that we will, as a nation, spend £40bn on line this year. It's even postulated that, by 2020, some 40% of our shopping will be done on line. Internet shopping has some obvious benefits. You don't get wet, greeted with indifference or trampled underfoot by bargain-fixated shoppers. It's easy to compare prices from different suppliers and deliveries are very secure. They'll tell you when your item is in stock, easily accept money-saving vouchers and even advise you when and if your auction site 'bid' is successful. Now that my family has entered the world of downloaded music, we hear a song on the radio that we like and, within ten minutes, it's on our iPod. The record token replaced by the iTunes voucher. Hassle replaced by reassuring ease. Problems replaced by solutions.

The online world presents itself as a soothing balm to the unhinged chaos of the high street experience, so is it time to sound the death knell for our high street retailers? Are our shops for the chop and our malls facing their final calls? How exactly should retail meet the challenge of the click clique? Or, when the retailer operates in the real and virtual worlds, how do they maximise profits in both arenas?

Instead of baulking at the apparent competitive edge being flexed by the online experience, retailers need to consider their own strengths. First of all, in spite of the economic gloom, there's every sign of yet another bumper Christmas for our high streets. John Lewis, The Home Retail Group and Woolworths are among those looking forward to their best pre-Christmas period ever and retail commentators are confidently predicting yet another record-breaking year.

Somewhere near to three million people are now employed in the retail industry and with nearly 300,000 businesses established in the UK we're hardly presiding over the death of an industry. Put succinctly, if John Lewis is planning to open another 20 department stores in the next 20 years, there must be plenty of opportunities for the discerning retailer out there.

Retail can offer a tangible experience, unlike its online competitors. You can touch and feel the merchandise, taste if you like, discuss the features of your purchase and try things on. It involves more exercise than going on line, even if you've only been tempted out of the house by the teasing aroma of fresh coffee. Psychologists argue that our 'hunter / gatherer' genetic origins are best suited to shopping and singles magazines reckon you can pull more effectively in a supermarket than anywhere else.

And yet, retail suffers from a malaise that rarely troubles the online world. It has an unfathomably low profile in this country. It may offer a complex, multi-faceted career, involving a combination of operational, management and sales skills. It provides experience of merchandising, design, customer service and financial skills and the job opportunities are there in their thousands. In any one year, for example, the Arndale Centre in Manchester has up to 2000 vacancies. There is no other career that best serves the dreams of the nascent entrepreneur, but you ask any parent if they'd like to see their kids pursue a career in retail ...

A friend of mine (and a proud advocate of UK retail) told me that her daughter wished to follow in her footsteps. Almost immediately friends and relatives telephoned to offer their commiserations. *Such a let down, you must be so disappointed.* The fact is that UK customer service is desperately poor and UK retail is tainted by association. But we're British customers, so we fear confrontation and remain tight-lipped in the face of contemptible service. As a worrying consequence, retailers have yet to find appropriate ways of getting us to provide them with the rich, detailed feedback they need to help them improve.

But it's not just our cultural idiosyncrasies that demean retail; it's the language we use, too. When someone finds themselves in a customer-facing position, we say they're at the 'front line' or the 'coal face'? How is that meant to motivate a youngster into thinking they've landed the number one career of choice?

Retail needs to develop a response on two levels. At the 'sharp end' (or so we insist on calling it) we need to instill a belief in seeing things from the customer's perspective. 'Walking in the customer's shoes' seems such a throwaway remark these days, but until high street retailers lose their internal fixation and start to develop different perspectives, customers will point those very shoes in a different direction.

More fundamentally, a concerted effort is required to raise the profile of retail and the emergence of the National Skills Academy and the proposed creation of locally-based retail skill shops certainly points in the right direction. Reaching out to shopping-centre managers, developers, retailers, schools, colleges and work providers, the concept aims to operate within a nationally agreed template of best practice.

Youngsters will get to see retail in a different, more positive light. They will see a clearly signposted path to an entrepreneurial career. Existing retail employees will have clearer opportunities for self-development and betterment within their chosen profession, while the large numbers of youngsters not in work or education, can start to fill the vacancies provided by this expanding sector.

Someone once said about restaurants: 'food always tastes better when it's served by someone you like.' That's not a concept the Internet can beat. So, by all means keep clicking, but let's stop putting retail down in this country and start recognising that today's shop girl is tomorrow's entrepreneur.

43

Very Cross Country (Part 2)

January 2008

I still remember the relief that flooded through my body when, at the age of 13, I came first in the school cross-country trials. The relief wasn't due to a love of running through frozen streams and over unforgiving cobbles, nor down to any particular athletic bent. No, it was simply due to the fact that, having proved equally inept at cricket and football, here was a sport where I thought I could do well.

You see, back in those days, sporting ineptitude was akin to declaring oneself interested in expressive dance. You didn't fit. You weren't one of the lads, which was especially ironic because the 'lads' rarely won cross-country races. They were usually gathered behind a bush, like delinquent hedgehogs, sneaking a crafty fag, or benefiting from the restorative powers of cheap lager, while I leapt over the finishing line like a gazelle in graceful flight.

Elsewhere school sport had a deeply traumatising image. Who can forget Brian Glover's domineering PE teacher in the film of Barry Hines' *Kes*, casually trampling over pupils as he emulated his heroes? Physical education was a militaristic separation of the strong from the weak and often a ritual humiliation of the latter. Even *Grange Hill*'s PE teacher looked like he would have been thrown out of the Gestapo for being too cruel.

The quality of facilities underlined the malaise. Apart from a pair of dangerous metal goalposts, a netball court and the ubiquitous plastic bibs, there was rarely more to appeal to the adolescent athlete. Any glance at the timetable would reveal football and cross-country in the winter and athletics in the summer. By athletics, please do not infer a comprehensive package of track and field activities, but 45 minutes of running around a field in a disorganised manner and a lecture on the dangers of javelins from a teacher whose only qualification for physical instruction was a close acquaintance with the pain barrier and a disturbing line in unfeasibly tight blue tracksuits.

Sport, it seemed, only existed to punish the awkwardly built but reward those less academically inclined (at my school at least). The possibility that there may be a link between competitive sport, personal development and growth was as distant and vague as physics then was to my adolescent mind.

To make matters worse the 80s and 90s were characterised by schools selling off playing fields to make up for a lack of funding, while political correctness saw that non-competitive, non-contact activities would be the only 'sport' to which any child could look forward.

Thankfully we now have a more enlightened view, with teachers speaking of a clear link between school performance and the physical and mental development obtained from participation in school sports. The Prime Minister announced some £100 million of additional investment as recently as July, building on 2003's National School Sport Strategy.

The aim of getting 75% of children taking part in two hours' school sport a week by 2006 has been exceeded and this extra cash aims to add a further three hours of sport a week for every single child. The Prime Minister is convinced. 'Watching sport is a national pastime. Talking about sport is a national obsession. But now we need to make taking part in sport a national characteristic,' he says, while critics note the lack of investment in providing sufficient PE teachers to meet the growing challenge. Gordon Brown may have one eye on the 2012 London Games, but it's especially gratifying to this ex-athlete to see his government start to support the link between sporting participation and academic achievement.

We have some notable Yorkshire-based examples of how well this theory can work in practice. Yorkshire-based journalist David Conn recently reported on the success of Bradford's Tong High School, a specialist sports colleague, where according to pupils' economic backgrounds, 29% of its pupils would normally expect to gain five A–C grade GCSEs. In 2006, 45% achieved the benchmark, thanks to a relentless commitment to the developmental powers of sport stretching back several years.

The task now is to complete the dismantling of our half-hearted attitude to sport in this country and create the support, commitment and passion for personal achievement that until now were most evident in countries like Australia and South Africa.

I can still conjure up the image of my breathless colleagues staggering home, the Benson and Hedges neatly concealed in their socks. And with my one moment of glory swiftly disappearing into the ether of my memory, is a fundamental re-focus on competitive school sport really imaginable?

An impromptu interview with my 12-year-old son provides a definitive answer. At his school in Halifax they play 'hoop ball' and 'mat ball': games which defy easy explanation, but which help to develop agility, balance and co-ordination. But there's always a running race too. Because it matters that someone gets the chance to win.

44

The Customer Strikes Back!
January 2008

January 28 2008 will prove to be a milestone in British customer service. Building on the success of a small-scale protest last year, the campaign group More Train Less Strain (MTLS) will carry out a ticket boycott in the South and South West of England. Commuters from towns stretching from Oxford to Bristol will refuse to carry a valid ticket for their journeys that day.

This unprecedented action has been prompted by a recent fare hike announced by First Great Western – one of the most crowded and least punctual services in the UK. 35% of FGW trains arrive late and even when they are on time, they're decrepit, crowded and often short of carriages. Faced with a 10% ticket price increase, MTLS has begged the Government to remove the franchise from FGW.

This action is significant because it is one of those rare occasions when the British are shaken from their apathy, realise the power of collective action and strike against the ruling classes ... er, railway companies. I may be getting carried away somewhat, but the MTLS invective calls to mind some historical facts, which when presented in the context of appalling customer service, should make us ashamed of our meekness.

After all, we only have rights as employees in this country because some brave individuals joined together, took the ultimate risk and unanimously threatened to withdraw labour. In the latter part of the 19th century, craftsmen's unions were replaced by industrial unions, where higher subs led to more concerted support for the working man. Finally, the exploitation of workers was met head on.

Had we taken the same approach to employment as we do to customer service in this country however, we'd still be living in slums and earning a shilling a day, getting a holiday to watch his Lordship pass by in his carriage, hoping for some spare change or a smile from her Ladyship.

In North America customers are renowned for their powers of confrontation and constructive feedback. I recently came across a photograph taken in a burger restaurant. Unhappy at the length of time he had to wait, a customer left, but not before using the ketchup bottle to write 'No Service. Waited 30 minutes' on the formica table top. And guess what? One of the USA's greatest achievements is the high profile enjoyed by customer service.

Back here in the UK, apathy rules. But think about it. When MTLS held their first ticket boycott earlier in 2007 First Great Western acquiesced. They took no action against those travelling without a valid ticket, for they knew what was likely to happen were they to intervene: quite simply, the possibility that they would have laid themselves open to several Trading Standards or Consumer Protection suits. After all, is it acceptable when service providers fail to show a duty of care to their customers?

Collective consumer action in this country is rare, but extremely effective. Remember what happened to Hoover in the early 90s or Ratners and their 'crap'? We can act decisively but fail to do so.

In our part of the country the recent floods exposed the chaos lying beneath the surface of our own public transport infrastructure. But one can sympathise with the service provider in such circumstances.

What cannot be excused, however, is the level of service endured by a friend of mine, who paid £300 for her family to visit London last weekend with our rail franchise holder. Upon discovering that the train was running one carriage short, her party were told their reservations had been transferred to another one. Arriving at the designated seat, she found passengers in situ who refused to move, claiming the seats were theirs. A group of lager-swilling morons sat opposite, mouthing obscenities for the rest of the journey – while the staff stood by.

I watched intently as a pair of Spanish tourists listened to the train manager's announcement as we left King's Cross the other day. Having explained which tickets were valid and which ones weren't (which, in itself, can take several minutes) our guests were wearing the look of people who might well take up arms if it meant re-establishing nationalisation.

Two friends recently bought new cars. Each bought a different model from a different dealership. But both had the same story to tell.

As the salesmen handed them their keys, they were told that they would receive a call asking for feedback on the service they had received. The salesmen then both asked for a favour. 'Could you say "excellent" as that'll get me my bonus?' And pray tell, how exactly is that supposed to ensure a continual stream of improvement data? Because organisations pay lip service to customer service in this country – and we generally stand by and let them.

And this is the moment when British Gas decides to emerge into the spotlight. On 15th January we were told that, with immediate effect, gas prices were to rise sharply. With a straight face British Gas announced that if they didn't pass on the increases they would make a loss. Our collective hearts bleed. We'll make a sacrifice for them, then, shall we?

Faced with an immediate 15% increase (and I stress the word 'immediate' as I seem to recall that when wholesale gas prices first fell, it took an age before this was reflected in our gas bills) some people, especially ones nearer the poverty margin, though officially safeguarded, may understandably feel more vulnerable.

Apparently it's all the fault of European energy markets and their failure to liberalise effectively. That must have been it. Surely our predilection for inaction had nothing to do with their keenness to get the bad news out.

But we still fail to act, perhaps distracted by the latest disappearance of Government hard disks, the dizziness induced by David Beckham's underpants or the excitement of next Saturday's early evening TV schedule.

I wish MTLS every success with their campaign – and let's see if we can't call upon the courage of our forebears, emulate our once famous tradition of dissent and start to demand better service in this country. Because right now, we *still* get the service we deserve.

45

Customer Service Nativity
December 2007

I like the phrase 'practising Catholic'. It seems to imply that, if you put your mind to it and apply yourself conscientiously, you can reach a state of expertise that brings its own rewards. For example, practise for five years and earn the right never to attend Benediction again. Add a brace of years studying in a seminary and lose the Holy Days of Obligation!

But having been brought up in the faith, for me the current season of goodwill is all the more special for it. Elsewhere commercialism may have taken over, but in the Bradley household, the crib makes its annual appearance and Daddy regales one and all with mysterious and exciting stories of the Nativity. The one the kids enjoy most is the Nativity Customer Service story. You mean you've never heard it? Then sit down, clutch your sherbet fountains to your chest and lend me your Wii. Er, sorry. I meant to say 'ears'.

Imagine if the Nativity had taken place in the UK, around now. Out in the Yorkshire Dales, Mary and Joe receive an email asking them to go on line and register for the census. It doesn't work, so they call their service provider. As recent research shows, it takes, on average, 17 minutes to speak to a human, so by the time they get through they're in a bad mood. 'It's no good,' says the assistant, in impenetrable English, sounding very far away (possibly Hull). 'You'll have to go to Leeds and sign on in person.' The pause that follows is as pregnant as his wife.

As no bus company can make money ferrying folk around the Dales, Joe has to kickstart his N-reg Polo and drive there. As the weather is closing in, he opts for a contingency and pre-books an evening at a local hotel. 'Just in case,' he tells Mary. 'We can take our Christmas cards with us and write them when we get there.' They stop for stamps, but discover the Post Office has been closed, as part of a strategic network review.

The journey is long. They spend the time spotting shop signs where apostrophes have been incorrectly applied and try to make their

SatNav work. When they finally arrive Leeds is busy and Mary is feeling the weight. They try to park at the Station car park, but the left turn that you have to execute to enter is so tight, Joe's wing mirror falls off. Mary tuts from the back seat.

Having queued for the Census, they're delighted finally to get to a clerk. 'I'm sorry for your wait,' she says. 'My weight?' Mary mistakenly hears. 'Thanks very much. I'm eating for two!'

Beyond that unfortunate opening remark the conversation is wordless. Until the end, at which point the clerk looks up with a forced smile: 'and is there anything else we can do for you today?'

'Call me a midwife,' retorts Joe, with a sigh. 'You're a midwife,' responds the clerk, to general dismay.

Having decided to stay in Leeds overnight, they opt for a relaxing afternoon, ingesting the aroma from the natural cosmetics store and having a Gingerbread latte and a mince pie.

At the newsagents, they queue for a scratch card. After ten minutes of queuing, they're told they're in the wrong queue. They start again, cursing under their breath. Joe's phone goes off. It's an automated message suggesting he consolidate his outstanding debts.

Next he gets a text. To 'thank him' his phone company is offering him a special new handset. Only trouble is, he has to sign up for a 36-month contract to get the extra benefits. Mary points out that they boil down to a more interesting font and a ring tone that sounds like a small rodent being sick in an echo chamber.

By now Mary's instincts have picked up the tell-tale signs. The baby is due. Time has flown and it's late. Amazing how much you can eat in a Chinese buffet when it's £5 a head.

At the hotel reception the girl has some bad news. They have over-booked and there's no room at the Inn. Joe says something obscene in Aramaic and asks for an explanation. The receptionist points out some small print at the bottom of the booking form and explains that it is standard industry practice. 'We can get a taxi to take you to a hotel in Knaresborough,' she helpfully suggests.

Joe and Mary decide to give up and drive home, but once into the Dales, the inevitable happens. They find shelter in a small village school at the end of a long narrow lane. Inside, the locals are preparing a Nativity play as the child arrives amongst streamers, hay and five-year-olds dressed as animals. The only witnesses missing are the shepherds. Their Dad is supposed to have them there by 7pm, but his SatNav has sent him the wrong way. Happily, two Argos deliverymen turn up, having carried a trampoline for two miles across open countryside. Donning tea towels and fluorescent safety jackets, they light up the scene.

The following morning the Three Wise Men arrive. The first two offer frankincense and gold, but the third shuffles around awkwardly. He's ordered some myrrh on line, but it hasn't arrived, in spite of an email telling him it was in transit. When this happens, he phones the provider, waits the standard 17 minutes to speak to a human – who doesn't have any record of his order – and ends the call with the promise of a voucher, 'for his inconvenience'. Sheepishly (appropriate in the circumstances) he now offers the voucher to Joe – a little wiser for the experience.

Hours later, the wise men go on line to plan the journey home and discover that there are speed cameras on the A65. Living up to their name, they choose a different route home. Joe reflects on the events of the last few hours as he composes his letter of complaint to the budget hotel chain. 'You know what,' he says to Mary, 'let's get a cheap flight to the Holy Land next time.'

46

Conclusion:
Conspiracy Theorists and Conscientious Hecklers

In this final section I've been unable to resist the temptation to pro-scribe some positive change for UK organisations, both retail and otherwise. Service undeniably has a low profile in this country, but until the root causes are properly acknowledged and a comprehensive 're-boot' takes place in our businesses, then we'll continue to be famous for our inability to serve customers (and poor dental hygiene).

Before I do that, it's worth sharing with you some of my more recent diary notes, recorded observations and diatribe in note form, as I think this continues to be a barometer of where we are right now, but also underlines the key ingredient missing in most organisations: the perspective of the customer.

I've avoided using the phrase 'voice of the customer' as this has become associated with the Six Sigma approach to lean management and improving the customer experience. I don't wish to criticise this particular philosophy, but it does take our eyes off the real prize: that of waking organisations up to the simple pleasures of taking a few steps in the customer's shoes.

It's my wholehearted belief that this simple act can be the catalyst for a cultural leap in organisations. Our internal fixation is not delib-erate, but a natural outcome of years spent 'under the bonnet' without ever driving the car.

I recall Kevin Costner, in Oliver Stone's fantastic conspiracy thriller, *JFK*, taking his colleagues on an early-morning walking tour around Deeley Plaza to explore just how President Kennedy could have been assassinated. They looked carefully at all of the evidence, which at that particular point was taking place several years after the event itself.

That walk produced the revelation that a tree that obscured the view from the Book Depository to the motorcade would have been in full foliage in November. Previously Americans interested in the events had been reassured that the tree would have been bare in the late Autumn and would have allowed Lee Harvey Oswald a free and unobstructed view of the President. Now they're not so sure – and so it is with the epiphany of the first walk in the customer's shoes.

Taking such a walk – and institutionalising it into your everyday behaviour – is just like the post-Christmas fitness push; something that takes time to feel natural, but which quickly purges your organisation of those extra 'pounds' of internal fixation.

Another benefit of repeat 'exercise' is that colleagues will come to see it as a natural work activity, rather than the extra-curricular nonsense that defines anything blessed with the title 'customer service workshop' these days. And once dipped fully into the customer experience, one begins to appreciate just how little traditional customer feedback systems contribute to the cause.

How reliably does a statistically significant high-volume survey truly reflect the emotional travails of today's UK customer? Sure enough, it's helpful in telling you who your customers are, but I suspect the truth of the emotional calamities being played out in businesses up and down the land is less likely to be revealed that way. Emotion, after all, defies easy measurement. Some songs make goose pimples appear on my forearms. But, curiously, when I play the same songs to my kids, they just feel nauseous.

The early-morning walking tour in Dallas can translate just as easily into any UK shopping centre, town centre or phone conversation. It's just the perspective that changes. Imagine what the woman inside your SatNav would say if she could give feedback on your driving? Being the customer gives you such a uniquely beneficial (and often entertaining) perspective.

Last week I attended an event at a local University at which the non-teaching management were trying to improve the student experience by identifying who their main customers were and what would be needed to improve current perceptions. Their moment of inspiration had occurred when they first mooted the idea. As they drafted how the day would look they made the decision to invite a small group of students and to ask them to appear on the day and describe their experiences of key 'moments of truth'. The early-morning walking tour would be taking place right there in the seminar room, the mirror held up and pennies dropping left, right and centre.

As it turned out, the students were masters of understatement, articulate and honest. Watching proceedings from the side of the room, I found myself spinning, Sam Tyler-like, back to 1981 and to my first days at Sheffield University. My Dad recollects turning up to drive me home one Christmas to discover that while many of my colleagues had packed their belongings into matching leatherette suitcases, I'd got all of my football shirts and trainers into 16 Gateway plastic bags and was standing proudly by them, like a particularly efficient sheepdog.

Even now, memories from those first few days at Sheffield are forming right in front of me. From the cheese and wine reception held by the Spanish Department to welcome all new students (a friend drove me there, but had to walk back) to that first clutching of the plastic pint glass and first goal for our football team Real Ale Madrid, these students' pictures of their own experiences were punching a hole in the clouds and allowing me a richly detailed reminder of my own past.

The session was facilitated properly. Rather than take a mix of observations, the 'walking tour' began with impressions on the admissions process, via Freshers' Week through to Graduation.

One student recalled the admissions experience with affection. Having attended an open day, he'd take away several hundred prospectuses (I'm assured that's the right plural. After all, I can't screw up on grammar in a section about education). This university offers a memory stick. The student illustrated his point perfectly by comparing the contrasting attributes of the huge pile of paper to his right and the tiny, portable device to his left.

Once contact had been made and a place sought, one student recollected how he'd received a Christmas card from the admissions department the winter before he joined. 'That was nice,' he concluded, but the understatement was evident: such a small gesture, but so enduring and so unique among so many underwhelming experiences, at a time when youngsters are letting go of the protection of home and family. Such a symbolic demonstration of care is worth a thousand website recommendations.

Other memories were less positive, but nevertheless clearly capable of offering insights into how things could continue to be improved, especially with the emphasis on 'ease'. For example, the campus is quite foreboding, complex and labyrinthine to the first-time visitor. Students therefore appreciate a map. The only problem is that one of the main student destinations on campus is a round building. So, unless you are approaching the building from above (and when I recall my own days as a student, that's not entirely out of the question), the distinction is less clear to the ambulant student. Only now did this particular 'moment of truth' emerge, thanks to this enlightened forum.

Accommodation, for students, is a chaotic and emotional roller-coaster. Most, if not all, students opt for a single room when choosing their accommodation. However, while the universities themselves are increasing the number of single rooms, there still remains the concept that strikes horror into the minds of those little fresh-faced freshers: the shared room.

One student, voice crackling with emotion, described how friendly the accommodation people were, and how helpful they'd been. Unfortunately, however, he'd ended up in a shared room, in spite of using the application form to denote himself clearly as a strange and quirky character. Again, another interesting insight.

Students are now vying with others to form the most anti-social picture of themselves, to ensure that the university's accommodation officers do not make the mistake of putting them in with someone who will soon believe they have strayed onto the set of *The League of Gentlemen*.

Some natural over-crowding is to be expected as every new year starts with the TV room, in this case, looking to one student like 'a refugee camp', but when asked to comment on how well the joint habitation had gone, he confirmed that they were now good friends and hit it off straight away.

Most of the dissatisfaction related to 'ease' of business. Students would queue to register and then to complete financial transactions, etc. Regularly, curtains would fall and 'closed' signs would be erected before the queue had gone. Occasionally, students would turn up to find the curtains already down, the distinct and faintly annoying silhouettes of administrators behind said curtains.

Happily, the students inconvenienced by the longest queue were able to provide their own therapeutic entertainment by berating a dodgy guitarist who was practising further up the line. The concept of 'hangover queuing' was also touched upon – sending an already disaffected group of 'customers' towards the edge of depression.

Library cards also provided some useful input. One student, who'd honed his ability to lose them to a high art, complained that he had to pay a £10 lost-card fee. The fact that this did not entitle him to a new photograph each time seemed unfair, though he was probably only worried that the original might turn up one day and reveal his pre-fresher Mum-prepared haircut.

Most pointedly, the conclusion of the discussion led to the students encouraging the staff to spend more time in the 'customer's shoes'. At this point, it was revealed that a couple of administrators had actually lived as students at the university for 2 weeks. That explained everything. The courage, inspiration and sheer common sense approach witnessed had evolved as a direct result of their findings.

My notes take me seamlessly from education to football, as my days of yore often did (and rarely in the opposite direction). Today I've been telephoning a Premier League football club to secure tickets for a match. We're doing this as part of the assessment work that we do for sporting organisations. It struck me that during a distinctly underwhelming experience, when the operator could not answer related questions about family areas and parking, nor was interested in making a connection, creating a positive, lasting 'first impression' or even idly contemplating an attempted 'cross sale' (membership, etc), there was still a chance that he'd score well on a mystery shopping call.

I hate mystery shopping. I believe the concept is one of the biggest hindrances to improving customer service in this country. There are several reasons why. Firstly, mystery shopping, which to my eyes, consists of several questions aimed at establishing that a certain number of pre-agreed internally-designed standards are being met, fails to acknowledge the fundamentally emotional nature of the customer experience.

Those usually recruited to carry out 'face-to-face' mystery shopping rarely have more than five or six boxes to tick and are never given the opportunity to move from 'employee' (which they are) into full 'customer' mode. They may have ticked boxes that are of little import to you or me and they certainly won't be asked the question: 'what is your impression of this organisation?' or 'how have your perceptions of this organisation changed since you visited?' Fair enough, those are the sort of questions that are contained within customer surveys, but with more bonuses tied to mystery shopping than customer service levels (by which I mean those that tie the emotional impact and subsequent perceptions and repurchase / advocacy intention to the experience), we're probably encouraging our people to do the wrong thing.

During the call to the football club it occurred to me that, yes, he had taken down my details, he had confirmed the terms and conditions, he had made a sale and he had answered promptly. He didn't give me any incorrect information either, but throughout the call I sank further and further into a fit of dislike, as warmth drained from the interaction like rats to a stinking skip (I like that one too).

It is possible that this operator was able to gain 4/5 on his mystery shopping report and yet for me never to wish to darken the club's door again. And yet, I found myself improbably calculating, he might have missed out on a few of the above 'necessary internal' points, say, scoring 2/5, but could have really made a connection, an emotional hook or created a memorable moment. Let me present you with two opening options.

Firstly, the operator picks up, introduces themselves and says, 'which game are you booking for?' or, secondly, the operator starts with a more general 'how can I help?' Clearly, in process terms, the first is the better option, as it fits the script through which you are to be shortly mangled. In reality, though, I prefer the second, as it sets the customer up to announce their general intentions, allowing the operator to create that memorable hook. For example, 'I'm thinking of bringing the family along for the first time,' leads to 'fantastic. I'm sure you'll have a great time. Now what can I do to make sure you keep coming back?' The sense of objectivity enjoyed by the employee who, for a short intense period of time, becomes the 'customer', is enhanced dramatically, even in the most unremarkable of circumstances.

Today we visit Marks and Spencer's in Leeds. In town to make a few purchases, we suddenly remember the need to buy some eggs. We enter the store, wander downstairs, locate the eggs, try hard not to look around us at the rest of the delicacies on display and make for the check-out.

Now while M&S might be improving as an organisation these days, the check-out experience, in my view at least, is as you would expect at most retailers: competent, polite and effective – certainly someway short of remarkable or memorable. Today, though, it is. The girl serving is deep in conversation with the previous customer – a woman of approximately the same age. I make the assumption that the customer is actually a staff member, they seem to be getting on so well.

It's our turn to approach. Feeling proud of having been able to resist the temptation of the epicurean feast behind us, we fall at the last hurdle, picking up a packet of those candy shrimps that I used to love as a kid. And a small chocolate egg with a vanilla fondant centre. And £10 cashback. There is no stopping us.

The girl smiles up at us and we have a friendly conversation, prompted by the choice of confectionery. She prefers Percy Pigs, which isn't a phrase you often hear at the typical British check-out. The conversation continues, smiles abounding. She takes one of the chocolate eggs (well, they are three for a pound), screws her face up at it and declares, 'I'm not sure how much this is. I don't normally do this job, you see.' Quickly she locates the price and processes the purchases as I draw my card through the Chip and PIN device.

I look behind me and the two customers in the queue are both smiling. Normally, this everyday interaction would be consigned to our mental recycling bins but today, we're all buzzing at something completely routine: warmth, humour, engagement and improvisation at a UK check-out.

So let's take a step back and look at this interaction from two separate perspectives. As a mystery shopping exercise, the elements that usually score the most (speed, accuracy, politeness) were not all there. There was a distinct delay as she keyed in my eggs (another phrase you won't hear again this year) and she clearly wasn't comfortable with all of the blinding technology before her. Nevertheless, in purely 'customer' terms, the interaction was spellbindingly perfect.

The fact that she was 'standing in' and not performing her usual role is key here. Though she may be M&S's number one employee in West Yorkshire, she's approaching a new job from a different perspective. Things are fresh, challenges are new and there's an infectious warmth about the experience of passing through her particular checkout. Had she been performing the job day in, day out, for several weeks, one might forgive a more anodyne interaction. One would not find it a problem and it would not affect one's patronage of the establishment, but the raw and 'uncut' nature of today's visit underlines the importance of giving people new perspectives. Fair enough, we can't be out on the streets looking at our competitors, but we can get different perspectives of the customer's view of us, by swapping roles and experiencing different parts of the organisation.

And before the HR managers' collective beats a path to my door with flaming torches, I'm not advocating a wholesale job 'mix-up' frenzy, but simply stressing the point that when people are absent, missing or employed elsewhere, customers benefit from the appearance of the replacement, while operational managers fret about the wrong data being keyed and the till not balancing.

The fact is, few of us would be thrown into paroxysms of joy at the emergence of a key piece of technology that streamlines the check-out process by a few seconds, but Marie's awkwardness with the system does not need to be redeemed by her natural affinity for customers. The awkwardness is just not relevant. By the way, I'm pretty sure she was called Marie, so if anyone at M&S is reading this, let her know what a good job she's doing.

Elsewhere recollections of any number of interactions reveal a prime concern with the process and an ad hoc, arbitrary attitude to customers. 'If I have the time to talk to you, I will. But I don't now, so shut up, pick up your shopping and leave, please,' would appear to be the subliminal message today.

The simplicity of the principle defies many organisations because they do not believe it is capable of being institutionalised, 'rolled out' or implemented. It defies the very fabric of our management structure – the need to organise and control. Such discoveries are more likely to be uncovered in an altogether different context: that of service leadership.

Creating the conditions in which customer experiences thrive continues to occupy the minds of conference organisers … sorry, senior executives everywhere. But that deliberate slip indicates how much of a 'golden fleece' the concept has become.

It's difficult to name one organisation that is perfect at the customer experience, but that's not a problem, since frequent imperfection offers service recovery an opportunity and, when well practised, this is capable of generating lifelong loyalty and stupendous levels of advocacy. Even leaders at businesses such as O2, Virgin Atlantic and First Direct would baulk at the suggestion that they are somehow perfect. And yet, it is the honesty of such leaders that defines an organisation that, more often than not, is likely to deliver something approaching good service.

Business perceptions of what is meant by service leadership are evolving with those advocating an employee-centred ethos currently occupying the centre ground. Develop a customer-focused culture, they say, built on strong employee engagement, and then you have a collaborative approach where both management and employees are pursuing the same goal. In some cases, the IT department is too, even if that stretches your credulity somewhat.

I agree with the principle of this approach. As John Timpson would say, turn your organisational structure upside down and the first thing you notice is that your customer-facing employees are the most important people in the business. Having met John a few years ago I was impressed by how far he'd taken this notion and how much 'freedom' had influenced ownership at the point of the customer experience.

Two points now concern me. Firstly (and obviously) that so few of the organisations we routinely experience on our travels appear to devolve authority to (or, more accurately, *trust*) their employees. That's no implicit criticism of John's approach, but a statement of reality. Something is making it hard or unpalatable for organisations even to contemplate this more empathetic, inclusive approach.

This leads me to draw another conclusion, which I set squarely at the heart of the positive future I'd like to see. John's business is close to customers and takes the time to walk in the customer's shoes (while repairing them, no doubt). There's evidence in their genetic make-up that they have spent time exploring service from their customers' perspective. Others fail to convert the opportunity presented by a customer-focused culture by failing to articulate it from the customer's viewpoint.

In practice, there may be service-related incentives, plenty of customer service training and even an annual employee awards night – and yet the DNA of the new approach is firmly 'internal', MBA-led perhaps. The leaders are those who have it in their gift to defy convention, step out of line and encourage these new necessary perspectives. So, for me, service leadership is defined by the following principles and activities.

Context is vital. Somehow amidst the maze of Chinese whispers that constitutes the majority of our internal communications mechanisms, the oft-repeated customer mantra becomes a tiresome cadenza, while the rhythm section of operational integrity distracts everyone with a tribal beat. The customer needs to sit before them and conduct the orchestra.

How organisations create a context for customer service depends largely on how it supports their revenue aspirations and now, in 2008, no one can argue against the resounding proof that an outstanding customer experience (even if focusing on recovery) delivers enduring levels of loyalty and advocacy. Bain & Company's Net Promoter concept may not be everyone's skinny vanilla latte, but it's prompted the LSE to investigate as recently as 2004 with the result that they, too, have concluded that it's possible to link levels of customer advocacy to business growth and annual sales performance – at least in the banking, automotive, telecoms and supermarket sectors. There are those who have expressed doubts about the scientific basis of Net Promoter, but I would offer a more fundamental observation – which is this.

Given that the figure is calculated by looking at your customer survey results, subtracting the total number of detractors from the 'fans' and ignoring those expressing no feelings either way, to produce what you hope will be a positive figure, it is imperative that the data is pure. It's at this point that we are being asked to trust that the measurement processes in the organisations in question are rigidly and robustly examined by an independent source, so that their veracity cannot be called into question.

But regardless of the concerns that you or I may have about the concept, it does give us one crucial benefit. It allows us to measure how good customer service is in our organisations – and it does it with one single figure. Research shows that this figure correlates directly to business growth and annual sales performance, but even where an element of doubt has crept in, its promotion across an organisation allows leaders to express service in measurable, numeric terms.

What I would like to see is this concept stepping out from behind the shadows into the public arena. There may be many conferences on the subject and much Internet-based hoo-hah (I've wanted to include that term for years), but it's absent from public debate.

Why is this significant? Well, my belief is that traditional customer measurement processes, survey mechanics, etc, fail to address two key issues which lie at the heart of the problem we face. While most organisations have abandoned the old annual survey in favour of more regular, even real-time, online surveying, for example, these advances are not being matched by any progress on transparency.

Undeniably, organisations are much more interested in our feedback than ever before. Just as I type this, an email drops in from Premier Inn asking me for feedback on my stay in their King's Cross hotel last Sunday evening. As it happens, I arrived late, cast aside clothing, showered, got changed quickly into the 'lounge suit', sprayed myself with pleasing aromas, attended a dinner, returned at 3 a.m, tripped over the aforementioned cast-aside clothing and slept. Not much to comment on, but I still remember the professional, almost studious welcome from the receptionist.

We're asked for our feedback. From the organisational perspective, this will allow them to convert our data into telling information that will help them pinpoint where changes and improvements will add the biggest bang for their buck. But let's spin that question around and ask it from the customer's perspective. What do we want? I think I'm on safe ground when I say that we'd like to see some sign of tangible improvement to the customer experience, in exchange for our feedback. It's seems a fair deal to me.

As a minimum, companies need to be more transparent with their customer feedback and introducing the concept of Net Promoter into the public arena will allow us to take more interest in the service performance of our major players. In previous ramblings I've mentioned the online wedding list agency whose customer feedback is expressed in real time by email and which appears unedited on their public testimonials page. Fantastic. I guess they're the sort of organisation that is going to try, at least, to give you a good experience. But they're in a small minority (possibly of one).

If our major banks, telecoms companies, supermarkets and car companies had their 'scores' more publicly on show, then not only would consumers be better able to judge their offerings, but the companies themselves would see customer service rapidly become core business – an objective that eludes all but the bravest nowadays.

I guess companies could point out that they transparently report their customer satisfaction figures when they announce annual results. The fact is they're effectively hidden from view, as the analysts sitting in the room with their double-shot lattes are only interested in the bottom line.

For our leaders, customer service is a little different. Prepare for an impenetrable analogy. It's like a child on *Dallas*. Yes, that's right, the small heir or heiress with the improbably bright blonde hair, over whose future unconvincing actors battle. Daddies fight to prove parentage, expressing undying love while Mommies try to remember who was implicated in their conception. But when finally in Pam or Sue Ellen's arms, the object of so much desire is quickly handed to a wordless Mexican extra and told to go and play.

I did promise it would be a little obtuse, but like an activated hand grenade, it's easy to talk about service in general terms, but when it falls into the hands of an individual leader, everyone runs for cover. That's because it's difficult for one leader to instill a focus on service without falling for the old 'back to the floor' routine. That's right, we'll send Frank off into the assembly department for a few days and all will be well.

The fact is employees only start to open up after several consecutive days' executive presence (and that's usually only to moderate their language). So re-anchoring the business around a key customer service figure takes the responsibility away from one and gives it to the rest of the business.

Unless this can be allied to practical exercises on 'the front line', whereby the leader appears, gives some context and asks for changes, promising to visit again at a future time (possibly unannounced), the chances of a culture change on the back of a visit from Field Marshall Sir Douglas Haig are small. But with some co-ordinated employee-led action to follow, you just might create a higher profile for service.

The complexities of introducing customer service as core business activity are many, but are more easily digestible when viewed from the customer standpoint. If we are to differentiate on the basis of the quality of the customer interaction and the strength of subsequent advocacy, then we need to focus on what directly influences that and work backwards. Context, skills, technical / product knowledge, attitude, customer focus, sales skills, recovery skills, humour, resilience and belief are all required. Easy? No.

But is local management focused totally on providing the conditions for these skills to thrive? Apart from attitude, which you can't train but have to recruit, every other one of these skills can be learned 'on the job', so the role of the line manager is critical. And yet, as I've argued before, managers are subject to real and imagined forces that lead them to focus on other things. Some rarely leave their laptops while others rarely arrive at the office. As I compile my continuing customer travelogue I see little evidence of management 'presence'. Now and again, when it does appear, it's like manna from heaven, relief in a dry continent or a cold towel on a sweaty forehead (I am the fourth Brontë sister).

Surely, if you agree with my illustration of some of the facets of an employee you'd like to do business with, then presence is a key factor. Even today, when buying my coffee in Prêt, the guy serving me asked me how my day was going. You just know that most people would only ask that question if they'd received recent encouragement to do so from a supervisor or manager – better still, if they'd seen their boss do exactly the same thing. In Prêt I would argue that it happens because there is a tangible customer-focused culture, but elsewhere?

Following presence, I recommend three tablespoons of *do as I do*. Even if for only a few minutes, role-modelling what customers expect is a key responsibility of managers – and that can usually only be done by doing the job.

Context-setting is essential. While some managers prefer to encourage their teams to come up with their own solutions, they tend to avoid confronting some of the bigger questions, like how do we improve service when there's no budget for it, or what can we do to make a real difference to the bottom line? The answer is time. You need to spend time with your team exploring the context, drawing out the contradictions, the challenges and the opportunities, framing all of this within the customer experience and encouraging the team to experiment and come up with new ideas and approaches.

You then follow this up regularly to help overcome initial shyness, offer support and information and give time and space for further discussion. Context setting is not showing them your targets and shouting at them until they achieve them. I'm not kidding either. I've been in shops while staff have been getting a 'right dressing-down'. Sometimes underwhelmed customers might acknowledge that it's probably been well deserved, but *not in front of us, please*.

You know that as sure as night follows day (and me receiving an unwanted phone call from some hysterical English graduate from Honolulu in the evening), coaching is going to form part of the management landscape and be a big part of creating the focus to which we aspire. Everyone accepts that it can work, but it's rarely raised above the level of necessary sideshow for the majority of employees, who try hard to forget that particular episode of *The Office*, when being pummelled for feedback on their current role and aspirations.

Coaching does require coaching skills – and managers don't come readily equipped with them. Curiously enough, though, it also requires time, presence and 'on the job' activity. If we were to focus our managers on providing customer-facing colleagues with these three gifts then the opportunities to make incisive contributions would soon outweigh the meaningless twaddle many of us associate with our own experiences of 'being coached'.

Hunting through my diaries for examples of tangible improvement in the customer experience, I come across an unusual little gem. But first, the reader will need to suspend disbelief while I announce that I am a member of a fitness club. Yes, that's right. I shoehorn my considerable thighs into my impressive running shorts and crash along at an ungainly 6 miles an hour on my little running machine. The iPod and adjacent TV (showing Sky Sports News) help take my mind off the work, although I once unconsciously swayed to the left in some kind of physical empathy with a sashaying winger on screen and ended up falling off the contraption and inventing a new and particularly painful gymnastic move.

Having retrieved my legs from the adjacent machine, I remembered that it's something else that happens there every time I drop by that makes my little heart leap. As I walk in and hand my membership card to the receptionist, he or she swipes it to produce an unpleasant photograph of me, taken after running 6 miles. I look like Marlon Brando in *Apocalypse Now*, but with less money and a much shorter life expectancy. Anyway, as the image appears on the screen and people in the vicinity cover their eyes, the receptionist, noting my name on the screen, says, 'Hi Mark. How are you today?' I love that. It takes so little effort, it's supported by the systems and it quickens your step (or at least increases mine from stationary to funereal) as you glide into the changing rooms and prepare for battle.

This takes me to the next facet of leadership that, according to my customer journeys, is not particularly evident: joint management and staff planning sessions. If our leaders are true to the concept of inclusivity at employee level and if they understand the role that employee involvement has in motivating and anchoring focus in the organisation, then it follows that planning should be a team operation.

Effective business planning has for too long been the preserve of management, as if their position on the hierarchical structure somehow bequeaths them a unique prescience. The reality is, however, that the team often 'know' the 'manor' better than they do. They're more able to look at the context, the broader strategy and point out the weak spots and unexpected opportunities, just as 'back to the floor' exercises can often uncover pointless damaging processes and procedures that staff 'must follow'.

Er, excuse me. The phone is ringing. I pick up. A pause. 'Are you aware …' a monotonous robotic female voice announces. 'Aren't you going to introduce yourself?' I say. 'That's not very nice. Here am I sat at my laptop and you don't have the decency even to introduce yourself. You and your *are you aware*!'

Yep, you've spotted it. It's another of these recorded outbound messages. Now I do accept that if the wording were to be altered considerably and a new focus on how we might spend the evening together were introduced, some customers would no doubt pay good money for that. But this practice infuriates me. Somehow my anger is only assuaged by my continuing to converse with her while she rattles off her pointless monologue.

I'm not going to spend time on the concept of rewarding the right behaviour, effort and direction, as this sounds too much like some weird Pavlovian experiment. Of course we humans respond, but what we respond best to is the belief that people appreciate your actions. I can easily conjure an image of a roomful of experts deciding whether vouchers or gifts would be best, when the first test should be whether employees are routinely thanked for what they do.

My reading of the situation in this country, based on countless observations, is that supervisors and managers are so tied to process (and sometimes their own profile) that employees are an afterthought. Recently, as I waited for some department store employees to stop their discussions and serve me, I watched as a manager approached. That had the effect. The chatter subsided immediately – with my transaction taking place in monastic silence, the manager looking on like a nightshift supervisor at a sweat shop. It would have been nice to attribute their new professionalism to the customer's presence, but I guess they just didn't like the manager.

Recent research has highlighted that improving customer service is globally the biggest challenge for CEOs and Chairpersons everywhere. While tacitly acknowledging that many have got it wrong, the message appeared to be that more imagination, creativity and commitment were needed from leaders to move customer service into the 'core business' position.

I'm restricting my perspective to that of the customer in this book – and I'm sure if leaders did too, they'd finally see the answers to some of these awkward questions. They'd step outside and start to look properly at the service their organisations deliver.

One final revelation that will appear at this point is one that may dismay fellow *Guardian* readers and those of a sensitive nature when it comes to political correctness. The fact is a great deal of customers are stupid, ignorant, badly behaved and undeserving of a good customer experience. You don't believe me. Then I invite you to get in your car (I know that's not politically correct either) and drive around your town for half an hour. You will encounter at least three other drivers who should be prevented from leaving the house – and one idiot who insisted on slowing down, while he was crossing the street on a red light, as if to challenge me to run him down. Had it not been for the epiphany that stirred me into using this analogy to back up my points about stupid customers, then I certainly would have finished the job. He was wearing an inscrutable look, somehow meant to convey his 'screw you' attitude. He ripped the heart out of that adjective. Inscrutable is the preserve of Eric Cantona, chipping Lionel Perez in the Sunderland goal and turning, like a bullfighter, to acknowledge the roars of the crowd. That's inscrutability.

I recall an evening at a Premier Inn in Birmingham, whose happy memories are dimmed by the recollection of the behaviour of a family who, upon finding their daughter wasn't feeling very well, decided to harangue the receptionist, like footballers around a referee – to follow the above analogy – blaming her for the child's imminent expiry. The language used, the inarticulacy, the rudeness and aggression denoted these customers as idiots too – and yet the receptionist managed (largely) to maintain her poise. To be fair, she let one put-down go at one point, but quickly rediscovered her professional calm. Had she looked up she might have sensed the invisible applause from the other families in the reception. The child, of course, was fine, but the parents' limited education had obviously been just enough to help them read an ambulance-chasing advert during *The Jeremy Kyle Show*.

Our social ills, our binge-drinking, vomit-lined streets and attitude-ridden, celebrity-hypnotised masses present enormous problems for customer-facing employees, for whom no day passes without them encountering someone too unhinged and dangerous to be even considered as a participant on Mr Kyle's programme. Is it any wonder that some employees are affected by these experiences and, somehow, that their frustration and anger manifests itself through indifference and defensiveness in front of all customers? It would be easy for me to point my finger at every organisation, as no one has really grasped the customer experience issue, but as often as not, I'm stood bewildered at the behaviour of other customers.

Customer service is therefore an output of a complex matrix of interacting elements, based on the principle of standing outside your organisation and looking in, and built upon the creation of a shared focus, where the customer experience is readily acknowledged to be 'core business activity'. And while you, as I, can probably feel an explanatory model coming on, let me summarise the principles that I believe all businesses will adopt once they spend sufficient time in the customer's crocs.

There needs to be reciprocal customer understanding, built on a transparent surveying mechanic, where visible improvements are promoted to customers, who in turn can see their commitment to provide feedback reciprocated in new improved experiences.

Convention will continue to resist change, so happy accidents must be followed up. For example, taking the hierarchical structure and turning it upside down reveals the key role of customer-facing employees. If they were regarded, for a month, as the external customer and you were serious about really impressing them, just how would things change for the better (clue: ask them)?

Values are always welcome and, as a customer, I like to see a company's intrinsic values reflected in my dealings with them. But values need to be customer-driven, recognisably valuable to them, rather than something dreamt up over a few lattes at the Costa bar in the staff canteen. Values also must be backed up with management activities that ensure they are the backdrop to all decisions, whether strategic, or the one you're making for the customer in front of you. The phrase *values-led organisation* sounds alluring, but in reality, we customers rarely see anything that remotely implies there's some moral fibre and humanity behind this faceless behemoth.

The service excellence industry in this country is alive and kicking and there are many good-quality conferences and events looking into the barriers to service, exploring change, sharing company case studies and making a real effort. But as a testament to the lack of transparency and trust in this country, customer service has yet to enter the public domain. If it were, we wouldn't have to pretend to look excited, just because a company has 'satisfied' customers. Check the Thesaurus and you'll find that not all definitions of the word are really what you should be purveying out there.

The advances in online communities and the success of organisations like More Train Less Strain, who have significantly altered the strategy at First Great Western, show that, if companies don't act and start to open up on how good their service is, then customers will pick up the standard and create even more havoc. I'm already planning to have tee-shirts with motifs such as 'I've seen your mystery shopping scores' and 'I want to be more than just satisfied'.

Central to this (and forgive the introduction of another train company) is perspective – and that, in my view, is the single biggest opportunity in front of us. I'm simply sharing my travels, anecdotes and thoughts.

I'm not writing a management manual. It all comes from putting yourself in the customer's footwear and spending significant time there. I first put these shoes on in 1999 and while the leather is starting to wear, the fog is lifting and if a positive future for UK service cannot easily be contemplated, the root causes of the current situation are now screamingly evident.

*

So, as I began, let me present my final few thoughts on a better future for British customer service by sharing my most recent diary entries, since they lay bare some of the bizarre idiosyncrasies of the challenge we face (and remind me to buy some new shoes).

Today is February 13th 2008 and I'm in London preparing to chair a conference in Holborn. For once, I breathe an air of confidence as I walk the short distance from the Tube to my hotel, just off Kingsway. The weather is incredibly clement for mid-February, reaching 16 degrees. I'm confident, because I know I won't have any problems with my business charge card. I did have a problem, but it's been resolved, hence my carefree demeanour.

Early last week I attempted to use my card to purchase some stationery. As I tapped in the four numbers, the cashier announced: 'Be careful, sir. The O is a bit touchy.' She was right. It didn't register. It meant that I had keyed in the wrong PIN. The result of this was an immediate and inexplicable attack of PIN psychosis. Suddenly my PIN number was a mystery. The temporary confusion had caused an entire branch of my financial lobe to malfunction. One further attempt failed.

Rather than risking a third and critical attempt (given that your PIN will be blocked if you incorrectly enter it three times), I opted for another card and took the sad story home with me. As I sat on the train, speeding north, I tried to re-invoke the magic number. It failed to materialise, causing me to wonder how I could do something for so long without remembering what I was doing. 'Simple,' explained my wife. 'Just ask anyone who's seen you driving.' Not helpful. But it was enough to jar my memory into an approximation of the number I'd forgotten. Confidently I typed in what I thought was the right number. Moments later – and to my considerable dismay at the experience – it was explained to me that I had failed again and my PIN was now blocked.

Having searched all over NatWest's website for a customer services number, I found it (embarrassingly) on the back of my card. I telephoned. Six minutes of automated apologies later, I explained my predicament to a courteous assistant who asked me for security details and explained that a reminder would be posted to me and would arrive within 2/3 days. It did. It arrived yesterday, prompting a large 'ah' of recognition in the owner. Which explains my confidence today, as I approach the hotel.

As is ever the case, hotels wish to insure themselves against you doing a runner, so they ask for your credit card details upfront. Proudly I present my card and nonchalantly glide over to the Chip and PIN device. But before I can extend my digit, the transaction has been declined.

'I'm sorry, sir,' comes the Eastern European accent. 'Yes, I know. I've been having problems with my PIN,' I retort. Deep in the receptionist's mind, a truer translation plays out. 'You're actually a vagrant who lurks around ATM machines and separates people from their cards – and I've just rumbled you.'

Dejectedly, I offer another card, while envisaging extended periods of dishwashing in this woe-begotten corner of Holborn. This time, it works. I ask for assurance that I can still pay with the charge card upon checking out, and seek the solace of my single room (with a faulty socket and an attractive view of bins – £213, not bad!).

In the room I contact my immeasurably better half to ask her to find the customer service number. 'It's on the back of your card,' she reminds me, perhaps offering an inkling of an insight into why it's generally accepted as dangerous for any financial institution to offer me any device whatsoever with which to settle bills and accounts.

I telephone at 13.51. I select the general enquiry option and the automaton advises, 'Your call is being placed in our queuing system,' and depression envelops the room like a tramp in a lift.

I begin to mark the number of times the system tells me, 'I'm sorry you've been kept waiting. One of our operators will be with you soon.' In the time that passes I begin to analyse the language that is being used. In some weirdly appropriate way it does match the robotic process in which I'm trapped. It's 'your call' not 'you' and they have 'operators' not 'people' or 'assistants'.

Worst of all I have been passively placed 'in our queuing system' – an innovation that should have been rendered redundant by any basic understanding of customer service. Nevertheless, I have to keep waiting. Five minutes later, after about twenty recorded apologies, I'm cut off, with a plaintiff series of three beeps. My temper is incredibly inclement for mid-February, reaching 100 degrees.

Taking a deep breath – with such a passion that passers-by struggle for Kingsway's remaining oxygen – I try again. This time I wait four minutes before finally speaking to someone who utters her introduction so quickly it might have been 'centipede horoscope and trouser press.' But she's helpful, adding competence to the courtesy offered by the previous assistant. She explains that I should have been told to visit a nearby ATM and 'unblock my PIN'. She apologises. I thank her and we end the conversation, as I reflect on the 10 minutes wasted.

Immediately I'm re-cast as the travelling customer, recording the ills of UK service: only a small disappointing experience, but one that magnifies what we endure on a daily basis.

This morning, my family dropped me off at Leeds railway station, like *Life on Mars*' Gene Hunt paying a visit to a nonce. Skidding in, a couple of cursory goodbye kisses and the sound of screeching tyres as they re-claim the in-car iPod and switch to something other than A-Ha, Neil Young or Wilco.

Leeds railway station must be experiencing an increase in traffic. Consciously, more of us are using public transport now, whether for the environment or for the horrors of our motorway network. The station has been enlarged in recent years and all the usual suspects, from Subway, via Starbucks to Burger King, have moved in like travelling folk to an empty field.

Ideally, your pre-journey moments could comprise a restful coffee and a glance through the *Yorkshire Post* (after all, it has some excellent columnists), while looking up at the departures board and wondering how romantic an afternoon in Mirfield might be. But under my unstinting microscope, there are obstacles still. I start at WH Smith, where I plan to purchase a magazine and a newspaper. I would like to avoid asking for a carrier bag, for the environment (but mostly because I can't open them). The lady offers one.

I contemplate the laptop bag I'm carrying and the anticipated circumstance of me having to carry my bag, the magazine and a cup of coffee though the ticket barrier, while displaying my ticket, and decide that without a third arm and an ability to contort, I'll need that bag. Ironically, she can't open it either. Steadfastly resisting the obvious trick of salivating onto her fingers and opening it with her moist digits thus, she offers it to me. Thankfully, the Lord has bequeathed sticky fingers to me as a matter of mutant alien family genes, so I'm able to open it and insert my purchases.

I move to the sandwich bar and peruse the menu. Having been on the slimfasts since being photographed leaving Ipswich Town's Club Shop and being later described as 'the Graf Zeppelin tethered to a small boy,' I'm perennially hungry. I opt for a Chicken and Leek Feuille and a Tall Latte, and ruminate on how we meekly accept that if something is given a foreign name, we will, like a bewildered flock of sheep, happily pay more for it. Were my repast described as a 'pasty and a milky coffee,' I would expect change from a pound. However, on this occasion, I get little from five.

I then have to negotiate the ticket barrier. Now this is an interesting phenomenon. Either they check your tickets on the train or check you in and out of the station. One or other process should be redundant, thereby saving money, time and resources and, presumably, improving service for travellers.

Here in Leeds, the manoeuvre required to complete this task usually stops people dead in their tracks as they try to extract their tickets from a wallet, with their tongue. Yorkshiremen muttering behind you leave you in no doubt that your cluelessness is ruining their day.

Strangely enough, as I've mentioned earlier in this book, the same ridiculous scenario is played out for anyone attempting to leave the car park at the side of the station.

Further ahead in London I find myself with a few hours to kill, the evening before the conference. I walk headlong into the dazzling brightness of the sparkling mid-February afternoon, the sun low, about to make its excuses and leave. Half-term tourists have claimed the streets and Covent Garden is shimmering with people, like a half-excavated termite mound. Buskers tune up as families hold ice creams like microphones, an impromptu street interview only moments away.

As the light fades into streetlights and pubs squeeze out their clients onto pavements, I start to think about eating (again). I've spotted a branch of Strada opposite my hotel. I recall hearing good things when this chain first made its appearance. Somehow I can visualise a sound write-up – the 'next-generation Pizza Express'? Something like that. Also, having perfected a *puttanesca* sauce at home, just short of drying out, tacky and unctuous, I quite fancied seeing what the restaurant version might be like.

At something like 6.30 I wander across the street into the restaurant. Downstairs it's busy. There are lots of couples, plus one woman dining alone, staring at a newspaper. I have brought the *Evening Standard* along too – a vital companion, a sign that you're not really a sad, abandoned old man with a pasta fixation.

'Have you a table for one?' I ask plaintively. The waitress smiles, looks around and catches the eye of a waiter descending the stairs towards us. 'Can you find a table for one upstairs?' she asks, in faltering English.

He turns and beckons me to follow him. I notice that upstairs is only half-full. Tables to my right are mostly occupied, but the area to my left is mostly untainted by human presence. I cannot see any 'reserved' signs. Although no tables are specifically laid out for one person, this establishment is opposite one of the better hotels in this part of London – and judging by the clientele, there are bound to be other solitary diners like me. At this point a third member of staff appears and starts to shake her head like a disapproving cowboy car mechanic. 'It's difficult,' she says in no-one's general direction.

'It's OK. I'll go somewhere else,' I say, picking up on her hesitation and intending to create some interest in allowing me to sit down. But they seem pleased that I have taken little persuasion. A fake sympathetic shake of the head later and I've gone downstairs and left the building.

As I leave, I pass the waitress who originally sent me upstairs. She throws me a quizzical look. A colleague of hers looks up. 'Thank you, sir,' he whimpers. My retort, not too far under my breath, shares the title to the B-side of Alberto y Lost Trios Paranoias' 70s hit 'Heads Down No Nonsense Mindless Boogie'. And it almost sounds like 'thank you'.

My long-suffering good lady receives a text from me announcing my general dismay, but in words she cannot repeat in front of anyone under the age of 53. 'Off to find a proper restaurant,' I end my diatribe. I recall previous nights alone in London. Fair enough, not finding a table upon which to dine is hardly despondency of the level of

Cathy Come Home, but it's not good enough, when there are tables a-plenty.

Ana reckons I should take a leaf out of my own book and actually stand up and be counted. 'Why didn't you say something?' she quite reasonably implores later during the evening as I dissect the experience over the phone. 'You're always criticising British customers for not speaking out and voting with their feet.'

A fair point. 'But I *have* voted with my feet,' I offer, by way of a tepid response to her chillingly effective argument.

'And,' the thought occurs to me, 'I *am* speaking out.'

'What do you mean?'

'Well, I may not have said anything at the time, but it's going in the book. So people can read about this restaurant and go somewhere else instead.'

'Can you do that? I thought you were told not to mention the businesses you were criticising in your first book. Lawyers and that.'

'I was. But if Fay Maschler and Jay Rayner can honestly criticise and still elude imprisonment, so can I. After all, it's only my opinion.'

'At least they generally get to taste the food. Unlike you.' Another fair point. But solitary dining is not impossible in London.

Previously, residing in the majestic comfort of the currently chaotic half-constructed Euston Premier Inn, I've wandered down Charlotte Street and found no end of eateries prepared to inflict the sight of solitary me in communion with my onion bhaji on their unsuspecting customers, leafing through *Mojo* like a 'once famous rock star'.

And so on we go. Today we discover that one of our local supermarkets has started to offer a foreign money service. That could be handy. We approach the till concerned and ask what, to most customers, would be a routine series of questions. 'Do you order the money or do you have it on the premises? What's the commission rate? And do we get reward points if we buy our money here?' The last question floored the assistant. He had a look on his face like someone in the audience of *Live Autopsy*. 'I, er, don't know.' Nice to know they've prepared their people well for that new initiative then.

Looking through my diary entries, I notice two emails from friends with a similar problem. Each of them went into their local bank branch to open an account for their children. Each of them was told it couldn't be done on spec, but that they would have to arrange an appointment. In each case, the appointment was two weeks away. Unsurprisingly, each opted to open their accounts elsewhere, even though the bank who let them down was the most convenient for each. And they say 'being easy to do business with' is one of the best descriptions of great customer service.

One other diary note – and an extensive one at that – was our involvement in BBC1's *Are We Being Served?* This programme ran throughout the summer of 2006, a kind of little sister to *Watchdog*, looking into the fabled low levels of British customer service. The family and I were recruited to do some 'undercover' work and this took us to the unlikely setting of North Wales – Rhyl, to be specific.

The idea was to experience lunch at a restaurant that research had identified as being somewhat poor on the service front. Memories are dimming now, but one typically British recollection stirs. We arrived early – at around 12 noon – and were among the first diners to order. To do this, you had to approach the till, order your food, pay for it, collect your cutlery and wait at your table for the food. Being early arrivals, there was no queue and we were able to order quickly. But by the time we were ready for a small dessert, the queue at the till was longer than a horse's face. I stood stoically in the queue, the hidden cameras trailing me from ten metres away.

What happened next was a little shameful, but I stepped out of the line, went to the drinks bar and asked if I could order the desserts from there. They acceded to my request, trying hard to stifle a look of horror as they realised procedures were being broken.

Everything was recorded and in a nice moment of redemption the restaurant chain committed to some meaningful changes. I couldn't stomach a return visit though.

In many ways it was reminiscent of recent train journeys. You can bet your bottom cheeks that the teaspoons, cups and saucers will be replaced, with military precision, some twenty minutes before the destination is reached. And yet, if in search of flexibility or assistance, no such rigour is observed.

British service and the retail customer experience are also in need of redemption. Improvements have certainly been noted and it's gratifying that, little by little, each sector is being lit up by the arrival (or re-invention) of a player with real customer virtues.

For it is these virtues that elude the vast majority, pointing to a deeper malaise. Perhaps the pursuit of excellence has got confused with the pursuit of money. It strikes me that if you pose the old cliché of what gets measured gets done, it's clear that by any metric, those who are pursuing money will stay until it's there and depart shortly afterwards.

I laughed heartily when one of our leading (how inappropriate an adjective) utilities announced recently that if they didn't put prices up, they wouldn't turn a profit (I paraphrase, but the implication was clear). God help us if they were to put customers before profit – and when did they pass that law that says you have to go out of business if you make an annual loss?

This got me thinking about how long organisations survive these days and thanks to one of *Business Week*'s excellent bloggers, we have the revelation that over much of the Western World, corporate bodies, on average, last just over 12 years before they expire.

Apart from the damage caused to the employees themselves, their communities, their suppliers and customers, only one significant constituency appears to survive, rising like a phoenix out of the ashes: the Chairman and CEO.

So why do companies die so prematurely? *Business Week* puts it succinctly: 'There is accumulating evidence that corporations fail because the prevailing thinking and language of management are too narrowly based on the prevailing thinking and language of economics. To put it another way: Companies die because their managers focus on the economic activity of producing goods and services, and they forget that their organizations' true nature is that of a community of humans. The legal establishment, business educators, and the financial community all join them in this mistake.'

One body is noticeable by its absence: customers. We allow this to happen and, by nature of our culture or our ignorance, we stand by complacently. It is therefore our duty to make every effort to identify those organisations who are, by the quality of the service they provide, nurturing a less blinkered, less money-oriented and more inclusive corporate being – one capable of sustaining a community, not a porcelain cash cow that explodes into a million pieces, after approximately 12 years, showering the few with riches and leaving the rest of us wondering what happened.

Successful communication is a two-way process. I send out and you receive. But three years on from my first tour of duty, an enduring indifference continues to blight the majority of our experiences as UK customers. There are two people in any conversation. There's only one here. No matter how much businesses pretend that they're customer-fixated these days, the clues tell us only one thing. This conversation you think you're enjoying? It's a monologue.

And as I close the laptop lid on another journey, the phone rings. This time it's not an automated outbound call, someone trying to tell me I've won a holiday or a sales call cunningly disguised as a request for feedback. It's my mate. He's a consultant and he's just been asked to a meeting by an organisation's Head of Communications. The description of his unsuccessful afternoon neatly underlines my continuing ire. The meeting had been called by the Head of Communications to explore a number of ideas, provided by my friend and his colleagues, aimed at creating an engaging, meaningful and entertaining video for employees.

Six attendees sank into oblivion as the host convincingly gave meaning to her role. The Head of Communications has to ensure that no communication takes place whatsoever – and, in the rare case that it does happen, she'll be there to ensure that it has no lasting effect.

As each idea was presented, her demeanour wouldn't alter. She sat stony-faced through several suggestions. 'This one won't work,' she'd say. 'If we do that, it would cost too much.' Another suggestion emerges. 'That'll appear too constructed,' she responded. Drawing a breath deeper than the Archbald Pothole in Pennsylvania, my friend continued through a list of diverse solutions. The inscrutability did not alter once. 'And that won't work because we shouldn't be going into so much detail.'

Filled with a desire to apply unreasonable amounts of pressure to her throat, my friend regained his composure and, mentally, tried to apply some meaning to his frustrating afternoon. In response to the long series of ideas, she had offered not one, but simply summoned rain clouds and emptied them on all and sundry, removing what little enthusiasm there was at the start of the meeting.

'Shall we go away and consider how else we could approach this?' my pal offered meekly, stepping backwards out of the room like a man discovering a box jellyfish in his bath.

In her own small way, the Head of Communications was correcting my notion - that the 'conversation' is only one-way. In her relentless determination to stand still, she's proving that, in reality, there's no one in this conversation.

No one sends out and no one receives.

I meet with members of the 'service excellence' community regularly. They are committed, passionate individuals who believe that their organisations can thrive by focusing on what matters most to their employees and their customers. The extent to which their dreams are becoming reality largely depends on how high up the organisational ladder their hopes are shared, but with awards schemes, competitions, and celebratory evenings, they're putting the message out that customers matter.

The problem is that we customers are not receiving this message. The existence of service excellence as a unifying concept for customers and organisations is strictly internal. A lack of transparency from organisations, most clearly evidenced by a failure to publicise openly just how well they are delivering what really matters to customers, troubles me. Transparency is all about honesty and honesty nurtures trust. We have no trust in the majority of organisations because we believe their commitment to the customer is simply 'lip' service, not real service.

We suspect – and all of the evidence points us this way – that leaders are only prepared to accommodate the real service excellence champions in their organisation, because now and again, it suits the PR machine to dredge up a 'happy customer' story.

Across the land, in shops, call centres, factories and offices, organisations say one thing but peddle another – and the physical manifestation of this is the desperate levels of service we all receive.

I am as guilty as the next one. My bank continues to underwhelm me, my broadband provider seems to thrive on treating customers with contempt, my government nationalises a bank because our Chairmen and CEOs are in a panic, but fails to display the same philosophical backbone when it comes to addressing our appalling public transport infrastructure.

And while all of this happens, we continue to stand by, dazzled by a two-for-one offer, hypnotised by a new sandwich filling, led down a scented aisle, choreographed into submission and conditioned to accept that culturally, we shouldn't expect great customer experiences, because we Brits just don't get it. Our curiously passive attitude to disappearing accountability and eroding levels of trust is clearly one of the main causes of the degrading of the customer experience in the UK today. But an alternative and increasingly compelling argument is forming.

Take a long walk in the customer's shoes and you'll see that it's all 'lip service'. True commitment to the principles of customer service excellence – transparency, honesty, trust and the creation of a mutually beneficial community of employees and customers with a shared focus on excellence – represents a step too far for the people making the self-enriching key strategic decisions.

Or perhaps that's being unkind. In reality, though, were they themselves to take a walk with the customer, the shocking revelation that all is not what it seems will almost certainly point to the mindset they should adopt, if they want their organisations to thrive.

But to paraphrase Martin Brampton, whom I quoted earlier in the book, our businesses want the most money for the least effort. Making customer service core business activity simply costs too much for leaders whose commitment lasts as long as it takes to achieve the particular level of personal enrichment they have earmarked for the current role.

To quote *Business Week*'s compelling argument: 'Companies die because their managers focus on the economic activity of producing goods and services, and they forget that their organizations' true nature is that of a community of humans. The legal establishment, business educators, and the financial community all join them in this mistake.' Strange though it may seem, most lawyers I know advise against naming 'offending organisations', even if the comments are based on my own experiences.

So the problem is cultural after all and, like all individuals trying to effect real change in their lives, the first few steps terrify us. It will be the case if we wish to address the problem of customer service in the UK, because we will need to take action.

Action on a personal basis will require an honest assessment of how our service relationships are meeting our basic needs as customers. If they are not, then we must take decisive action and seek a service provider who has a notion of what it takes. We must make clear what is and what is not acceptable and we must hold senior executives to account when a basic level of service is not provided.

Where we can acknowledge that the greater good will be achieved by group pursuit of action, we should continue to support the communities who have created havoc for those banks wishing to levy unreasonable charges and led to real change for commuters in the South West of England. It takes courage for the British to say 'this is not acceptable,' such is our conditioning to accept poor service. But now that people are banding together to make a stand, it would be a pity if we weren't able to complete the task and bequeath a better customer experience to the next generation.

Dr Johnson once said that 'every man thinks meanly of himself for not having been a soldier.' Well, since our companies have proven themselves incapable of doing what's right, we must ensure that regret does not come to characterise our dotage.

When we give good 'word of mouth' we wield our most potent weapon. We are capable of propelling any number of businesses to success as much as we can consign failing ones to industry's recycle bin. We now need to bring our 'word of mouth' closer to the incident that created our opinion in the first place, overcome our national shyness and tell people exactly what is and is not acceptable.

Each and every day, someone, somewhere will be asked 'is everything OK?' by a passing employee. So, by becoming a conscientious heckler, answering 'no, actually,' and constructively explaining why we are disappointed, we may enter senectitude safe in the knowledge that we saw the Emperor naked and created a service revolution at the same time.

www.ardrapress.co.uk